PRODUCT
LEADERSHIP

Other Books by Robert G. Cooper

Winning at New Products:
Accelerating the Process from Idea to Launch

Portfolio Management for New Products
(with Scott J. Edgett and Elko J. Kleinschmidt)

PRODUCT LEADERSHIP

Creating and Launching Superior New Products

ROBERT G. COOPER

PERSEUS BOOKS
Cambridge, Massachusetts

Library of Congress Catalog Card Number: 98-86946

ISBN 0-7382-0010-7

Perseus Books is a member of the Perseus Books Group
Jacket design by Suzanne Heiser
Text design by David C. denBoer
Set in 10.25/13-point Palatino by Nighthawk Design

    6 7 8 9-DOH-02 01 00

Find us on the World Wide Web at
http://perseusbooks.com

Perseus Books are available at special discounts for bulk purchases in the U.S. by corporations, institutions, and other organizations. For more information, please contact the Special Markets Department at HarperCollins Publishers, 10 East 53rd Street, New York, NY 10022, or call 1-212-207-7528.

To the three ladies in my life . . . my wife, Linda,
and my two daughters, Barbara and Heather

Contents

Preface

This book is aimed at senior executives, leadership teams, and senior managers who want to become leaders in product innovation. And who doesn't? Over the past decade, I've been privileged to give presentations to a great number of CEOs and leadership teams of businesses, both in North America and in Europe. What never ceases to amaze me is how mystified they are by product development. Their intentions are good, but they don't seem to quite know what to do in order to help their businesses get a steady stream of winning new products—and big winners—to market.

No executive today is unaware of the strategic need for winning new products. As one senior person put it, "Ten years ago, all you had to do was demonstrate positive profits. That's not enough anymore. Now Wall Street seems to expect great product innovations along with profits." And so the pressure is on virtually every leadership team to deliver great new products. The new corporate motto is "innovate or die."

The trouble is, that's not so easy. Where does one start? Leading your business's product innovation efforts is quite a new challenge for many leadership teams. Thus many senior people appear somewhat at a loss. Perhaps the problem is that, until recently, product development was "an R&D thing," effectively taken care of by the technical community in the company. No longer. Now product development is a business-wide activity, and one where the leadership team of the business must be front and center, clearly in charge . . . indeed, *leading* the charge!

This book shares some of the same thoughts as my popular book, *Winning at New Products: Accelerating the Process from Idea to Launch.* That book, whose second edition was published in late 1993, focused mostly on the need to implement a *Stage-Gate*™ new product process, the details of such a process, and how to implement. It went on to become the most poplar book on new products ever, and indeed is perhaps why, today, some four years and 35,000 copies later, 60 percent of U.S. industry has adopted some form of a *Stage-Gate*™ process.

The current book moves above the tactical level, however (*Stage-Gate*™ and its details is largely a tactical process). In *Product Leadership*, I outline the critical success factors—those factors that distinguish leading businesses and blockbuster new products from the also-rans. These factors are based on decades of academic research that we have conducted. Not surprisingly, I outline the need for a *Stage-Gate*™ new product process—after all, *Stage-Gate*™ has served leading companies well this decade. And I provide you, the leadership team, with enough detail to understand what this process is and does. But I go beyond the *Stage-Gate*™ process of my other book, and also highlight what's new here: the 6Fs of a third-generation new product process.

The current book moves into new areas too, well beyond the *Winning at New Products* book, because there's more to product leadership than just implementing an effective product development process. And since 1993, our research has progressed and uncovered new findings in areas such as benchmarking business's new product performance (what distinguishes successful businesses) and new product portfolio management methods. Indeed, *Product Leadership* is predicated in part on the results of our most recent benchmarking study that uncovered the three cornerstones to excellent new product performance:

- new product strategy—do you have a well-thought-out new product strategy for your business, complete with defined goals, arenas, attack plans, and deployment breakdowns?
- the right resources, properly allocated—is project selection, resource allocation, and portfolio management up and running effectively in your business?
- a high quality new product process—do you have a *Stage-Gate*™ process in place and working well?

Get these three cornerstones right, and you're 90 percent on the way to becoming a leader!

Effective resource allocation is one of the three cornerstones of successful businesses in product innovation, so I devote several chapters to this topic. Project selection and effective gatekeeping is part of resource allocation, and is also a critical task for the leadership team of the business. Indeed, *gatekeeping* and making the gates work is one of the most important roles that senior management plays in successful businesses. Portfolio management is also a topic that has come of age, is fundamental to resource allocation, and is one way that the business's strategy is manifested. An entire chapter is dedicated to portfolio management, simply because this too is where the leadership team of the business must lead: they are the "portfolio managers" of the business.

Strategic issues—namely developing new product strategy for your business, one that spells out your goals, strategic arenas, and attack plans, and then gives direction to project selection and resource allocation—is another cornerstone of performance. It too is an important topic of the current book. Again, the senior people must lead here and have an active part in the crafting of their business's new product strategy, and so a chapter is devoted to this topic.

A number of people helped me in the writing of this book. My two closest colleagues are Professors Elko Kleinschmidt and Scott Edgett, both at McMaster University's Michael G. DeGroote School of Business. We do much of our research together, and we have co-authored numerous articles and a very recent book (*Portfolio Management for New Products*, Perseus Books, 1998). Many of the thoughts and ideas that appear in the current book have been reviewed and discussed with these two close colleagues, and hence their ideas permeate my book. Both world-class scholars in this field, they have been invaluable in the preparation of this book. I thank each of them. Two other close colleagues are in Europe: they are Jens Arleth, senior partner in U3 Innovation Management (a Copenhagen new products consulting firm), and Alec Pettit, managing director of New Product Consultancy (Ricksmansworth, near London, U.K.). We do much work together, and as leading practitioners, they bring a practical orientation to my thinking. In their consulting practices, they have tested many of the theories and practices highlighted in the book, and have also made valuable suggestions. For example, the *ProBE* diagnostic tool, in Appendix A, was developed jointly with Jens Arleth.

Others who have influenced the shaping of this book, either via testing concepts or making suggestions that have found their way into the book, or providing valuable examples, are (alphabetically): Dr. Ed Bartkus, formerly of Rohm and Haas, Martin Brennan of Reckitt & Colman UK; Tony Brophy of Guinness Ireland Group; Bob Davis, formerly of Procter & Gamble, now with Market Facts; Larry Gastwirt of Vantage

Consulting and the Stevens Institute, N.J.; Norm Heyerdahl of Fluke; Karen Kraziano and Bob Wood of Rohm and Haas; Leslie Littel of Transitions (PPG); Bill Rodger of Decyma Consulting, Kathryn Sachse and Marg Kneebone of the Royal Bank of Canada; John Schneider of Prochem Ltd.; Lee Stewart of Hallmark; and Per Velde of Telenor (Norway).

I would also like to thank my daughter, Barbara, who while in the employ of our consulting company, Product Development Institute Inc., collected ideas, did library research for me, and proofread many of the chapters. My youngest daughter Heather also helped out on some of the typing. Finally, I thank Kathy Ball, librarian at McMaster's Michael G. DeGroote School of Business, who assisted in library research work.

I would also like to acknowledge the generous financial support for the research that underlies this book. *Product Leadership* is very much a fact-based book. Indeed, my colleagues and I have amassed probably the largest database in the world on new product launches and new product business performance. So the book has decades of research as its foundation. But academic research needs funding, and I sincerely thank those people and businesses who generously donated, without seeking anything in return. Special thanks to: William Brennan, Esso Chemical Canada (Exxon in Canada), who has sponsored our research for over a decade; Lawson Mardon Packaging Company, now headquartered in Switzerland (and especially Larry Tapp, formerly CEO, who funded my research chair); Sally Ginter of Dow Chemical, who supports the research; and Dr. Chris Bart, Director, Innovation Research Centre at McMaster University, whose grants also help fund the work.

1

Winning Is Everything

In war, there is no prize for the runner-up.
—Omar Bradley, U.S. General

New Products Warfare

Companies everywhere are engaged in a new products war. The battle-fields are the marketplaces around the world for everything from consumer electronics to new engineering resins, from potato chips to computer chips.

The combatants are the many companies who vie for a better position, a better share, or new territory on each battlefield or marketplace. They include the large and well-known combatants—the IBMs, Procter & Gambles, GEs, Du Ponts, and 3Ms, as well as an increasing number of foreign players—BASF, Sony, ICI, JVC, and Siemens. More recent entrants have gained prominence in the past few decades because of new product victories: Microsoft with computer software, Glaxo with pharmaceuticals, Hewlett-Packard with laser printers, Northern Telecom with telecommunications equipment, and Intel with computer chips.

The costs of this warfare are enormous. By the 1990s, the cost of R&D in the G-5 countries* had exceeded *one billion dollars per day!* That's far higher than the cost of any recent military war.[1] And as much as 5 percent of national economies are devoted to this new products

*The United States, Japan, Germany, Great Britain, and France.

1

warfare.* Other, not so obvious costs are the many victims of this war—the companies that simply disappear or are gobbled up by the victors.

The weapons of this war are the thousands of new products developed every year in the hope of successfully invading chosen marketplaces. But most new product attempts fail. Increasingly the quest is for weapon superiority—seeking product differentiation in order to secure a sustainable competitive advantage. Positioning plays a key role too, as combatants deploy their troops to secure an advantageous position on the battlefield. They use tactics such as frontal assaults, outflankings, and even attempts to reposition the enemy.

The combatants have their shock troops that lead the way into battle—the sales teams, advertising people, and promotional experts. The cost of these shock troops is enormous (it costs Procter & Gamble more than $100 million to launch a new brand in the United States). But the battle is often decided by the unsung heroes—the infantry—the many engineers and scientists in R&D labs and engineering departments around the world—less glamorous and less visible, but at the heart of almost every victory.

The Generals Decide on the Strategy

As the senior executives, you are the generals. It is you who plan and chart direction, and attempt to define a *business* and *technology strategy* for your business. You generals speak in terms of strategic thrusts, strategic arenas, and the need for strategic alignment. Sadly, many generals have not really grasped the art of new product or technology strategy very well. So, as is often the case with ill-defined strategy, the battle is won or lost tactically in the trenches by the shock troops and infantry. As a result, you generals must also be concerned about tactics as well—about the details of how the battle will be fought. This means that the generals must ensure that the right processes are in place to make the tactics happen, namely, *an effective new product process*. Finally, generals concern themselves with *resources*—about how many resources to commit to product development, and about where to deploy them—to which battlefields or arenas of strategic focus.

---

*For example, the United States spends about 3 percent of its GNP on R&D. We estimate, from our studies, that about half of this R&D goes to product development (as opposed to process development and improvements, and other technical activities). For every dollar spent on new product R&D, about another two dollars are required for marketing, capital, and production expenditures.

Winners and Losers

As in any war, there are winners and losers. The winners are those firms, such as Merck, 3M, Microsoft, and Hewlett-Packard, who have an enviable stream of new product successes year after year. There are losers as well: General Motors, who for the past decade or so, failed to launch new products that captured the consumer's interest (while Chrysler, given up for dead in the 1970s, rebounded with the K-car and Minivan, and has hit the market with one winning new product after another in recent years). Sometimes the defeat is so great that the combatant collapses and simply disappears. Apple Computers, once the leader in PCs, is now facing difficult times. Although there are many reasons for Apple's problems, its unsuccessful *Newton*, the much-heralded handheld personal digital assistant, symbolized Apple's slide. Remember the *Newton*: it could read handwriting as data entry. But the product didn't work: it was unable to read up to half the handwritten input. Users quickly became frustrated, and the word got out. Sales never materialized, and Apple was finally forced to withdraw the product.

It's War: Innovate or Die

As the twenty-first century begins, this new products war looms as the most important and critical war the companies of the world have ever fought. The message to senior people is this: innovate or die! Winning in this new products war is everything. It is vital to the success, prosperity, and even survival of your organization. Losing the war, or failing to take an active part in it, spells disaster. The annals of business history are replete with examples of companies who simply disappeared because they failed to innovate, failed to keep their product portfolio current and competitive, and were surpassed by more innovative competitors.

Profitability and Speed

In winning at new products, as in warfare or war games, the goal is victory—a steady stream of profitable and successful new products. On this new product battlefield, the ability to mount lightning attacks—well-planned but swift strikes—is increasingly the key to success. *Speed is the new competitive weapon.* The ability to accelerate product marketing ahead of competition and within the window of opportunity is more than ever central to success. And so this book is about more than success;

it's about how to get successful products to market, and in record time. There are major payoffs to speeding products to market:

- *Speed yields competitive advantage.* The ability to respond to customers' needs and changing markets faster than the competition, and to beat competitors to market with a new product often is the key to success. But too much haste may result in an ill-conceived product, which has no competitive advantage at all!

- *Speed yields higher profitability.* The revenue from the sale of the product is realized earlier (remember: money has a time value, and deferred revenues are worth less than revenues acquired sooner); and the revenues over the life of the product are higher, given a fixed window of opportunity and hence limited product life.

- *Speed means fewer surprises.* The ability to move quickly to market means that the original commercial assumptions are probably still valid, and that the product as originally conceived is more likely to meet market requirements. The short time frame reduces the odds that market conditions will dramatically change as development proceeds. Then consider the *seven-year development effort* incurred by some U.S. auto companies: here, market requirements, market conditions, and the competitive situation are likely to have changed considerably from beginning to end of the project.[2]

So speed to market is a preoccupation throughout this book but *not at the expense of managing the project properly.*

There is a dark side to speed. Our studies of hundreds of new product winners and losers show that there is a strong and positive connection between speed and profits; but the connection is anything but one-to-one. Many of the actions project teams take in the interest of saving a little time often have the exact opposite effect, and in some cases, destroyed the profitability of the venture. So, I will never recommend cutting corners in haste or executing in a sloppy fashion in order to save time—it just doesn't pay off. In short, speed is important, but it is only one component of our all-important goal of profitable, big new product winners.

Fact-Based Management

Military principles are based on facts—facts gathered by military historians and strategists who have studied countless wars and battles since the beginning of time. This book and its prescriptions are also very much fact-based. Since the 1970s, my colleagues* and I have investigated almost 2,000 new product launches and hundreds of companies. The goal: to uncover what winners do differently from losers; what the common denominators of successful new products and businesses are; and what distinguishes the top performers.

▶ Some of our studies have focused on *individual new product projects* (we call these the *NewProd project studies*). Two recent investigations that I often cite include: a study of 203 new North American industrial new product projects consisting of 123 successes and 80 failures; and a study of 103 North American and European new products from the chemical industry.[3] In both, multiple gauges of product performance—profitability, market share, meeting objectives, and so on—were measured; similarly, many characteristics of the project—from the nature of the market to how proficiently the project team executed key activities—were gauged, and then correlated with success in order to identify those factors that distinguish the big new product winners.

▶ Some other studies looked at the business or company, rather than individual projects, and asked the broader question: why are some businesses so much better at new products than others? We call these the *benchmarking studies*. In the most recent one, which I often refer to, business units' new product performances were gauged on 10 metrics (such as percentage of sales from new products; or return on investment [ROI] on R&D spending), that were then reduced to two key dimensions: *profitability* and *impact*. The drivers of business units' new product performance were then identified.[4]

Depending on the type of study—at the project level, or a study of business units—the success factors uncovered are somewhat different. However, regardless of the study, the fundamental question was always the same: what makes for a winner?

These studies have been widely published (they have resulted in over 75 publications in leading journals); they have an international focus;

---

*I do not claim credit for all the research work. My colleagues, whom I have worked with, and whose research findings are part of this book, include: my immediate colleagues and co-researchers, namely Professors Elko Kleinschmidt and Scott Edgett; and others I have worked with (in alphabetical order), namely, Professors Ludwig Bstieler, Roger Calantone, Ulrike de Brentani, Chris Easingwood, and Chris Storey.

and together they represent the most comprehensive studies in new product management practices undertaken to date.[5] It is on this research foundation that the current book has been constructed.

Key Points for Management

New products is a war, no longer just a game. Victory in this war ultimately decides the fate of your business. Key questions to ponder:

▸ Do you and the other members of the leadership team of your business recognize that you are indeed at war, and that this war merits your undivided time and attention?

▸ Are you leading your business the way generals would run their warfare operations; for example . . .
  • have you mapped out a strategy for this war—a new product and/or technology strategy?
  • have you defined the battlefields or strategic arenas where you wish to fight?
  • have you thought about tactics—about the details of how new products should be brought to market?
  • and is speed—lightning attacks, fast mobilization—a key ingredient in your battle plan?

If not, you're not quite ready for this war. So read on and prepare yourself.

The Role of Senior Management

You Are the General

This book is for you, the generals of industry: the CEOs, general managers, managing directors, VPs, and directors who aspire to lead their businesses to victory in the new products war. Your duty as a member of the leadership team of your business is to *lead*. And what could be more important these days than to lead the new product charge? More than most business endeavors today, this effort will shape your business strategy and will determine your company's fortunes.

The trouble is, some generals have not been trained for the new products war. And that's where this book provides some guidance. In the first few chapters, we outline the critical success factors in product innovation—those factors that our research finds consistently distinguish successful businesses—the victors—from unsuccessful businesses in the new products war.

The Biocides business unit at Rohm and Haas in Philadelphia is one of the winners. The business was born in the 1970s, the result of a stunning new product success in biocidal agents (biocides are chemicals that prevent bacteria, fungi and other biological organisms from growing; most nonedible liquids, from paint to papermill fluids, contain minute amounts of biocides). Since this first new product, the business has gone from strength to strength; and today, it is one of Rohm and Haas's most successful and profitable businesses. The secret to that profitable growth is one new product and new application winner after another.

The business's general manager, Howard Levy, has led the business from its inception. Howard has never forgotten what won the first battle, and so he has continued to emphasize new products as a leading edge of his business strategy. His was the first business at R&H to implement a formal new product process—a template designed to drive products to market quickly and successfully. Howard and his leadership team play a key role in project selection and new product portfolio management; they also focus directly on the business's new product strategy, having mapped out a technology and market strategy to guide the innovation effort.

The point is that the leadership team must recognize that product innovation is a business priority, and that they must lead here.

Cornerstones of Performance

Speaking of victors, here's a preview of the three success factors or cornerstones of new product performance that emerge from our studies (Figure 1.1):

1. Having a *new product strategy for the business* (it was surprising in our recent benchmarking study how many businesses simply lack a new product strategy altogether!).
2. Having the right *resources*, sufficient resources, and most important, deploying your resources wisely—to the right strategic arenas and projects.
3. Having a *new product process* that works—a template or tactical road map to drive new products to market quickly and successfully.[6]

Figure 1.1   Three Cornerstones of Performance

Reprinted with permission from R. G. Cooper & Kleinschmidt, E. J., "Benchmarking firms' new product perfromance and practices," *Engineering Management Review* 23, 3, Fall 1995, 112–120. © 1995 IEEE.

I introduce these three proven cornerstones of success to underscore the fact that each of these drivers, and hence success, is within the control of the leadership team of the business. Note that the Biocides management group takes a direct and close interest in all three areas. We'll spend much more time on each of these three cornerstones, and also look more closely at our benchmarking results. The point I make here is that *you can control, manipulate, and alter* these key new product parameters—strategy, resources, and tactical roadmap or process—and in so doing, *you dictate the new product outcomes for your business.*

The trouble is, too many business leaders seem not to be terribly interested in their responsibility to product development: a "hands-off" management approach. They talk the talk—about how important product development is—but often fail to walk the talk . . . for example, fail to make the needed resource commitments, or distance themselves from key new product decisions. Perhaps it is because senior people are so focused on short-term, day-to-day issues; or maybe you view product development as a bit of a mystery; or you assume that product development is "an R&D thing," and "those techies" or scientists will take care of it.

Wrong on all counts! Fast-paced, successful product development is perhaps the *most important challenge faced by today's companies.* So it is most important that you leaders get involved; you must understand the critical success factors, and how you manipulate each; and, most important, you must indeed lead!

I am always surprised when I see senior management failing here. A senior management meeting had been called to discuss product development in a major utility company, where management had proclaimed that new products and services were the key to the future in their deregulated market. About half the senior people were absent, including the marketing VP. Some fairly lame excuses were made for most absentees. My response to this dismal showing was direct: "What on earth could be more important than your future . . . more important than making decisions about what product and service offerings you will offer—in effect, decisions about the fate of your company in the marketplace?" There was silence, because everyone in the room knew that *nothing was more important,* that some senior people had become sidetracked by urgent, but not important issues. And they were shirking their leadership responsibilities.

Senior Management in Winning Businesses

Businesses whose senior managements are strongly committed to and very much involved in their new product efforts do much better, according to our benchmarking studies.[7] Such businesses with greater senior management involvement in new products boast much higher impact efforts (for example, new products impacted strongly and positively on the business's sales and profits) and also a very positive overall success rating.

Businesses where senior managements lead their new products efforts, and in so doing, achieve superlative results, are ones where:

- senior management is *strongly committed* to new products and product development.
- management commits the *necessary resources* to achieve the firm's new product goals.
- senior management is *closely involved in the project Go/Kill* and new

product spending decisions—they have a central role in the new product project review process and in resource allocation decisions.

At the project level, in our studies of hundreds of new product projects, one conclusion is that top management support is critical to getting individual new product projects to market. Without top management support, there is much less hope of securing the needed resources and approvals to proceed. This comes as no surprise. Perhaps more provocative is that top managers support failures with almost equal frequency as they do successes! That is, executive-sponsored projects don't do so well: they get to market alright, but their success rates are fairly average.

A very clear picture for senior management emerges from our research: You must lead, but not micro manage. Don't get caught up in the trap of overinvolving yourselves in the day-to-day management of individual new product projects, or of driving your own "pet projects" to market. It's often tempting to do this, but *that's not leadership* and *it's not your role!*

Rather, your role is very much that of an enabler—to set the stage (but not necessarily be an actor, front and center); to be a behind-the-scenes facilitator; and to create an environment that fosters product development.[8] This sounds like a worthwhile personal goal, but what does this mean in practice? Here are the key ingredients of new product success that studies have uncovered and that have a direct bearing on your actions and your leadership:

1. **You must embrace a long-term commitment to product development.**[9] This is especially difficult in a world where a short-term, financial focus seems to dominate. Look beyond a one-year time horizon and ensure that resources are committed for the longer term (not off again, on again), and that your development portfolio contains a certain proportion of longer-term and platform projects (not just quick, one-year hits).

2. **Then, develop a vision, objectives, and strategy for your new product effort driven by (and linked to) your business's corporate objectives and strategy.** Most business leaders have new product goals alright (for example, "By the year 2005, 32 percent of our revenue will come from new products"); but they don't have a clue how they'll achieve this goal—there is no new product strategy for the business!

3. **Install a systematic, high-quality new product process in your business, and practice discipline, following the principles of the**

process. Many firms do indeed have systematic new product processes, such as *Stage-Gate*™ (almost 60 percent of firms).* Move toward a *third-generation* new product process (15 percent of firms have).[10] But most important, demonstrate that you're committed to the process by your actions, not just your words. Ironically, time and time again, the first ranks to "break discipline" are usually the senior people! They circumvent the process with their executive-sponsored projects; they consistently miss gate meetings; they fail to make timely Go/Kill decisions or ignore the gate criteria altogether; and so on.

4. **Next, make available the necessary resources.** Again this is difficult given the desire to boost short-term profitability. Recognize that if new product success is the goal, there is no free lunch here: our studies clearly show that businesses that commit the money and people on average are blessed with much higher new product performance—profitability, successes rates, and so on. And pay special attention to resource deployment or allocation—where the money is spent.[11]

5. **Finally, foster innovation in your organization.** Create an innovative, positive climate for product development—one that supports, rewards, and recognizes new product efforts in your business. Empower project teams, and support committed champions: act as godfathers, sponsors, or executive champions for major new product projects.

We'll be revisiting each of these five themes as this book unfolds, providing practical direction for you and your leadership team here. But note these five themes—they are what characterize successful businesses when it comes to new product results.

New Products: The Key to Corporate Prosperity

Before you embark on your journey toward more successful product innovation, first consider why there is all this emphasis on new products. Back in the early 1970s, when I began this research, my literature review revealed that there was *hardly anything* written on the topic. Why, then,

*The term *Stage-Gate*™ was coined by the author in the 1980s, and is a trademark of RG Cooper and Associates Consultants Inc., a member company of the Product Development Institute (PDI).

have the 1990s ushered in an unprecedented period of preoccupation with product innovation and getting new products to market?

Simple! New products are your future: they are vital to the success and prosperity of your corporation. The period of downsizing that characterized the mid-1980s to early 1990s is over: senior executives are beginning to sober up to the reality that *no corporation ever shrank itself to greatness.* As we move into the next millennium, the growth game is on—faster than ever. Front and center in this growth game is the desire for new products—successful, significant, winning new products. Driven by rapidly advancing technologies, globalization of markets, and increasing competition at home and abroad, effective new product development is emerging as *the major corporate strategic initiative* of the decades ahead. Those corporations that succeed at new product development will be the future Mercks, HPs, 3Ms, and Microsofts; those companies that fail to excel at new products will invariably disappear or be gobbled up by the winners.[12]

Impact on Sales and Profits

New products now account for about 32 percent of company sales, on average, up significantly from the 1980s. (Here I define a product as "new" if it has been on the market by that company for five years or less.) New products have a similar impact on corporate profits: in the period from 1976 to 1981, new products contributed only 22 percent of corporate profits; this *has grown to 30 percent* in the 1990s. That is, profits from new products account for almost one-third of the bottom line of corporations![13] On an industry-by-industry basis, while some high-technology industries approach 100 percent of sales and profits from new products, even mature industries are remarkably close to the mean values here.

The Best Really Shine

These percentages are only averages, and thus understate the potential. What CEO wants to be average! A minority of firms do much better than average, according to a recent PDMA's best practices study.[14] These 22 percent of firms—the Best—are compared to the Rest. The Best . . .

- have 49.2 percent of sales derived from new products (versus 25.2 percent for the Rest);

- see 49.2 percent of profits derived from new products (versus 22.0 percent for the Rest); and
- start with 3.5 ideas to achieve one winner (versus 8.4 ideas for the Rest).

The point is that stellar performance is attainable in new products warfare: these firms model the way.

Exceptional Profits

New products are also very profitable, on average. A study of 203 representative new product launches in U.S. businesses reveals that approximately two-thirds are considered to be commercial successes.[15] And these winning products do exceptionally well (see Figure 1.2 and Table 1.1):[16]

- return on investment is astounding: the average ROI for successful new products is 96.9 percent;
- new products pay off very quickly: the average payback period is 2.49 years; and
- they achieve an excellent market position: the average market share in their defined target markets is 47.3 percent.

Averages don't tell the entire truth, because as might be expected, a handful of very big winners skew the results. So consider the median values, which are almost as impressive:

- 50 percent of successful new products achieve a 33 percent ROI or better;

Table 1.1 Profitabilities of New Products

	Average Values		Median Values	
	Successes	**Failures**	**Successes**	**Failures**
Return on Investment (%)	96.5	8.3	33	3
Payback Period (years)	2.49	65.1	2	20
Market Share (%)	47.3	12.4	35	2

Note: These are the same numbers shown in Figure 1.2, but in table format here.

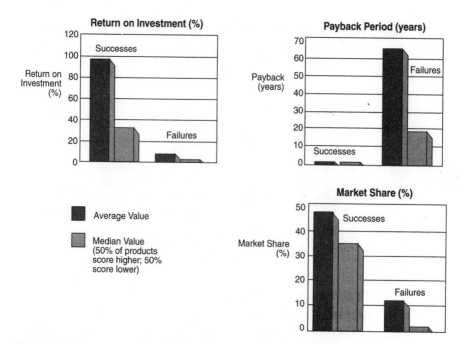

Figure 1.2 Profitability of New Products: Successes vs. Failures
Source: Cooper & Kleinschmidt, endnote 15

- half have a payback period of two years or less; and
- half achieve a market share in excess of 35 percent.

Not all the new ventures studied are winners, however; so these exceptional performance results must be tempered with the cost of failure. And in this study, about one-third are unsuccessful launches. But even factoring in these losses, product development must be considered a very profitable undertaking overall.

Impact on Investment Value

Why is product innovation so important these days? One factor is the financial market, which seems to dominate corporate behavior. An annual *Fortune* survey rates top U.S. corporations on a number of criteria, including "value as a long-term investment." Using data supplied by *Fortune,* I studied various predictors of investment value. The results are provocative. *The single strongest predictor of investment value is "degree of innovativeness of the company."* A typical industry relationship—how innovativeness affects investment value—is shown for the chemical industry in Figure 1.3; other industries showed much the same relation-

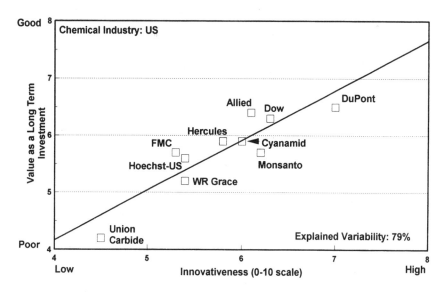

Figure 1.3 Impact of Innovativeness on Value as a Long-Term Investment

R.G. Cooper, "Stage-gate systems: A new tool for managing new products." Reprinted from *Business Horizons* 33, 3, May–June 1990. Copyright 1990 by the Foundation for the School of Business at Indiana University. Used with permission.

ship. The conclusion is that product innovation is not only important to remain competitive in the firm's marketplace; it also seems to be important to financial markets in determining the worth or value of the company as a long-term investment, and hence to the cost of capital to the firm.[17]

A recent *Fortune* survey lists the most admired major corporations in America.[18] In the top 10 are firms such as Coca-Cola, Merck, Microsoft, Johnson & Johnson, Intel, Pfizer, and Procter & Gamble. Coincidentally, all of the most admired companies are the top one or two firms in their industries in terms of *innovativeness*. In the same *Fortune* issue, another article entitled "Secrets of America's Most Admired Corporations" reveals that *new ideas* and *new products* are the key: to be genuinely admired, these businesses posses a common quality—"that ingredient is innovation, and all the top companies embrace it passionately."[19]

Huge Amounts at Stake

Research and development expenditures are also impressive. In the United States, R&D expenditures recently reported amounted to $166 billion annually, or about 2.54 percent of the gross domestic product

(GDP). In Japan and Germany, R&D spending is similarly high at 2.94 and 2.37 percent of GDP, respectively.[20]

Certain industries, noted for their growth and profitability in recent decades, spend heavily on R&D. For example, the software industry spends almost 20 percent of sales on R&D; the computer communication equipment industry averages 12.5 percent of sales on R&D; pharmaceuticals averages 11.5 percent; and chemicals averages almost 7 percent (see Table 1.2 for an industry breakdown).

The Drivers of Innovation

New products are clearly the key to corporate prosperity. They drive corporate revenues, market shares, bottom lines, and even share prices. But why is product innovation speeding up so much, and why is so much more emphasis being placed on your product innovation track record? One recent book even likens the innovation phenomenon to the *international arms race* between 1950 and 1990.[21] Here are four drivers of product innovation identified by senior executives.[22]

- *Technology advances:* The world's base of technology and know-how increases at an exponential rate, making possible solutions and products not even dreamed of a decade or so ago. What was science fiction and featured on "Star Trek" in the 1970s—for example, hand-held computers or micro (nonintrusive) surgery—is suddenly a technological reality today.

- *Changing customer needs:* Marketplaces are also in turmoil, with market needs and wants, and customer preferences changing regularly. The company that seemed omnipotent only a few years ago suddenly falls from favor with the consumer. Witness IBM's current problems, as corporate customers have shifted their desires dramatically away from mainframe computers (IBM's traditional strength) to much smaller computers and LAN servers in recent years. In other markets, customers have come to expect new products with significant improvements. We consumers have become like kids in a candy shop: we see what is possible, and we want it.

- *Shortening product life cycles:* If you have the impression that the world is moving much faster, it's not that you're getting older—it really has speeded up! A study done by A. D. Little shows that product life cycles have been cut by a factor of about 4 over the past 50 years (see Figure 1.4).[23] Your new product no longer has a life of

Table 1.2   20 Largest R&D Spending Industries (U.S.)

Industry	R&D Spending (millions $) 1997	R&D $ as % of Sales	R&D as % of Margin	Annual R&D % Growth (1997 vs. 1996)
Aircraft	2,183	4.2	24.4	−4.6
Chemicals and allied products	6,593	5.9	14.7	8.2
Computer and office equipment	20,938	6.1	15.8	4.5
Computer communication equipment	3,449	12.5	21.5	20.0
Computer peripheral equipment	2,240	6.3	14.9	11.7
Electronic equipment	11,212	4.8	16.6	4.2
Electronic computers	3,449	4.6	18.2	8.7
Food and kindred products	3,595	1.4	4.3	5.8
Household audio and video equipment	7,657	6.2	23.4	8.9
Motor vehicle parts, accessories	1,928	3.2	15.7	5.9
Motor vehicles and car bodies	28,316	4.7	26.3	8.7
Petroleum refining	5,254	0.5	2.2	4.8
Pharmaceuticals	25,562	11.5	16.3	11.6
Phone communication, radio-telephone	24,504	4.8	10.6	2.0
Photographic equipment and supplies	3,569	6.5	11.2	3.6
Prepackaged software	11,506	19.9	26.8	17.9
Radio, TV, broadcast, communication equipment	5,344	9.1	28.7	15.3
Semiconductor, related devices	9,897	8.2	17.7	13.1
Special industry machinery	2,102	10.3	22.6	21.0
Telephone equipment	9,207	9.8	29.3	13.7

Source: *R&D Ratios & Budgets,* June 1997 edition, Schonfield & Assoc., Lincolnshire, Ill.

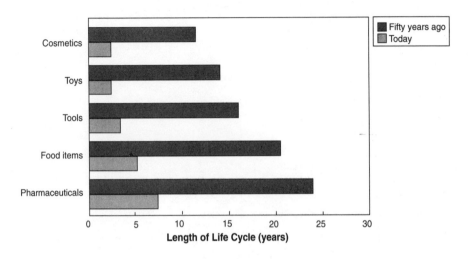

Figure 1.4 Decreasing Product Life Cycles
Source: A. D. Little as cited in von Braun; see endnote 1.

five to 10 years, but within a few years, sometimes even months, it
is superseded by a competitive entry, rendering yours obsolete and
necessitating a new product. This has placed much pressure on
businesses and their managements. For example, in one leading
electronics firm in the United States, as product version number 1 is
hitting the market, its replacement, product version 2, is already in
the Development phase, and product version 3 is waiting in the
wings for a Go-to-Development decision.

▶ *Increased world competition:* Your business now has access to foreign
markets like never before, but at the same time, your domestic market has become someone else's international one. This globalization
of markets has created significant opportunities for the product innovator: the world product targeted at global markets. It has also
intensified competition in every domestic market. Both factors
have sped up the pace of product innovation.

A quick review of all four drivers of product innovation reveals that
none is likely to disappear in the next decade or two. Technology advances will continue to occur; so will changes in market needs and demands; world trade and globalization of markets march on, spurred by
trade agreements and the creation of free trade zones; and competition
will drive life cycles to become even shorter. Product innovation will be
even more critical to corporate prosperity in the years ahead than it has
been in the recent past.

Key Points for Management

Management must lead, because new products are your key to business prosperity. Consider . . .

- the high-profit impact that new products have (or should have) on your sales and profits.
- the impact that innovativeness has on your business's valuation or share prices.
- where your future sales and profits will come from.

Compare yourself to industry averages: 32 percent of sales and 30 percent of profits. But who wants to be merely average? The top performers do much better than this, so this should be your goal: 49 percent of both sales and profits!

Next, think about how profitable successful new products are—the spectacular ROIs, paybacks, and market shares achieved by winning new products. Very few other investments in your business offer these high rewards and returns.

Next there are financial markets to consider. Not so long ago, a steady and profitable business was what *Wall Street* valued. That is still true, except increasingly the investment community is looking for growth and a solid new product track record. This investment community cannot be ignored: they determine your share price, your price earnings (P/E) ratio, and ultimately your business's cost of capital.

Don't forget the resource commitments. If your business is typical, chances are you're already spending a lot on new product development. But are you spending enough? Compare yourself to the norms in Table 1.2, but recognize that R&D spending is only 35 to 40 percent of the total cost of product innovation. There are also marketing, production, and capital expenditures.

Finally, as you look to the future, consider the drivers of innovation in your industry: technology advancing at an ever increasing pace; rapidly changing customer needs; shortening product life cycles; and increased world competition. None of these four drivers is about to disappear; indeed, in the next millennium, expect these four drivers to be stronger than ever.

So take charge of your business's innovation efforts. The payoffs are too huge, and the costs too great to be ignored.

Warning: It's Not So Easy to Win

No one said this would be easy. In new products warfare, one always faces a dilemma. On the one hand, you recognize that new products are critical to your business's long-term success. They keep your current product portfolio competitive and healthy, and in many companies, provide you with long-term and sustainable competitive advantage. The problem is that product innovation is fraught with dangers and pitfalls: boasting a steady stream of successful new products is no small feat.

The hard realities are that the great majority of new products never make it to market. And those that do face a failure rate somewhere in the order of 25 to 45 percent. These figures vary, depending on what industry and on how one defines a "new product" and a "failure." Some sources cite the failure rate at launch to be as high as 90 percent. But these figures tend to be unsubstantiated, and are likely wildly overstated. According to Crawford, who has undertaken perhaps the most thorough review of these often-quoted figures, the true failure rate is about 35 percent.[24] Our own studies concur: we find the average *success rate* of developed products* to be about 67 percent. But averages often fail to tell the whole story: this success rate varies from a low of 0 percent to a high of 100 percent, depending on the company![25]

Other studies point to the difficult times faced by new product managers. A PDMA study reveals that new products have had a success rate of only 59 percent at launch over the past five years.[26] The Conference Board reports a median success rate of 66 percent for consumer products and 64 percent for industrial goods (defined as success in the marketplace after launch).[27] Booz-Allen & Hamilton cite a 65 percent success rate for new product launches.[28]

Regardless of whether the success rate is 55 or 65 percent, the odds of a misfire are still substantial. Worse, the figures cited above don't include the majority of new product projects that are killed along the way, long before launch, yet involve considerable expenditures of time and money.

The attrition curve of new products tells the whole story. One study reveals that for *every 7 new product ideas, about 4 enter development, 1.5 are launched, and only 1 succeeds.*[29] Another investigation paints an even more dismal picture: for every 11 new product ideas, 3 enter the development phase, 1.3 are launched, and only 1 is a commercial success in

---

*That is, projects that emerged from the Development phase. Note that many projects are killed during Development or before.

the marketplace (see Figure 1.5).[30] The most recent PDMA survey reveals a 7-to-1 ratio.[31] The bad news continues. An estimated 46 percent of all the resources allocated to product development and commercialization by U.S. firms are spent on products that are cancelled or fail to yield an adequate financial return.[32] This is an astounding statistic when one considers the magnitude of human and financial resources devoted to new products. But a minority of firms (30 percent) do achieve an enviable 80 percent success rate: that is, 80 percent of the resources they spend on innovation go to new product winners. These few firms show that it is possible to outperform the average, and by a considerable margin.

Key Points for Management

How well is your company faring in the new products war? Do you even know? Most companies cannot provide fact-based statistics on success, fail and kill rates, on the proportion of resources spent on winners versus losers, or other key performance metrics. When was the last time you went golfing with serious golfers, and they turned to you and said, "Let's not keep score!" Serious players keep score. Do you?

Keep score in the new products war. Key statistics to track include:

- success versus failure rates at launch.
- attrition rates: what percent of projects continue at each stage (or gate) in the process?
- proportion of resources devoted to winners versus losers versus killed projects.

In Chapter 4, which deals with the new product process, I provide you with a list of "in-process" and "post-process" metrics to help you keep score here.

What's New about a New Product

Serious players keep score in new products warfare. But in order to keep score, one first must have a definition of what counts as a new product. One of the problems with some of the scores cited above is that they include different types of new products: for example, the attrition rates

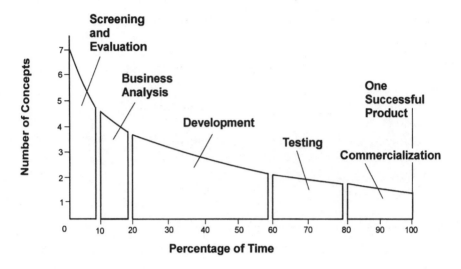

Figure 1.5 The Attrition Rate of New-Product Projects
Source: Averaged over results from several studies: see endnotes 13, 22, 30. Most heavily weighted on [30].

for truly innovative new products are much higher than for extensions and modifications of existing company products.

Defining Newness

How does one define a "new product," " innovativeness," or "newness"? There are many different types of new products. "Newness" can be defined on two dimensions:

▶ *new to the company,* in the sense that your business has never made or sold this type of product before, but other companies might have. Nonetheless you must still incur the costs of development and launch, and face all the risks associated with a new initiative.

▶ *new to the market* or "innovative": the product is the first of its kind on the market. This is the traditional definition of "new product"; but if you adhered to this definition alone, you'd exclude much of the product development effort that takes place within your business.

Categories of Newness

Viewed on a two-dimensional map, as shown in Figure 1.6, six different types or classes of new products have been identified.

1. *New-to-the-world products:* These new products are the first of their kind and create an entirely new market. This category represents

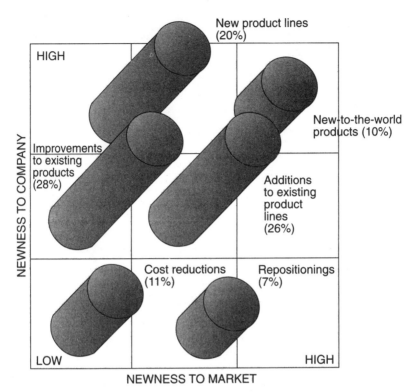

(Height of cylinder denotes number of introductions relative to total)

Figure 1.6 Categories of New Products

Reprinted with permission of Booz-Allen & Hamilton from *New Product Management for the 1980s* (New York: Booz-Allen & Hamilton, 1982).

only 10 percent of all new products, according to a Booz-Allen & Hamilton study.[33] Well-known examples include the Sony Walkman, the first home compact disc player, and 3M's Post-It Notes.

2. *New product lines:* These products, although not new to the marketplace, nonetheless are quite new to the particular firm. They allow a company to enter an established market for the first time. For example, Canon was not the first to launch an office version of a laser printer; Hewlett-Packard was, with its LaserJet. When Canon did introduce its version, it was clearly not an innovation, but it did represent a new product line for Canon, with all the investment that entailed. About 20 percent of all new products fit into this category.

3. *Additions to existing product lines:* These are new items to the firm, but fit within an existing product line the firm makes. They may also represent a fairly new product to the marketplace. An example is Hewlett-Packard's introduction of its LaserJet-6, a more

up-to-date and powerful version of its laser printers. The printer is a new item within the LaserJet line, and its added features and resolution made it somewhat novel or "new to the market." Such new items are one of the largest categories of new product—about 26 percent of all new product launches.

4. *Improvements and revisions to existing products:* These "not-so-new" products are essentially replacements of existing products in a firm's product line. They offer improved performance or greater perceived value over the "old" product. These "new and improved" products also make up 26 percent of new product launches. For example, Mobil Chemicals produces modified polyolefin plastics. A significant percentage of its R&D effort goes into product "tweaks"—that is, modifying existing polymers in order to respond to a changing customer requirement or a competitive threat.

5. *Repositionings:* These are essentially new applications for existing products, and often involve retargeting an old product to a new market segment or for a different application. For years, aspirin (or ASA, as it is known in some countries) was the standard headache and fever reliever. Superseded by newer, safer compounds, ASA was in trouble. But new medical evidence suggested that aspirin had other benefits. Now aspirin is positioned, not as a headache pill but as a blood clot, stroke, and heart attack preventer. Repositionings account for about 7 percent of all new products.

6. *Cost reductions:* These are the least "new" of all new product categories. They are new products designed to replace existing products in the line, but yield similar benefits and performance at lower cost. From a marketing standpoint, they are not new products; but from a design and production viewpoint, they could represent a significant technical undertaking. They make up 11 percent of all new product launches.

Most firms feature a *mixed portfolio* of new products. The two most popular categories, additions to the line and product improvements or revisions, are common to almost all firms, according to Booz-Allen & Hamilton. By contrast, the "step-out" products—new-to-the-world and new-to-the-firm product lines—constitute only 30 percent of all new product launches, but represent 60 percent of the products viewed as "most successful."

Sadly, many firms stay clear of these two more innovative categories: 50 percent of firms introduce no new-to-the-world products, and another 25 percent develop no new product lines. This aversion to "step-out" and higher-risk products varies somewhat by industry, with higher-technology industries launching proportionately more products that are innovative. New evidence indicates that some higher-risk products, namely, new-to-the-world products, may not be quite so risky: they have excellent successes rates and exceptional profits when successful. This occurs in part because such step-out products tend to be bold innovations with significant competitive advantage; additionally, they are recognized as challenging projects, and management and the project team is able to rise to the occasion—an excellent job is done.[34] By contrast, new product lines to the firm are the opposite: they are assumed to be lower risk, but actually result in lower success rates and mediocre profits on average.

Another Way of Defining a "New Product"

An alternative definition of a "new product"—and one effectively used by Hallmark (cards), GTE, and SC Johnsons Wax—relies on the notion of *commercial risk*. Thus, any change to the product that is *visible* to the customer/consumer, and hence creates a risk to the brand, business, or franchise, is considered to be a new product. This includes genuine new products, line extensions, line additions, and repositionings; but it excludes cost reductions (that are invisible to the customer), process improvements, fundamental research, and maintenance projects.

Recent data from industrial product firms in moderate to high-technology businesses are shown in Figure 1.7 and compared to industry at large.

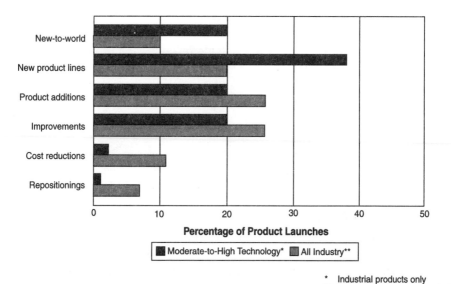

Figure 1.7   How Innovative Are New Products?
Source: see endnotes 22 and 34.

Note the importance of the two most innovative product categories to firms in moderate to high-technology industries: a total of 58 percent of new products launched, compared to 30 percent in all industry.[35]

Key Points for Management

First, arrive at an agreed-on definition of "what is a new product" in your business. Most businesses count at minimum the top four types of products in Figure 1.6. Another definition is "any change in the product that is visible to the customer and hence creates risk to the business"—see previous page. Now that you've defined a new product, you can start keeping better and consistent score.

Next, review the new products that your company or business has introduced in the past five years. Make a complete list. Then categorize them according to the six types in Figure 1.6. Questions to consider include:

1. What is the split of projects by type (percent breakdown)? Does it differ much from the all-industry averages shown in Figure 1.7? Why?
2. What is the breakdown by product type in Figures 1.6 and 1.7 in terms of total resources spent . . . that is, to which types of products has the money and effort been devoted?
3. What is the breakdown by sales and profits . . . that is, which types of products are generating the revenues and profits? What is the success rate by type?
4. Is your current breakdown or split the desirable one? What should be the split of new products by type in Figures 1.6 and 1.7?

An Introduction to the Game

In this chapter, you've seen that winning at new products plays a critical role in determining your business's fortunes. You've also had a quick glimpse at the three cornerstones that distinguish the victors in this new products war. And I've challenged you and your leadership team to play the role of generals and to lead here. Some of the key elements of your leadership role were outlined.

You have also witnessed some of the risks in product innovation: the high odds of failure and significant rates of attrition. But recall that when successful, winning at new products has significant payoffs. Keeping score is an important facet of your war plan, so I laid out a method to help categorize new products in order that the scores can be more comparable. And, finally, you saw some par values or norms for these scores for different types of new products—from the truly innovative to the not-so-new.

In the next chapter, we begin to take a hard look at the evidence. Key findings from our own research, that probes both businesses and projects, are highlighted in Chapter 2. Here you'll learn the common denominators of the top performers and gain insights into what senior management should do. Six critical success factors that focus largely on the new product process are outlined in Chapter 2. Chapter 3 continues with this theme, and introduces seven additional critical success factors, which deal more with strategic issues, and also presents factors important in selecting winning new product investments. These two chapters reveal that there are clear patterns to success, and indeed, that new product success is both predictable and controllable.

Chapter 4 focuses on one of the critical cornerstones of superior performance, namely, the *new product process* itself. Here, the *Stage-Gate*™ process, developed by the author and implemented successfully in hundreds of leading firms worldwide, is outlined. Before you say, "But we already have a new product process in our company," wait! Most such processes either are poorly designed (they lack the vital ingredients of a high-quality process), or they simply haven't been installed well. In this chapter, you'll find out what the requirements and ingredients of a successful new product process are, and, without going into too much detail, gain a solid overview of the *Stage-Gate*™ process, including the third-generation process . . . certainly enough to direct its implementation (or overhaul) in your own business.

Sufficient resources and *effective resource allocation* is a second key cornerstone of new product performance. Chapters 5 and 6 focus on resource issues and on resource allocation decisions. Here senior management has a vital role, since you *are* the resource allocators. Chapter 5 looks at effective gatekeeping—how to make the gates in the new product process work. Note that the leadership team of the business is usually the main gatekeepers in the process; and this chapter is about how you can make more effective gate or Go/Kill decisions on individual projects. Chapter 6 moves to the broader resource allocation topic, namely, *new product portfolio management*, looking at all projects together and as a portfolio of investments.

Chapter 7 considers the third equally critical, but often overlooked, cornerstone of new product performance, namely, *developing a new product strategy for your business*. It's fine to have a new product process—that's how we move the ball down the field (Chapter 4). It's proper to speak about resources and their allocation—that deals with players: how many and what tasks they're assigned (Chapters 5 and 6). Ultimately, however, you must face strategic questions as well: in which arenas should you play the game, and how should you enter each or play the game in each?

The final chapter, Chapter 8, provides an executive summary and wrap-up: an overview of the entire book and a quick listing of the key messages and calls to action.

So read on! Ready yourself for new products warfare: first, witness the critical success factors in the next few chapters, and then how they can and should be built into your business so that you, too, can be a *big winner* at new products.

2

What Separates Winners from Losers: The Critical Success Factors

Those that cannot remember the past are condemned to repeat it.
—**George Santayana, American philosopher**

I am the master of my fate;
I am the captain of my soul.
—**W. E. Henley, Invictus.**

Learning from Past Victories and Defeats

What are the critical success factors in product development—those factors that consistently separate winning products from losers, winning teams from the also-rans, and high-performing businesses from the less stellar ones? The results of our investigations into hundreds of businesses and several thousand individual new products provides many insights:

One of the top performers investigated is a little-known sea food company in Nova Scotia, Canada, called National Sea Products. I select this company as an example, because only a few years ago, the firm faced extinction due to a ban placed on Atlantic cod fishing off the east coasts of the United States and Canada. Besides owning a large fishing fleet, including factory ships, and a number of fish-processing plants, the company's other main asset was its *Highliner* brand name in Canada, under which it sold its packaged frozen fish products in supermarkets.

And so, solutions were sought. Faced with the loss of its main source of supply, the company needed new products badly. An executive-sponsored task force was set up to design and implement a *new product process*—one that incorporated best practices and would translate new product ideas into commercial launches quickly and effectively. The process worked admirably, and within six months, new products—frozen foods and dinner entrées based on other fish, chicken, vegetables, and so on—began to appear on supermarket shelves under the *Highliner* name.

Concurrently, the president, Henry Demone, worked on a *new product strategy* for his business. Like any general, he mapped out his battlefields: branded retail product in Canada; private label in the United States; and food service (hotels, restaurants). He decided priorities across markets, and for each market, how much to spend on R&D (deployment of resources). And finally, for each market, his executive committee agreed on a winning strategy. For example, for retail-Canada, the strategy was to be the innovator: new frozen food products, innovative, top-quality, responsive to emerging consumer food trends, fast to market, and leveraging the well-known *Highliner* name. Other strategies were adopted for food service and private label.

Finally there was the question of *resources*. Even though financial disaster loomed, the company increased its financial commitment to product development. A formal new products group was established—marketing, R&D, brand management, process engineering—dedicated 100 percent to new products. This commitment was remarkable, first because the company was not that large, and second, because most everyone else was downsizing at the time!

The effort worked. The company today is in solid shape; the brand has been strengthened; and National Sea boasts an enviable stable of successful new products. As we stand back and assess how management executed this coup, we see that what National Sea's executives did, perhaps unwittingly, is put in place *the three cornerstones* of high-performing product developers: *strategy, process,* and *resources.*

Indeed, *these three cornerstones* distinguish the higher-performing business units (see Figure 2.1).[1] This is the central finding of our most recent benchmarking study. This study of hundreds business units considered 10 different measures of new product performance, including percentage of sales by new products, success rates, impact on the firm, and overall profitability of the business's total new product efforts.[2]

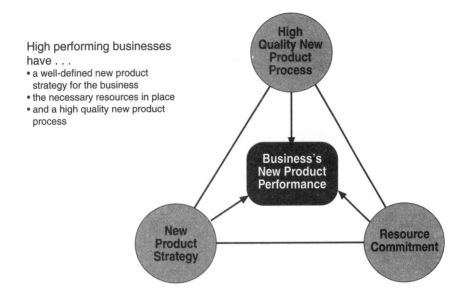

High performing businesses have . . .
- a well-defined new product strategy for the business
- the necessary resources in place
- and a high quality new product process

Figure 2.1 The Three Cornerstones of Performance

Reprinted with permission from: R. G. Cooper & Kleinschmidt, E. J., "Benchmarking firms' new product performance and practices," *Engineering Management Review* 23, 3, Fall 1995, 112–120. © 1995 IEEE.

Then, almost 100 practices and characteristics of these businesses were probed in order to determine what drives high performance.

Here are some details of the three cornerstones of performance—the common denominators of the top performers (see Figures 2.1 and 2.2):

Cornerstone #1: A High-Quality New Product Process

Does your business have a superb new product process or roadmap to guide and speed new products from idea through to launch? The top performers do. Merely having a process does not make the difference, however. It is the nature of that process, and whether it possesses key success ingredients, that makes all the difference. Some of these success factors that top performers build into their processes include emphasizing the up-front, predevelopment homework; building in the voice of the customer throughout; demanding sharp, early product definition; having tough Go/Kill decision points where projects really do get killed; and highlighting quality of execution throughout. More on these elements of a winning process later in the chapter. The new product

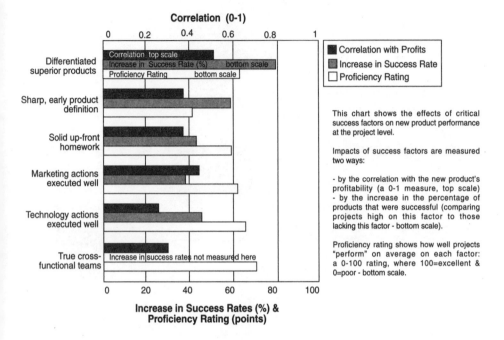

Figure 2.2 Critical Success Factors at the Project Level (NewProd Studies)
Source: NewProd studies, endnote 3 in Chapter 1.

process implemented by our example company, National Sea Products, met and exceeded these criteria—an excellent process, in our judgment. Most firms' new product processes in our studies are not!

Cornerstone #2: A Clear and Well-Communicated New Product Strategy for the Business

Do you have a clearly articulated new product strategy for your business? If so, you're in the minority. But businesses that boast such a strategy do better, according to the benchmarking results. Having a new product strategy for the business means:

- ♦ There are clear goals or objectives for the business's total new product effort; for example, what percentage of sales or profits new products will contribute to the business.
- ♦ There are clearly defined arenas—specified areas of strategic focus, such as products, markets, or technologies—to give direction to the business's total new product effort.

- Specified resources are allocated or deployed against each arena (for example, how much will you spend on product development in market A versus market B; or on technology platform X versus Y?).

- A strategy for how to attack or win in each arena is defined (for example, whether you'll be a niche player, or low-cost provider, or value-added competitor; whether you'll be the innovator or fast follower, and so on).

- The strategy has a long-term thrust and focus, including some long-term projects and platform initiatives (as opposed to a short-term plan and a portfolio of quick hits and incremental projects).

- And finally, the role of new products in achieving the business's goals and the new product strategy for the business are clearly communicated to all who need to know.

Again, National Sea's president had crafted a new product strategy that met most of the above criteria. Sadly, most of the companies in our benchmarking studies are found lacking here too. I'll come back to new product strategy, what it is and how to develop it, later in the book (Chapter 7).

Cornerstone #3: Adequate Resources for New Products

There is no free lunch in the new products war! Some companies in our studies had cut product development efforts—R&D and marketing money and staff—to the bone in an attempt to produce short-term profits. The longer-term effects are, however, very negative. Top performers commit the needed resources; specifically:

- In top-performing businesses, senior management has devoted the necessary resources—people and money, marketing and technical—to achieve the business's new product objectives. By contrast, average and poorer performers tend to be very short on resources and dedicated players. Marketing resources devoted to new products is a particular area of weakness.

- R&D budgets are adequate—judged to be sufficient in light of the business's new product objectives.

    In our benchmarking studies, one medium-sized firm that produced instruments had a clearly articulated goal of being the "number one firm in our industry in terms of product leadership and innovation." A closer look at R&D spending reveals that the firm spent about *half the industry average* on R&D as a percent of sales. There is a serious disconnect between stated goals and spending levels! This type of wishful thinking was far too prevalent among our sample of businesses.

▸ Finally, the necessary people are in place and have their time freed up for new products. The latter is an important point: often people are designated to be on product development teams, but they are not dedicated—they have their "real jobs" too (for example, marketing and operations people). And time was rarely freed up to enable these people to participate in new product projects as fully as they should have. The resources are there in theory, but not in practice!

Key Points for Management

The three cornerstones of successful product development, according to our benchmarking studies, are:

- having a superb new product process for driving products to market quickly and successfully;
- having a defined new product strategy for the business—one that directs the business's new product efforts; and
- having the necessary resources in place—quality and quantity.

Each of these success drivers can be activated by you, the leadership team, and each is a key component of performance.

The rest of this chapter focuses on the *new product process* and on the success factors that make up this process. The challenge this chapter poses is this: deal with this first cornerstone, and overhaul your new product process—but be sure to build in the success factors we outline as this chapter unfolds.

Subsequent chapters deal with the two other cornerstones: resources and strategy.

The #1 Cornerstone: A Quality New Product Process

A *high-quality, superb* new product process is the strongest common denominator among high-performance businesses . . . more powerful than having a new product strategy for the business, or even having the right resources in place (although the three cornerstones of success are intimately connected, and the symbionic effect of all three acting together yields the most positive results—see Figure 2.1).

A word of caution here. The mere existence of a *formal* product development process has absolutely *no effect* on performance, according to the benchmarking studies. There is no correlation at all between merely having a formal process and performance results. The message is this: those companies who mistakenly believe they can "go through the motions" and reengineer their new product processes (usually amounting to documenting what they're already doing!) are in for a big disappointment. Having a process doesn't seem to matter; rather it is *the quality and nature of that process*—building in best practices—that really drives performance.

Six Critical Success Factors
in a Superb New Product Process

1. Management emphasizes doing the up-front homework in the process—both market and technical assessments—*before projects move into the Development phase.*
2. The new product process emphasizes a strong market orientation, and builds in the voice of the customer throughout.
3. A high-quality new product process includes sharp, early product definition, before Development work begins.
4. There are tough Go/Kill decision points in the process, where senior management really does kill projects.
5. There is a focus on quality of execution, where activities in new product projects must be carried out in a quality fashion.
6. The new product process is compete or thorough, where every vital activity is carried out—no hasty corner-cutting here! But the process is also flexible, where stages and decision points can be skipped or combined, as dictated by the nature and risk of the project.

Consider now the *ingredients* of such a superb new product process, and the message they convey to you in senior management:

*1. Management emphasizes doing the up-front homework in the process—both market and technical assessments—***before projects move into the Development phase.**

Too many new product projects move from the idea stage right into Development with little or no assessment or up-front homework. Why?

Because senior management allows it to happen, and because senior management has not mandated or embraced a new product process that demands that solid up-front homework be done! Homework includes those many activities that occur before Development begins: initial screening; market, user and competitive studies; technical and manufacturing appraisals; and financial analysis.

The results of this "ready, fire, aim" approach are usually disastrous. In our NewProd projects studies, inadequate up-front homework is a major reason for failure.[3] Poor market analysis and a lack of market research—moving directly from an idea into a full-fledged development effort, and failure to spend time and money on the up-front steps—are familiar themes in product failures.

By contrast, more homework prior to the initiation of product design and development is consistently found to be a key factor in success. Our research shows that the quality of execution of the predevelopment steps—initial screening, preliminary market and technical studies, market research, and business analysis—is closely tied to the product's financial performance. Successful new product projects have over 1.75 times as many person-days spent on predevelopment steps as do failures. There's more: solid up-front homework drives up new product success rates by 43.2 percentage points and is strongly correlated with performance (see Figure 2.2); and projects that boast solid up-front homework achieve 2.4 times the success rate and 2.2 times the market share as those with poor homework.[4]

Not convinced? There's even more evidence: our benchmarking studies reveal that homework is a key ingredient in a high-quality new product process, and is significantly and positively correlated with performance. More specifically, businesses that consistently build in the up-front homework in projects prior to Development have both more profitable and higher-impact new product efforts than do other businesses (see Figures 2.3 and 2.4).[5] The far right column in Figure 2.4 shows results for those 20 percent of projects that featured superb up-front homework; the left column reveals results of the 20 percent worst projects in terms of homework. The differences are clear. Note also that there are diminishing returns to doing homework—this is not a straight-line relationship, so one must be careful to avoid overkill here.

The clay business is hardly the place where you'd expect to find rampant innovation. Yet even here, solid homework led to a great new product winner, namely, *Opacitex*. Opacitex is a new clay, developed by English China Clay in Atlanta, and aimed specifically at the

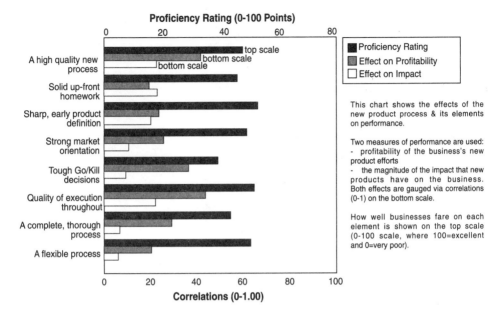

Figure 2.3 How the New Product Process Affects Performance
Source: Benchmarking studies, endnote 4 in Chapter 1.

newsprint industry. It is Opacitex that enabled newspapers, such as *USA Today,* to feature a very white and opaque sheet—one that displays color printing well, and can be printed in color on both sides. Prior to Opacitex, newsprint was almost see-through and off-white— a dirty gray/brown in color. Only fine paper—the kind we use in our offices—was white and opaque. But fine paper and the clay used to make it white, bright, and opaque was far too expensive for the newsprint business.

The story begins in 1986, when an astute marketing specialist at ECC, Eddy Turner, heard that newspaper publishers were hinting about the desire for a white, opaque sheet but *at no extra cost.* "That's not possible," was the typical reply. But Eddy persevered, and began to do his homework:

- He undertook a thorough market analysis of the newsprint industry, and ascertained the volume potential—that part of the market that might benefit from a white sheet.
- Next he worked with his technical people, who undertook a preliminary technical appraisal to see if there were indeed

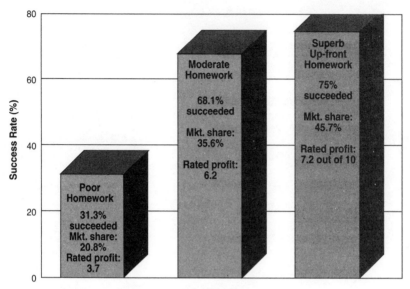

Rated profit: a 0-10 rating, where 10=exceptional, 0=major loss.

Figure 2.4   Impact of Good Up-Front Homework
Reprinted with permission from: R. G. Cooper & Kleinschmidt, E. J. *New Products: The Key Factors in Success.* Chicago: American Marketing Assoc., 1990, monograph.

possible technical and manufacturing options: the concept of using a low-value waste by-product from an ECC processing plant was proposed.

- A preliminary market study, involving visits to numerous newsprint mills, pinned down the requirements for the product. The required paper had to be white and opaque, but not to the degree that fine paper was. The customer wish list was developed. This study also enabled a preliminary "value-in-use analysis" whereby Eddy determined that if clay could replace fiber in the final sheet, then depending on how much fiber was replaced, and the current cost of fiber, the clay had significant and positive economic value to the user. The "values" were calculated for each potential customer (newsprint mills) and potential pricing and economics were assessed.
- More technical homework ensued: some preliminary experiments to show that a possible product that met the customer requirements was technically feasible from the waste stream and at the right cost.

- Next a *concept test* was undertaken. The proposed product—in concept form—was taken to newsprint mills for their reaction. Note that the product *had not yet been developed*, yet Eddy was able to assess market reaction. Intent to purchase was established, and the study also confirmed the exact product requirements and user economics.

All that remained was for Eddy to prepare a business case founded on facts. The management decision, based on Eddy's solid business case, was "Go-for-Development." The project was a big success and indeed changed the face of the newspaper business in North America. But had it not been for the solid homework in the early phases of the project, the economics never would have worked—the key was the value-in-use analysis on users—and the project never would have been approved for Development.

The emphasis that the Japanese place on the planning stage of the new product process is described by Havelock and Elder: Japanese developers make a clear distinction between the "planning" and the "implementation" phases of a new technology initiative. The objective of planning is complete understanding of the problem and the related technology before a Go decision is made. It is reported to be an unrushed process that might look agonizingly drawn out to Western eyes.[6]

A lack of up-front homework seems to be the rule in product development, however. Indeed, most businesses confess to serious weaknesses in the "up-front" or predevelopment steps of their new product process. Pitifully small amounts of time and money are devoted to these critical steps: 7 percent of the money and 16 percent of the work effort. The benchmarking studies score the average quality of up-front homework across businesses at a very mediocre 57.5 points out of 100. (In our studies, businesses rated their proficiencies on each of the performance drivers on a 0 to 100 point scale; here 100 was "excellent" and 0 meant "very poor.") Similarly, in the NewProd projects studies, quality of execution was rated on a zero-to-ten scale for each of 13 key tasks. The results:

- quality of execution across homework or predevelopment tasks is mediocre at best (see Figure 2.2); and

- successful teams undertake superior up-front homework (more time, money, and effort; also better-quality work) and execute the early-stage marketing actions much better than do teams that fail.

The predevelopment, up-front homework activities are important because they qualify and define the project. They answer key success questions such as:[7]

- Is the project an economically attractive one? Will the product sell at sufficient volumes and margins to justify investment in development and commercialization?
- Who exactly is the target customer? And how should the product be positioned?
- What exactly should the product be to make it a winner? What features, attributes, and performance characteristics should be built into it to yield a product that will delight the customer?
- Can the product be developed and at the right cost? What is the likely technical solution and what are the technical risks? And how will it be produced and delivered, with what risks, and at what costs?

Some managers seem skeptical about the need for this vital homework because they're in too big a hurry: "More homework means longer development times to market!" is their excuse. This is a valid concern, but experience shows that homework pays for itself, not only via higher success rates, but also yields reduced development times. The result is faster to market:

- First, all the evidence points to a much higher likelihood of product failure if the homework is omitted (see Figures 2.2, 2.3, and 2.4). So the choice is yours: *fast failures* or thoughtful successes!
- Second, better project definition—the result of sound homework—actually speeds up the development process.[8] Many projects are poorly defined when they enter the Development phase: vague targets and moving goalposts. This is usually the result of weak predevelopment activities: the target user is not well understood, user needs and wants are vaguely defined, and desired product features and performance requirements are cloudy. With a poorly defined product and project, R&D or design people waste considerable time seeking definition, often recycling back several times as project parameters change.
- Third, rarely does a product concept remain the same from beginning to end of the project. The original idea that triggered the pro-

ject is seldom the same as the product that eventually goes to market. Given this inevitable product design evolution, the time to make the majority of these design improvements or changes is not as the product is moving out of Development and into production. More up-front homework anticipates these changes and encourages them to occur earlier in the process rather than later, when they are more costly. The result is considerable savings in time and money at the back end of the project, and overall a more efficient new product process.

Key Points for Management

Take a hard look at your new product process. If homework is typically lacking (it usually is!), then you have no one to blame but yourselves. *Homework doesn't get done because senior management doesn't demand it!* I find that either senior management has failed to establish a process to ensure that the right homework is done, or does not follow the discipline of that process.

The solution: overhaul your new product process. Be sure to build a detailed homework stage (or two) into your process—a homework phase that results in a business case based on fact rather than speculation. These initial screening, analyses, and definitional stages are critical to success. As a member of your business's leadership team, resist the temptation to allow projects to skip over these vital up-front stages, and don't approve an ill-defined and poorly investigated project moving into the Development phase. Insist that solid up-front homework be undertaken—more on this in Chapter 4.

---

2. *The new product process emphasizes a strong market orientation, and builds in the voice of the customer throughout.*

Successful business units, and teams that drive winning new product projects, pay special attention to the voice of the customer. New product projects that feature high-quality marketing actions—preliminary and detailed market studies, customer tests, field trials, and test markets, as well as launch—are blessed with more than double the success rate and 70 percent higher market shares than those projects with poor marketing

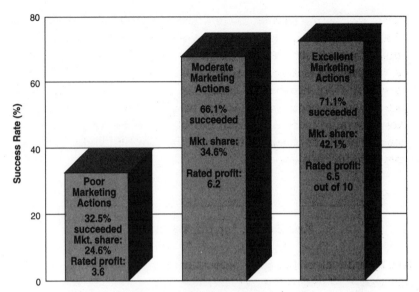

Rated profit: a 0-10 rating, where 10=exceptional, 0=major loss.

Figure 2.5 Impact of a Strong Market Orientation (Voice of Customer)
Reprinted with permission from: R. G. Cooper & Kleinschmidt, E. J. *New Products: The Key Factors in Success.* Chicago: American Marketing Assoc., 1990, monograph.

actions (see Figure 2.5). Further, a strong market orientation increases success rates by 38.6 percentage points and is strongly correlated with new product performance (NewProd projects studies[9]). In our benchmarking studies, a process that emphasizes the customer and marketplace via market studies, market research, concept tests, competitive analysis, customer field trials, and so on, is significantly correlated with the profitability of the business unit's total new product efforts.[10]

Transitions Optical, a joint venture between PPG Industries of Pittsburgh, Pennsylvania and Essilor International, Paris, has a stunning success in the eyeglasses market with its *Transitions III* plastic lenses that adjust to sunlight for prescription eyewear. Extensive market research revealed that consumers were unhappy with the traditional product. This 20-year-old competitive technology was perceived as heavy, for older people, and "worn by farmers." But the concept of variable-tint eyewear—whose tinting changes to accommodate bright sunlight or darker rooms—was appealing. Market research was undertaken in numerous countries to *identify customers' needs* in this lucrative market. The research showed that consumers were looking for lightweight, modern, variable-tint eyewear, whose tinting changed quickly; at the same time, the lens had to be really clear when worn indoors. PPG, a world leader in the production of glass and coatings, was capable of developing the photochromic technology, and Essilor possessed the distribution network. But would the proposed product be a winner? To find out, numerous *concept tests* were undertaken with the proposed product—shopping mall interviews and focus groups of consumers—to confirm customer liking and purchase intent, not only in the United States, but in France, Germany, and the United Kingdom. When *Transitions III* was launched in the mid-1990s, it proved to be *right on* for the market, and very quickly achieved the leading market share. Sales are still growing at 25 to 30 percent yearly.

A failure to adopt a strong market orientation in product innovation, an unwillingness to undertake the needed market assessments, and leaving the customer out of product development spells disaster. It's like a broken record: poor market research, inadequate market analysis, weak market studies, test markets, and market launch, and inadequate resources devoted to marketing activities are common weaknesses found in virtually every study of why new products fail, including our own.

Sadly, a market orientation and customer focus are noticeably lacking in many businesses' new product projects. The marketing actions are among the most weakly executed in the entire new product process, according to both the NewProd and the benchmarking studies. Witness the mediocre scores recording marketing actions (Figures 2.2 and 2.3). These same investigations reveal that relatively few resources and little money are spent on the marketing actions, particularly those that occur in the early stages of the project. Finally, whether businesses build in the voice of the customer and in a quality fashion scores a mediocre 61 points out of 100 in our benchmarking studies.

In one major chemical company, a new product benchmarking analysis of all of its business units revealed a common deficiency: a lack of marketing input in new product projects. A meeting of business unit general managers very quickly identified the reason why: a lack of marketing people. For every 60 scientists, it was estimated *there was only one marketing person;* and often this one person had not been formally trained as a marketer. A resource audit, which looked at typical projects and required tasks, revealed that for this company, the ideal ratio was about *one marketer for every four scientists* . . . not the 60:1 current ratio! Management is now acting on a commitment to dramatically increase the number of marketing professionals.

The message is clear: spare no effort in building the customer or user into your new product process. This means right from the beginning of the process, namely, *ideation:* 75 percent of all successful new products see the idea come from the marketplace. Companies must devote more resources to market-oriented idea generation activities, such as focus groups and panels of customers; market research to determine customer need areas; using the sales force to actively solicit ideas from customers: and developing close or partnering relationships with lead users.[11]

Next, the customer must be *an input into product design*, and not just an after-the-fact check that the design is satisfactory. Too often, market research, when done at all, is misused in the new product process. It tends to be done as an afterthought: after the product design has been decided and to verify that the proposed product indeed has market acceptance. If the results of the market study are negative, most often they are conveniently ignored and the project is pushed ahead regardless. The mistake is clear: market research must be used as an input to the design decisions, and not solely as an after-the-fact check. Investigations to determine users' needs, wants, and preferences and to identify competitive product strategies, strengths, and weaknesses provide insights that are invaluable guides to the design team before they charge into the design of the new product.

Even in the case of technology-push new products (where the product emanates from the lab or design department, perhaps the result of a technological breakthrough or a technology platform project), there still should be considerable marketing input as the technology is shaped into a final product design. That is, following the technical discovery, but before full-fledged development gets under way, there is ample opportunity to research and interact with the customer to determine needs and wants, to shape the final product the way the customer wants it, and to gauge likely product acceptance.

The customer is also an integral facet of the project during the Development phase. Seeking customer inputs and testing concepts or designs with the customer is very much an interactive or "back-and-forth" process. During the Development phase of the project, and after the market research is done, *constant and continuing customer contact* remains essential. Keep bringing the customer into the process to view facets of the product as the prototype or final product takes shape, via multiple iterations of "build and test" or rapid-prototype-and-tests. For example, develop rapid prototypes, working models, or facsimiles of the product as early as possible to show to the customer in order to seek feedback regarding market acceptance and needed design changes. Don't wait until the very end of the Development phase—the field trials or user tests—to unveil the product to the customer. There could be some very unpleasant surprises!

Finally, as the project moves toward commercialization, ensure that rigorous customer tests (perhaps even test markets or trial sells) are built into your process, along with a properly resourced, well-planned Launch phase.

Key Points for Management

Stand back for a moment and consider the process I've just described above, where the customer is an integral part of the Development effort: ideas from the marketplace; market research to understand customer needs and problems so as to flesh out the design; market research to test the proposed product concept before Development begins; rapid prototype-and-test iterations all the way through Development; and solid field trials and test markets prior to Launch.

Are your business's new product projects done this way? Or do yours resemble the typical hit-and-miss approach: you know the customer, so there's no sense researching her needs; only you know the technology, so there's no way you can bring the customer into the Development phase; and so on. If you have a lopsided new product process, one that is dominated by technology and excludes the customer, first, probably you are underperforming; and second, the solution is within your grasp! Start thinking about putting in place *a rigorous, balanced new product process*—one that strikes the right balance between *technology push* and *market pull*. (Later in Chapter 4, we'll see such a process.) And make sure that the needed marketing resources are in place.

---

3. A high-quality new product process includes sharp, early product definition, before Development work begins.

A failure to *define the product*—its target market; the concept, benefits, and positioning; and its requirements, features, and specs—before Development begins is a major cause of both new product failure and serious delays in time-to-market.[12] In spite of the fact that early and stable product definition is consistently cited as a key to success, businesses continue to perform poorly here: the benchmarking studies reveal a modest quality score for the product definition step of 66.8 points out of 100—hardly stellar performance (Figure 2.2).

Our research finds a strong and direct link between sharp, early, stable product definition and success. The benchmarking studies show clearly that sharp, early product definition is significantly correlated with both the profitability and the impact of the firm's total new product efforts. In a similar vein, the NewProd projects studies demonstrate a very strong impact of product definition on performance: early and stable product definition enhances project success rates by 59.2 percentage points; such well-defined projects have 3.7 times the success rate and 1.6 times the market share as those which lack definition; and product definition is significantly and strongly correlated with performance (Figure 2.3).

We're not alone, however: Crawford implores managers to include a "protocol step" just prior to the Development phase, where the requirements of the product are clearly spelled out and agreed to by all parties involved in the project.[13] Getting the product definition right was also uncovered as the key to success in an internal study undertaken by Hewlett-Packard:[14] "The most frequent cause of missed project schedules is unstable product definition. Most (85%) of the manufacturing cost of a product is determined before the design begins."

Some companies undertake excellent product and project definition before the door is opened to a full development project. This definition goes *well beyond a technical definition* (for example, product specifications); it includes:

- specification of the target market: exactly who the intended users are.
- description of the product concept and the benefits to be delivered.
- delineation of the positioning strategy (including the price point).
- and a list of the product's features, attributes, requirements, and high-level specs (prioritized: "must have" and "would like to have").

Some more caveats: This definition is based on facts, the result of solid up-front homework and a strong early customer involvement; it is signed off by all project team members to demonstrate total alignment of all relevant functions; and it is signed off by you, the leadership team of the business, to demonstrate buy-in and functional alignment at the top of the business.

Milltronics is a medium-sized company, and a world leader in the field of instrument manufacture (specifically, process instruments that use ultrasonics for distance and depth measurement). Dave Bignall, the CEO, was convinced that new products were taking too long to move through the Development phase, in part because the product definition was vague at the outset and too many changes were incorporated partway through Development. An audit of past projects was undertaken, and his hunches were proven correct: product definition, early in the game, was clearly a problem.

Dave then led the charge to implement a formal new product process to overcome this and other problems that had been identified. Foremost in the resulting process is a Definition stage, which immediately precedes the Development phase. Vital technical and marketing activities are laid out in this stage to ensure a well-defined product, and one whose specs are not likely to keep changing all the way through Development.

Milltronics's Definitional Step

The second homework stage in Milltronics's new product process is labeled "Definition." Here are some of the key actions:

The marketing people on the project team are required to "define the *winning product concept:* a unique superior product with value to the customer; in the language of the customer & emphasizing customer benefits; and outlining *must* and *preferred* product characteristics (prioritized)."

Concurrently, and with marketing input, the technical team members must "develop Product Specs, including number of models & options."

The key deliverables to the Go-to-Development gate are a defined target market, product benefits, a preliminary marketing plan, including pricing, a set of frozen product specs, and the results of a concept test done on users—signed off by the project team and based on facts.

Projects that have such sharp, early, fact-based definition prior to Development are both more successful and speed to market faster. Here's why:

- ▶ Building a definition step into the new product process forces more attention to the up-front or predevelopment activities. If the homework hasn't been done, then arriving at a sharp definition that all parties will buy into is next to impossible.

▶ The definition serves as a communication tool and guide. All-party agreement or buy-in means that each functional area involved in the project has a clear and consistent definition of what the product and project are and is committed to it: there is functional alignment and consistent priorities across functions.

▶ This definition also provides a clear set of objectives for the Development phase of the project and the Development team members. With clear product objectives, Development typically proceeds more efficiently and quickly: no moving goalposts and no fuzzy targets!

Note that one of the biggest time wasters we uncovered in our NewProd studies is changing product specs. The scenario is this: the project team thinks they have a pretty good idea of customer requirements, so they skip through the homework phase, define the product on paper, and proceed into Development. Much later in the game—perhaps after the prototype or sample has been developed, and during the field trials— the team is made aware of a number of new features or performance requirements that *suddenly must be built into the product*. And so the project must back-track, the product is redefined, and three more months are added to development. It's like trying to score a goal in soccer, but someone keeps moving the goalposts. Note that these new design requirements *aren't really new*; they could have been discovered near the beginning of the project had the team taken the time early on.

Key Points for Management

Sharp, early product definition follows from solid homework and customer involvement (above). When overhauling your new product process, build in a *product definition stage* or phase, as HP has, where the necessary research is undertaken to arrive at a winning and stable product definition. Following this stage, incorporate a *definitional checkpoint or gate* into your process much as Milltronics has, where the leadership team of the business reviews and signs off on the product/project definition. Make it a rule for your management team: no project enters Development without a product definition, based on facts, agreed to by the project team, and signed off by you, the senior management team.

4. *There are tough Go/Kill decision points in the process, where senior management really does kill projects.*

Projects tend to take on a life of their own! In too many companies we investigated, projects move far down the process without serious scrutiny: once a project begins, there is very little chance that it will ever be killed—the process is more like a *tunnel* than a *funnel*. The lack of tough Go/Kill decision points means too many product failures; resources wasted on the wrong projects; and a lack of focus. The result is many marginal projects are approved, while the truly meritorious projects are starved.

Some companies we investigated had implemented *new product portfolio management,* and one of their first revelations is that their portfolio of projects stinks! The truth is that many new product projects in most businesses' portfolios are either . . .

- unfit for commercialization: they are simply bad concepts—a weak market, no fit with the company, or no competitive advantage; or
- low-value projects—projects that can deliver only marginal value to your business.

But new product resources are too valuable and too limited to allocate to the wrong projects. The desire to weed out bad projects, coupled with the need to focus limited resources on the best projects, means that tough Go/Kill and prioritization decisions must be made.

A new product process that features tough Go/Kill decisions is a critical but often missing success ingredient, however. Having tough Go/Kill decisions is strongly correlated with the profitabilities of business units' new product efforts (benchmarking studies). Sadly, tough Go/Kill decision points is *the weakest ingredient* of all process factors studied, with a very poor score of only 49.0 points of out 100 across all businesses.[15] Further, in the NewProd projects studies, for 88 percent of projects investigated, the initial screen is deficient (the decision involves only one decision maker, and/or there are no criteria used to make the decision); 37 percent of projects do not undergo a predevelopment business or financial analysis; and 65 percent do not include a precommercialization business analysis.[16] The fact is that most of the critical evaluation points—from initial screening through to precommercialization business analysis—are characterized by serious weaknesses: decisions not made, little or no real prioritization, poor information inputs, no criteria for decisions, and inconsistent or capricious decision making.[17] In many cases, managers confessed that projects simply aren't killed once they're into Development: projects become like "express trains, slowing down at the stations but never with the intention of stopping until they reach their final destination, market launch."

Often the problem of poor project evaluation boils down to a lack of good criteria against which to judge projects: what is a "good" project? The many studies into success and failure provide insights into what criteria to use. New product success is in fact *fairly predictable:* certain project characteristics consistently separate winners from losers, and in a strong way. These characteristics can and should be used as criteria for project selection and prioritization. But most managers aren't aware of these criteria, or aren't familiar with the various effective screening techniques that all but guarantee better Go/Kill decisions. So the Go/Kill decision usually boils down to a financially based one, which of all methods yields the worst results![18] That's why I devote an entire chapter to the topic of gatekeeping, making better Go/Kill decisions, and what criteria and methods to use (Chapter 5, "Effective Gatekeeping").

Specialty Minerals in Allentown, Pennsylvania, a spin-off company from Pfizer, has developed a unique scoring scheme that management uses both for making Go/Kill decisions on projects at gates as well as for portfolio management. The company uses a five-stage, five-gate new product process. At each gate, the project is judged by management on seven factors:

- Management Interest*
- Customer Interest
- Sustainability of Competitive Advantage
- Technical Feasibility
- Business Case Strength
- Fit with Core Competencies
- Profitability and Impact

These factors are scored at gates on 1–5 scales, and the total score is used to make Go/Kill decisions on individual projects. Management is very aware that overuse of financial criteria (for example, using Net Present Value [NPV]) is problematic: they argue that reliable financial data are simply not available at the very point in a project's life when Go/Kill and prioritization decisions are required. Additionally, management desires a rigorous gate decision tool that employs the appro-

*Modified slightly from Specialty Minerals' exact list.

priate criteria, and in a quantitative fashion, which their scoring model does. Finally, to check that the result is really a funnel, the project attrition curve is displayed—a plot of number of projects passing each gate versus gate number (see Figure 1.5).

Key Points for Management

When you overhaul your new product process, build in a tough Go/Kill gating mechanism. Typically there are about five gates in the average new product process. That's why we call the recommended process a "Stage-Gate" process: stages are preceded by gates.

If you currently have a new product process in your business, chances are you have *milestone review points* but not gates. Milestone reviews are like gates with no teeth. Milestone review points are comfortable meetings, where the progress of the project is discussed and suggestions made—a "feel good" information update. Gates, by contrast, are where you, the leadership team, review the project in depth and decide whether you wish to continue to fund it: gates are very much Go/Kill decision points; they are tough and rigorous; and projects really do get killed! Focus is the result.

The goal is to move from a *tunneling process*—where projects are rarely killed—to a *funneling process*—where mediocre projects are culled out at each gate and resources are focused on the truly meritorious projects. To build tough gates into the process, you need:

- a definition of *deliverables* to each of the four, five, or six gates— what information is required by management in order to make an effective, timely decision;
- specification of who the gate decision makers or *gatekeepers* are (typically the leadership team are the gatekeepers from Gate 2 or 3 on in a five-stage process); and
- delineation of the *criteria* against which the project will be judged—these criteria are the basis for the Go/Kill and prioritization decisions.

Gates and gatekeeping are vital topics, and an area that is the domain of the leadership team of the business. More on this in Chapter 5.

5. *There is a focus on quality of execution, where activities in new product projects must be carried out in a quality fashion.*

New product success is very much within the hands of the men and women who lead and work on the project. Certain key activities—how well they are executed, and whether they are done at all—are strongly tied to success. In our NewProd projects studies, quality of execution of key tasks stands out as the major driver of performance: note the high correlations and effect on success rates in Figure 2.2.[19] Pivotal activities that decide outcomes include undertaking preliminary market and technical assessments early in the project; carrying out a detailed market study or marketing research prior to product design; performing a detailed business and financial analysis; and executing the test market and market launch in a quality fashion.

Quality of execution of key tasks and activities throughout the new product process is emphasized in top-performing firms. This is one of the most important ingredients of a quality process, with strong correlations to both profitability of the business's total new product efforts, as well as significant correlations with impact, according to the benchmarking studies.[20]

There is a quality crisis in product innovation. No, not the usual product quality problems, but rather serious weaknesses in the way projects are carried out. Quality of execution is mediocre on average, however—a quality rating of about 6 out of 10 in our projects studies. Similarly, the benchmarking studies find the mean score for quality of execution to be a modest 64.5 points out of 100 across all businesses. When was the last time that you, as an executive, accepted a quality score of 6 out of 10, and thought this was good performance? It isn't—these are terrible scores, but typical, and may very well be true of your business too. In short, our studies reveal that key activities don't happen as they should, when they should, or as well as they should; and success and profitability suffer as a result.[21]

Incidentally, one of the underlying reasons for poor quality of execution is not that project teams and leaders are ineffective, but that there are too many projects in the pipeline—factor #4 above, a lack of focus. The end result of no focus and too many projects is that quality work on these projects begins to suffer.

The message is this: the best way to double the success rate of new products in your business is to strive for significant improvements in the way your product innovation process unfolds. Management and project teams must develop a more disciplined approach to product innovation. The way to save time and money is *not* to cut corners, execute in a hurried and sloppy fashion, or cut out steps. This is false economy: it results in more time and effort spent later on the project, and results in a higher failure rate.

One more point: you, the leadership team of the business, are the gate-keepers at the key checkpoints or gates in the process, and hence you are in effect the *quality controllers* of the process. This is an important role for senior people: spotting and halting projects that feature poor-quality work. The VP of Innovation at Hoechst-U.S. expressed it this way:

> "As a member of the executive and also a key gatekeeper, I view my role, not so much as judge and critic, but more as a *quality assurer.* When project teams present their projects to the leadership of the business at gates, I ask enough penetrating questions to assure me and my colleagues *that the information being presented is based on facts* (not on hearsay and speculation) and the result of quality work."

> "How? Simple. I select some so-called vital facts, for example, sales projections for years 1, 2 and 3. And I ask the question: 'How did you get these numbers . . . where did they come from?' And I listen to the answer very carefully, especially to the nature, quality, and effort that went into developing these numbers. From these questions and answers, I can then assess whether or not this team is doing a quality job."

Key Points for Management

When overhauling your new product process, make *every effort* to build in best practices at *every stage;* focus on quality of execution throughout; and set high standards at gate checkpoints, where deliverables are scrutinized, with gates becoming the quality-control checkpoints in your innovation process.

Some managements become concerned that emphasizing quality of execution *adds time to projects.* Our research shows that this is *not true:* indeed, quality of execution is one of the key drivers of cycle time reduction. Remember: no one is advocating postponing decisions or leaving projects in a queue awaiting perfect information; the message is that taking the time to do a quality job saves time later. Make "doing it right the first time" a rule in your business's new product process. As a senior gatekeeper, *you* are the *quality controller;* ultimately you dictate the quality of execution of your business's new product projects!

6. *The new product process is compete or thorough, where every vital activity is carried out—no hasty corner-cutting. But the process is also flexible, where stages and decision points can be skipped or combined, as dictated by the nature and risk of the project.*

This success factor follows closely from #5 above—quality of execution. Many companies had discovered that not only was the *quality* of work lacking, but in some cases, the *work was lacking altogether.* In our benchmarking studies, the mean score here is a very mediocre 54.3 points out of 100. That is, key tasks, such as market analysis, business assessment, and customer or user research, were simply not done at all!

A thorough and complete process is critical to success, however. Completeness is correlated significantly with profitability of businesses' new product efforts, while an analysis of activities undertaken versus success rate across projects reveals a dramatic negative impact of deleting key activities and steps in the process. For example, skip the detailed market study, forget about the business case, and drop out the customer test, and you just increased the odds of failure of the typical project by a factor of three![22]

At the same time, avoid building in bureaucracy and time wasters. Here I define bureaucracy as "work that adds no value." One pitfall some firms encounter when they do reengineer their product development process is the failure to build in flexibility. Instead of being a template or roadmap, the "formal process" becomes a straitjacket beset with bureaucracy (the benchmarking studies reveal some problems here: a mean "flexibility score" of 63.0 points out of 100).[23] For example, there are requirements for forms to be filled out, deliverables to be delivered, and tasks to be done; and these are done regardless of whether or not they are needed. Note that process flexibility is significantly correlated with positive profits (see Figure 2.3), while yet another study of firms' new product processes revealed flexibility to be a key yet often-missed success ingredient.[24] So don't become a slave to your process. Here's how:

In a flexible process, stages can be collapsed, gates combined, and long lead-time activities moved ahead. The point is that these decisions to *streamline the process* are made consciously, ahead of time, and at gate decision points, rather than on an ad hoc, spur-of-the-moment basis. And they are made for the right reasons, where the risks of streamlining (for example, omitting a stage or activity) are weighed against the costs.

Procter & Gamble has built commonsense flexibility into its new product process:*

"Flexibility

It is acceptable to overlap the beginning and ends of succeeding phases provided that we understand the risks involved and have agreed at the previous decision checkpoint. In addition to overlapping phases, you may need to find ways to cut corners to meet business needs. You need to recognize that cutting some corners is far riskier than cutting others. The key is to identify the determinants of success for each initiative and give them all the attention possible.

Corners Not to Cut

Concept Development—If the concept is weak or flawed in any significant way, the project is almost guaranteed to fail no matter how high the quality of subsequent steps.

Product and Process Development—The product you take to market must be distinctive and superior to deliver the full promise of your concept.

Copy Development—Starting a test market or [market] expansion without sound, tested [advertising] copy in hand is very risky, and carries a low probability of success."

Key Points for Management

When designing your new product process, error on the side of thoroughness. Flexibility and short-cuts can be built in, especially for lower-risk projects and when the risks of omission are understood. But for significant and higher-risk projects, adopt and adhere to a disciplined, thorough new product process.

When overhauling your new product process, be sure to provide for flexibility. Remember, the new product process is *a risk management model:* it is simply a series of steps designed to gather information to reduce uncertainty and thereby manage risk. Thus, strict adherence to every stage, step, activity, and gate in the "formal process" depends on the risk level of the project. The rule is this: the higher the risk, the fewer the detours allowed. And, as noted in P&G's roadmap, there are certain steps—such as development of the concept and development of the physical product itself—that one does not cut corners on.

---

*Taken from P&G's *Product Launch Roadmap for Success.*

Make a High-Quality, Superb New Product Process a Top Priority

A high-quality new product process clearly pays off. Businesses that boast superb new product processes—ones that incorporate the six success factors listed above—are rewarded with superior performance: they outscore the other firms on 10 performance metrics, ranging from new product success rates to profitability, according to our benchmarking studies.[25] In particular, these businesses' total new product efforts meet sales and profit objectives more often, and have a strong positive impact on businesses' profits. Additionally, those new product projects that feature the six success factors of a superb new product process (above) are far more successful—typically more than double the success rates, and close to double the market shares.[26]

If your business does not have such a process, or if your process is flawed, then you're missing out on one of the obvious success drivers, and one that is within your control.

Key Points for Management

The message is clear: a vital cornerstone of new product success is having a high-quality new product process. Start by undertaking a thorough audit of your business's new product process. For example, select a handful of past projects and perform a postmortem or *retrospective analysis* to see what happened—whether your process was working or not.

In particular, judge your own business's new product process against the six ingredients of a superb process outlined in this chapter—factors that are proven to correlate with success. Recall that these success factors include:

1. Solid up-front homework, both market and technical, before the Development phase begins.
2. A strong market orientation and attention to the voice of the customer throughout.
3. Sharp, early product definition, before Development begins.
4. Tough Go/Kill decision points in the process, where projects really are killed.
5. A focus on quality of execution—key activities carried out in a quality fashion.

6. A compete or thorough process, but also a flexible process, as dictated by the nature and risk of the project.

Check your business against these six criteria. If your process falls short on some of them, consider a total overhaul of your new product process. Chapter 4 portrays a model of an excellent process—one that you might want to use as a standard.

3

The Keys to Victory: Seven New Critical Success Factors

Winning isn't everything . . . it's the only thing.
—**Vince Lombardi, U.S. football coach**

We Sometimes Miss the Obvious

Is having a well-oiled new product process all there is to winning big at new products? Not at all! The previous chapter highlighted six success factors that focus on *process*—doing the up-front homework well, building in the voice of the customer, getting sharp, early product definition, making tough Go/Kill decisions, and so on. All these success factors are ingredients of a high-quality new product process—something I encourage you to implement in your business. But there is more to success than *a solid process, proficient execution, or brilliant tactics.* In this chapter, we explore seven other critical success factors—ones uncovered in our NewProd projects studies and our benchmarking investigations, which are not related to process, but nonetheless are vital to success.[1] Some of these are fairly well known, but our investigations continue to reveal *major gaps* between actual and ideal practice here.

Seven Additional Critical Success Factors

1. Top-performer firms have put in place the needed resources to undertake new products: that is, senior management has made the *necessary resource commitment, and kept it.*
2. It's almost too obvious, but a dominant success factor is having a unbeatable product: a superior product; a differentiated product; and a product that delivers unique benefits and better value to the customer.
3. The right organizational structure, design, and climate are key factors in success.
4. Look to the world product: an international orientation in product design, development, and target marketing provides the edge in product innovation.
5. Leverage your core competencies. Synergy with the base business and its strengths is vital to success; "step-out" projects tend to fail more often.
6. Market attractiveness is a key criterion for project selection and prioritization.
7. Speed is everything! But not at the expense of quality of execution.

1. Top-performer firms have put in place the needed resources to undertake new products: that is, senior management has made the necessary resource commitment, and kept it.

Adequate resources is one of the three cornerstones of superior performance: resource commitment drives both the profitability of the business's total new product efforts, as well as the impact that this effort has on the business (see Figures 2.1 and 2.3).

There are *three main facets of resource deployment* that top performers have in common:[2]

1. In top-performing enterprises, senior management has devoted the necessary resources—people and money, marketing and technical—to achieve the business's new product objectives. By contrast, average and poorer performers tend to be very short on resources and have few dedicated players; marketing resources devoted to new products is a particular area of weakness.

   Senior management often fails to heed the simple adage that *there's no free lunch here.* In an effort to overcome weak new product performance, management sometimes looks for quick fixes and resort to a *reengineering exercise.* The problem is that you can reengineer all you want—for example, design brilliant game plans—but that won't make up for a lack of players. Other businesses turn to *strategic planning exercises* as the solution to their weak new product performance. But often the resulting strategy and goals are hollow ones, simply because they are not backed up with the needed resources. And so another well-intentioned initiative flounders. As one manager eloquently stated: "Even the best game plan in the world comes to nothing if there aren't players on the field!"

A lack of resources continues to plague new product projects, and is often the culprit underlying *poor quality of execution:* there simply aren't the necessary people in place nor the time available to do a quality job. The result is that corners are cut, activities are done in haste, tasks are left out . . . and the results are predicable. One frustrated new product project leader at her company's technology conference exclaimed: "I don't deliberately set out to do a bad job. Yet, when you look at the job that the project leaders around here do, it's almost as though our goal is mediocrity. But that's not true . . . we're good project leaders, but we're being *set up for failure*. There simply isn't enough time and not enough people or the right people to do the job we'd like to do!" She went on to explain to senior management how insufficient resources and budget cuts coupled with too many projects were seriously jeopardizing the way key projects were being executed. She was right! The point is: *the resource commitment must be aligned with the business's new product objectives, strategy, and processes* for positive results.

2. R&D budgets are adequate—judged to be sufficient in light of the business's new product objectives.

   This is just another facet of the resource question, but with a specific focus on *technical budgets*. R&D spending devoted to product development, measured as a percentage of sales, is by far the *strongest determinant of the impact* of the product development effort, according to our benchmarking studies.[2] Thus, metrics that capture performance magnitude or impact, such as the popular measure, "percentage of sales by new products," are driven by the magnitude of spending. The message is clear: if your performance goal is to have a high-impact new product effort—for example, to achieve a high percentage of your business's sales from new products—then increased R&D spending is the most obvious lever to pull. The relationship isn't one-to-one, but it is strong!

3. Finally, the necessary people are in place, and have their time freed up for new products.

Senior management approves projects, and goes through the motions of assigning people to them. The problem is: the assigned people are often expected to work on another six projects, or in the case of marketing and manufacturing people, to do "their real job" in addition to the new product project.

Some enlightened firms, however, are taking steps to overcome this deficiency. At Alcoa's Knoxville packaging division, for example, when a project's action plan is approved at each gate review, the plan spells out resource commitments, people, and their time allocation. Assignments of personnel to specific projects are made realistically, and in full awareness of their other duties and obligations. But this division is an exception: most businesses fail to deal adequately with the allocation of people to projects, and people are simply overassigned so that projects are indeed set up for failure.

The point is that merely having a sound new product process does not guarantee success. There must be players on the field as well—not just part-time or Saturday afternoon players, but full-time, dedicated resources. Many projects simply suffer from a lack of time and money commitment. The results are both much higher failure rates and longer times to market.

This resourcing success factor, at first glance, is a little too obvious. But many managers don't get the message. As the competitive situation has toughened, companies have responded with restructuring and doing more with less. The result is that product innovation, rather than being treated as an investment, is viewed as a cost that must be reduced. And so resources are limited or cut back. At the same time, market pressures have increased the need for new products, and so more projects than ever are in the pipeline. And the result approaches *pipeline gridlock.*

This short-term focus regarding resources takes its toll. Recall from the previous chapter how badly certain vital activities, such as market-oriented actions and predevelopment homework, are highly under-resourced:

▶ A strong market orientation is missing in the typical new product project. And much of this deficiency is directly linked to a lack of marketing resources available for the project. Only 16 percent of the average project's total costs go to marketing actions, and most of these are at the back-end or Launch phase of the project. Note that successes have more than twice as much money spent on marketing activities (other than the Launch) than do failures.[3]

▶ Similarly, predevelopment or up-front homework also receives pitifully few resources: approximately 7 percent of the cost of the average project goes to these pivotal front-end activities. These extra resources pay off, however: successful new products, on average, have more than twice as much money spent on the homework phases than do failures.[4]

Key Points for Management

Is your new product effort adequately resourced? Telltale signs that it's not include the following:

- projects seem to take forever to get to market.
- vital up-front homework isn't done, and business cases seems to be based more on guesswork than facts (as an aside, take a hard look at just how much time and money is spent on the pivotal homework phase for your business's typical project);
- market information seems badly lacking, and the voice of the customer is not built into projects as it should be (again, review just how much marketing effort really goes into your projects; and whether there are enough marketing people, with time freed up, to do what is needed);
- there are problems moving the typical project into operations/manufacturing and Launch or roll-out (largely because these groups—manufacturing, operations, and sales—are not involved in the project until too late); and
- overall, quality of work seems substandard and not what it should be.

If these symptoms exist, likely the problem is simply a lack of resources—trying to do too much with too little. Top performers put the resources in place! Having a solid new product process, the first cornerstone of success, is only part of the answer. So too is having an articulated new product strategy, another cornerstone. But unless the process and the strategy are properly resourced with people, time, money—and the commitments kept—don't expect stellar performance.

The time is ripe to undertake an *audit of resource adequacy,* and the impact that this is having on performance. In the previous chapter, I suggested selecting a few past projects and performing a *postmortem* on these. Continue this postmortem, but now with a focus on resources: Are there enough resources? Are they the right ones? And what is the impact?

Next, have a *resource requirements assessment* undertaken. Here's how. Look at your new product goals—for example, percentage of sales by new products. Then translate these goals into numbers of major and minor Launches per year over the next five to 10 years. Then translate Launches into numbers of projects at different stages in your new product process (be sure to consider the attrition curve—Figure 1.5). Finally, reduce this to numbers of people. You may be shocked to discover the gap between *resources required* to achieve your goals versus *resources actually in place*. This may explain why your new product performance is deficient and why projects take so long.

2. *It's almost too obvious, but a dominant success factor is having a unbeatable product: a unique superior product; a differentiated product; and a product that delivers unique benefits and superior value to the customer.*

The one vital success ingredient, and coincidentally, which most firms fail to address, is the *product itself*. One of the top success factors we uncovered is delivering a *differentiated product* with *unique customer benefits* and *superior value for the user*. This one factor separates winners from losers more often than any other single factor! For example, our NewProd projects studies show that such superior products have five times the success rate, over four times the market share, and four times the profitability as products lacking this ingredient.[5] Just how vital a unique, superior product is can be seen in Figure 3.1. Here the really differentiated and superior products achieve a stunning 98 percent success rate at Launch (the bar on the right). Contrast that to the 18 percent success rate achieved by the me-too, tired, copycat products (the bar on the left).

Seven ingredients of a unique, superior product with real value for the customer

1. Meets customers' needs better than competitive products.
2. Is a better-quality product than competitors' (however the customer defines quality).

3. **Has unique benefits and features for the customer.**
4. **Solves customers' problems with competitive products.**
5. **Reduces the customer's total in-use costs (better value-in-use).**
6. **Has highly visible benefits for users.**
7. **Is innovative or novel—the first of its kind on the market.**

Note that product superiority is defined in the eyes of the customer!

This result should come as no surprise to product innovators. Apparently it isn't obvious to everyone, however: a number of studies point out that "tired products" and "me-too" offerings are the rule rather than the exception in many firms' new product efforts. The NewProd investigations reveal that much time and energy is devoted to projects that fail to score high on this number one success factor. The two most common failure scenarios we encountered are:

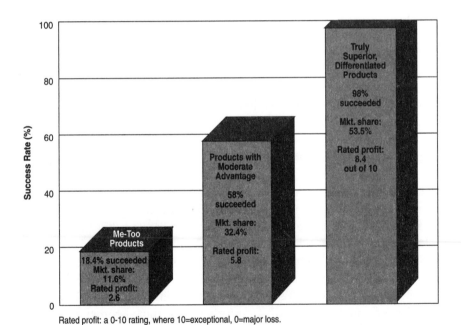

Rated profit: a 0-10 rating, where 10=exceptional, 0=major loss.

Figure 3.1　Impact of Product Superiority—Differentiated Products with Unique Benefits

Reprinted with permission from: R. G. Cooper & Kleinschmidt, E. J. *New Products: The Key Factors in Success.* Chicago: American Marketing Assoc., 1990, monograph.

- Copycat projects that yield boring, undifferentiated products with no new benefits for the customer; often these projects are the result of a rushed effort to get something out to market quickly in the mistaken belief that "we'll get our fair share of the market."
- Technology-driven projects, where the business's internal technical community decides what the customer wants; the engineer, scientist, or designer then builds a monument to himself or herself—a great technological achievement—and wonders why thousands of customers stay away.

Surprisingly, very few businesses can point to specific facets of their new product methodology that emphasize this one vital success ingredient. Often, questions such as "is the product strongly differentiated from competitors'?" or "does it offer the customer unique benefits?" are noticeably absent as screening, project selection or program prioritization criteria, while rarely are steps deliberately built into the process that encourage the design and delivery of such superior products. It's almost as though the process architects—the people who reengineered the new product process—were content to design a process destined to yield mediocre products! Even worse, the preoccupation with cycle time reduction and the tendency to favor simple, inexpensive projects actually penalizes projects that lead to product superiority.

At a technology conference in a major U.S. food company, I was approached by the head of technology of one of the company's better-known divisions. He was quite proud of his newly conceived product innovation process, and asked me to give it a quick review.

The next morning, I asked him to tell me about his division's most successful, recent new product Launch. He went on to describe a snack food product that most Americans know well, and when I asked him why it had been a success, he replied: "Because it was really a dynamite product—it was unique, differentiated . . . good value for money . . . really delighted the customer."

My reply was: "Exactly. You've just hit upon the number one success factor we find in our many studies—a differentiated product that offers unique benefits and superior value to the customer. Now, let's go through the documentation in your new product process, and you show me where you've built in this critical success factor into your methodology."

Both of us pored through his process document, page by page. At the end, a somewhat embarrassed technology director exclaimed:

"It's not here . . . I can't believe it. The most important success factor is not even mentioned in our process!" He was right: nowhere in any of his process stages were there activities, tasks, or practices designed to yield a unique, superior product; nor did any of the Go/Kill or prioritization criteria at gates score more points for such projects. Product superiority was *noticeably absent* from his process. Unfortunately, the majority of new product processes I am asked to critique share the same deficiency.

The challenge the product developer faces is to ensure that the seven elements of product superiority are built into each and every new product project (see list on page 64, "Seven ingredients of a unique, superior product"). In short, the seven ingredients of product advantage become personal objectives of the project leader and team, and must be molded into the game plan.

But how does one invent or build in product superiority? Note that superiority is derived from design, features, attributes, specifications, and even positioning. Here's an illustration:

Fluke Corporation of Seattle is well noted for its innovative products in the field of hand-held electrical measurement instruments. A strategic decision to diversify into new markets led to the creation of the Phoenix team—a project team whose mandate was to deliver a superior product or two in a market outside of the firm's normal scope, namely, in the chemical industry.

Facing a totally new market, the project team had no one in the company to turn to. So they began their voyage of discovery with some prework, namely, project planning, synectics (innovative team process training), and a review of the trade literature (magazines). The first team visit was to a chemical industry trade show in Chicago, followed by a few field visits to nearby chemical plants. The plant field visits were not based on sophisticated market research methodology—it was simply spending an afternoon in the control room, chatting with and observing the ultimate customer, the plant instrument engineers. The project leader calls this "fly on the wall research"; others might call it "anthropological research" or "camping out."*

---

*"Camping out" is the term that Hewlett-Packard uses to describe this immersion research, whereby the project team or designers spend much time with customers, really learning the customers' operation, needs, problems, and so on.

After some 25 site visits, the project team acquired a good understanding of the instrument engineer's problems and needs. One fact that was observed was the amount of equipment the engineers needed to carry out to the plant merely to calibrate common instruments, such as pressure or temperature gauges. Every gauge and brand, it seemed, needed a different calibration instrument. Second, observation revealed that after the engineer had calibrated the gauge, he then took readings and recorded them on a clipboard. After calibrating a number of gauges, the engineer returned to the control room, and then typed into his computer all the hand-recorded readings from the field—a time-consuming process.

You've probably guessed what the Phoenix team's new product became:

- a universal calibration instrument that could calibrate any gauge in the plant (this was made possible via the use of software rather than hardware in the hand-held tool); and
- an instrument that recorded the readings in the field—the user simply keyed in readings, which went into the tool's memory; and on returning to the control room, downloaded these directly into his computer.

The Documenting Process Calibrator, "the one field calibrator that does its own paperwork," went on to become a great success—another example of what results from really understanding customer needs, and designing a superior product in response to these needs.

An important point here is that "product superiority" is defined from the customer's standpoint, not in the eyes of the R&D or design departments. More than unique features are required to make a product superior, however. Remember: features are those things that cost you, the supplier, money. By contrast, benefits are what customers pay money for! Often the two—features and benefits—are not the same. So in defining "unique benefits," think of the product as a "bundle of benefits" for the user, and a benefit as something the customer views as having value to him or her.

The definition of "what is unique and superior" and "what is a benefit" is from the customer's perspective; it must be based on an in-depth understanding of customer needs, wants, problems, likes, and dislikes. Recall the prescriptions in success factor #2 in the previous chapter—building in the voice of the customer.

Key Points for Management

Seek differentiated products that offer unique benefits to the customer and provide better value for money. This is not a quest for the impossible; rather, there are many steps and actions that you must insist be built into projects to achieve this goal:

- user needs-and-wants studies, much like the Fluke example;
- competitive product analysis—to understand what you need to better; and
- constant testing of the product as it takes shape—concept tests, protocept tests, rapid-prototype-and-tests, and so on.

At gate and project review meetings, keep asking questions: How is this proposed new product better? What are the unique benefits? And what has the project team done to gain insights in order to design a product that will delight the customer?

Speaking of project review or gate meetings, have you considered what criteria you should use to rate and rank projects? Well-run gate meetings use criteria, and I'll be providing a good list of screening or project scoring criteria in Chapter 5. However, if product superiority and the seven elements that comprise it are strongly correlated to profits, doesn't it make sense to use these seven items (see pp. 64–65) as criteria against which to rate and rank projects?

---

3. *The right organizational structure, design, and climate are key factors to success.*

The evidence is compelling: investigations into new product success consistently cite interfaces between R&D and marketing, coordination among key internal groups, multidisciplinary inputs to the new product project, and the role of teams and the team leader. Successful new product projects feature a balanced process consisting of critical activities that fall into many different functional areas within the firm: marketing and marketing research, engineering, R&D, production, purchasing, and finance, to name a few. Maidique and Zirger's study of new product launches in high-technology firms reveals that a critical distinguishing factor between success and failure is the "simultaneous involvement of the create, make, and market functions."[6] Similarly, analyses of Japanese successes emphasize their attention to manufacturability from the start of development efforts, the location in one place of engineers, designers, and manufacturers, and the conception of management unconstrained by traditional American functionalism.[7]

Our NewProd projects studies show that projects undertaken by empowered, cross-functional teams are more successful.[8] And our benchmarking studies reveal that successful businesses pay special attention to the team structure, as follows:[9]

▶ All significant projects have an *assigned team of players*. That is, people are specifically assigned as team members. Here most businesses fare modestly well, with a mean score of 67.2 points out of 100, according to the benchmarking studies. Many firms have heeded the call for formally designating project team members; but in others, it wasn't clear just who was on the project team and who wasn't!

▶ These assigned players are *a cross-functional team*—from R&D, marketing, manufacturing, engineering, and so on. Businesses are getting the message here (score: 72.8 points out of 100).

▶ All significant projects have a *defined and accountable team leader*—a person who is responsible for seeing that the project makes progress. Businesses also do well on this success ingredient, scoring a positive 75.5 points out of 100.

▶ Project leaders are *responsible* for the project *from beginning to end* (as opposed to being responsible for only *one phase* of a project; or having project leadership change hands many times during a project's life). Here business units receive a poor score on average: 55.3 points out of 100.

▶ The team leader *is dedicated to one project* at a time (as opposed to trying to lead many projects, or having myriad other assignments). This is a *particularly weak ingredient* of team quality, scoring a dismal 34.8 points out of 100. Simply stated, team leaders are *spread too thinly* across too many projects or have too many other duties to run projects effectively!

▶ High-quality teams interact and communicate well and often, with *frequent project update meetings,* progress reviews, and problem resolution sessions. The best teams have short but weekly meetings to ensure that the entire team is up-to-speed. Teams received mediocre ratings here, on average (57.3 points out of 100).

Key Points for Management

Design your organization for product innovation. Product innovation is not a one-department show! It is very much a multidisciplinary, cross-functional effort. Organizational design—how you organize for new products—is critical. Except for the simplest of products and projects—line extensions and product updates—product innovation must cut across traditional functional boundaries and barriers.

How well does your business fare on the important team factors? Consider the six arrow list items above—the ones found to be closely linked to better performance—and rate your own project teams in your business. This can be done informally, or perhaps as part of the post-mortem on projects I suggested above.

One answer is to design and implement *a new product process* that deliberately cuts across functional boundaries and forces the active participation of people from different functions. Make every step or stage in the process a multifunctional one. Resist the temptation to have a "Manufacturing Stage" or "Marketing Stage," where a single department or function owns the stage. That is, your new product process must build in different tasks and provide checks and balances that require the input and involvement of these various functions.

> For example: a project cannot proceed into a full-scale development effort until a detailed market assessment has been completed, and until a manufacturing appraisal is complete. Without the active participation of both manufacturing and marketing people, the project does not get released to development—it goes nowhere!

A second and equally important answer lies in *organizational design.* What type of organization structure brings many players from different walks of life in the business together in an integrated effort? In short, how do you take a diverse group of players and turn them into a team? It's clear that the traditional functional organizational structure does not suit many of the needs of product innovation. Indeed, functional approaches—where the project is divided into functional segments, and each functional department handles its piece of the project—leads to the lowest new product performance.[10] Tom Peters argues strongly in favor of project teams: "the single most important reason for delays in development activities is the absence of multifunction (and outsider) representation on development projects from the start."[11] He continues: "The answer is to comingle members of all key functions, co-opt each function's traditional feudal authority, and use teams."

More Key Points for Management

Move to a team approach that cuts across functional lines. The three approaches that appear to work best are:[10]

- *Balanced matrix:* Here, a project manager or team leader is assigned to oversee the project and shares the responsibility and authority for completing the project with the functional managers: there is joint approval and direction.
- *Project matrix:* A team leader is assigned to oversee the project and has *primary* responsibility and authority for the project. Functional managers assign personnel as needed and provide technical expertise: functions become the "resource providers" here.
- *Project team:* A project manager is put in charge of a project team composed of a core group of personnel from several functional areas. The functional managers have no formal involvement or authority. Here, the team works outside the traditional organizational structure. This approach is best used for major and very complex projects.

A dedicated and empowered project leader is essential for timely, successful projects. The leader must *have formal authority* (this means shifting authority from functional heads); and the leader and team must be empowered to make project decisions, and not be second-guessed, overruled, or "micro managed" by the functional heads or senior management.

All three organizational approaches work well with a formal new product process in place. The transfers of authority and responsibility from functional managers to the team leader and team take place at the gate or Go/Kill decision meetings. Here, the functional bosses are the gatekeepers, and in approving projects, they *also approve the transfer of their resources* (people and money) to the project leader and team.

For the team to work well, team members must communicate effectively with each other. Often they don't!

> In an audit of a business's new product effort, where project team members were interviewed, we were shocked to find out that some project team members were not even aware of the status of their projects. In one instance, the project had been cancelled about one week previously, and some team members did not even know yet! In another, key funding decisions had been made and only some team members were aware. And these teams were relatively small!

To promote such communication, ideally, team members should be located close to each other. "Physical proximity is one of the keys to good teamwork," is the conclusion of studies done in a number of firms. 3M reports that physical distances beyond 100 meters thwarts team interaction severely. Co-location is one solution: team members from different functions in the company are relocated in one area or department. A team office is another solution. Another is to rely on frequent but quick team meetings, and where all absentee team members are sent notification of the decisions made. Improved electronic communications have helped overcome the physical distances that plague some project teams, so make these tools available via information technology (IT) to your project teams: group software (such as *Lotus Notes*); project management software (such as *Microsoft Project*); teleconferencing and videoconferencing capabilities; and e-mail, Internet, or Intranet. Be sure to provide training on these new technologies: in far too many companies we studied, the tools were available but team members failed to exploit them fully due to a lack of knowledge of how to use them! And speaking of training, do provide training to your team leaders on how to lead a team, and to team members on how to participate as team players.

Keep the team small and dedicated. Although many people may work on a project during its life, the *core team* should number no more than eight people, according to studies done at AT&T. The ideal number is five to seven, and where possible, core team members should be *dedicated* to the project 100 percent of their time! From my observations of hundreds of project teams, I would far rather have a team of two or three full-time people (that is, 100 percent dedicated to my project) than a team of 10 half-time people. Why not the team of 10? First, I never get my 50 percent of their time. Second, they lack ownership—they have other important things going on. And finally, communication is a nightmare. Give me the small, dedicated team any day!

The final organizational ingredient essential to making this multifunctional team work is *climate and culture*. The climate must reward and encourage creativity and innovation. For example, 3M provides cash awards to about 10 percent of its employees annually for doing innovative and creative things. Milliken has a *hall of fame*, whereby individuals and teams are publicly recognized for their contributions to innovative projects.

At the same time, the climate must avoid punishment for failure. The only way to ensure no failures is to take no chances. So, if failures are punished, expect little in the way of risk taking and entrepreneurial behavior.

Additionally, the resources must be available to enable people to do creative and innovative work. Some companies have a deliberate policy to make resources available to innovators. 3M allows its technical people 15 percent of their time to work on their "unapproved" pet projects; Rohm and Haas allows technical employees to have 10 percent "scouting time" to do their own projects; and many successful new product projects have been initiated as "boot-strapped" projects using spare time and spare money.

Key Points for Management

Senior management must set the stage for effective project teams.

1. Provide the means for good team communication:
   - small, dedicated teams
   - physically close to each other or via co-location or a team office
   - electronic communication facilities and IT support (with training)
   - team training—for members and the leader
2. Provide the right climate and culture:
   - reward and recognize teams and team members
   - avoid punishment for failure
   - provide resources for creative work: time off or scouting time; boot-strapping money and facilities

---

4. Look to the world product: an international orientation in product design, development, and target marketing provides the edge in product innovation.

We uncovered a number of different strategic approaches for dealing with the domestic-versus-international strategy issue. The six-cell matrix, bounded by product and target market, helps compartmentalize the various strategic options your business has (Figure 3.2):

◆ *Product Design:* You have three choices:

1. *strictly domestic design.* Here the product is designed to suit the domestic market. If international sales are anticipated, this domestic design is modified/adapted to the foreign market after the domestic Launch.

   Alternately, you can build in the international requirements at the outset. There are two "international approaches" to product design:

2. *global:* develop a "one-size-fits-all" product—a "world" or "global" product. But given national differences, this is often difficult. Even Coca Cola uses different product formulations, depending on the geographic market!

3. *glocal:* develop a single product that has multiple variants, each variant designed to accommodate different geographic markets. The advantage here is that products can be tailored to local needs, but that economies of scale are achieved—a

	Domestic Product Design	International Product Design: Global or Glocal
World Target Market	Too few case examples	★ 84.9% successful (17.2% of cases)
Nearest Neighbor (Regional) Target Market	45.5% successful (6.7% of cases) ✗	★ 78.1% successful (18.3% of cases)
Domestic Target Market	43.1% successful (31.1% of cases) ✗	61.5% successful (23.7% of cases)

★ Stars indicate the best places to operate: international product design (global or glocal designs) in world or nearest neighbor (regional) markets.
✗ Crosses indicate the worst place - domestic product design, domestic target markets.

Figure 3.2 Impact of an International Orientation on New Product Success Rates
Reprinted with permission from: R. G. Cooper & Kleinschmidt, E. J. *New Products: The Key Factors in Success.* Chicago: American Marketing Assoc., 1990, monograph.

single development program and one project team, a single technology, and perhaps even consolidated manufacturing.

▶ *Target Market Choice:* Again you have three choices:

1. *domestic.*
2. *regional or nearest neighbor.* For a Danish company, this would be "Scandinavia" or "all Europe." For a U.S. firm, this might be "North America" or "Americas."
3. *world* (or perhaps "industrialized world").

Which strategic approach works best? The 3 × 2 matrix in Figure 3.2 reveals five possible cells or options, and in our studies, projects were found in all seven five. But which were most successful and profitable? Here the evidence is clear. International products—either global or glocal—targeted at world and regional export markets are the top performers (the starred sections of Figure 3.2). By contrast, products designed with only the domestic market in mind, and sold to domestic and regional export markets fare more poorly. The magnitude of the differences between these international and exported new products versus domestic products is striking: differences of two- or three-to-one on the various performance gauges. Not only do international products do better abroad; they also do better in the home market—almost double the domestic market share versus domestic products. Why? Because, by competing against the world (rather than just at home), the standards of excellence are increased, and the project team is forced to rise to the occasion.

The comfortable strategy of "design the product for domestic requirements, capture the home market, and then export a modified version of the product sometime in the future" is myopic. It leads to inferior results today; with increasing globalization of markets, it will certainly lead to even poorer results in the years ahead. The threat is that your domestic market has become someone else's international market: to define the new product market as "domestic" and perhaps a few other "convenient countries" severely limits one's market opportunities. For maximum success in product innovation, the objective must be to *design for the world* and *market to the world*.

This international dimension is an often overlooked facet of new product game plans, or one that if included, is handled late in the process, or as a side issue. In most North American firms' new product processes we study, the international facet is either not even mentioned in the process, or it crops up late in the process. For example, international inputs are often sought after Development begins, while international product testing and test markets follow well behind domestic ones, almost as an afterthought. European firms, by contrast, appear somewhat more sensitive to this international dimension.

A major implication of this need to adopt a global orientation is the design and implementation of a *global new product process* and *organizational structure* to handle such projects. This global requirement increases the complexity of product development considerably; it means that, more than ever, firms must adopt a *systematic* and *consistent* new product process. This global new product process is one that both domestic and international units utilize, and that integrates actions across national borders and regions. Here are the key ingredients of a transnational new product process:

▶ Build in international checks early in the process and project—for example, determining whether other units around the world want to become involved in the project, and to what degree. For example, Guinness, the Irish brewer, builds in a *International Alert* early in its new product process to solicit international interest (from other Guinness companies) in new developments.

▶ Incorporate international commitments into the process—for example, which business units commit to paying for what. And what volume and price commitments must be made by international units at different gates.

▶ Rely on international project teams: team members may reside in different countries and different tasks may even be undertaken in different countries. For example, Reckitt & Colman, the U.K. consumer products firm, utilizes project teams that cut across countries, and in some cases, across continents.

▶ Require international market research and customer contact: market studies and field trials in a variety of countries are built into the game plan. For example, Lego, the Danish toy maker, undertakes multiple concurrent market studies and market research on a new Lego product in many countries, all coordinated from Denmark.

▶ Utilize global criteria for Go/Kill decisions to replace the traditional domestic ones (for example, if a project has global potential, it scores higher on certain criteria than does a domestic project). Reckitt & Colman use a scoring model for project selection and prioritization at gate meetings; projects that are "world" score more points than "Euro-products," which in turn score more than "domestic" projects. Thus international projects are favored in the overall prioritization scheme.

▶ Structure global or regional gate meetings (for example, does each region make a Go/Kill decision on the project; or is this done globally via a single global gate meeting?). For example, Reckitt & Colman have moved from country-specific Go/Kill gate meetings to international category teams, which make the Go/Kill decisions across multiple countries and regions.

Key Points for Management

Your business has options when it comes to the international dimension. Figure 3.2 outlines these options in terms of target market and product design. Recognize that, on average, international products—global and glocal—aimed at export markets (region or world) are the most profitable. So at least consider these in your repertoire of possible approaches.

In order to be able to exploit all options in Figure 3.2, you must adopt an international approach to new product development. In practice, this means:

- developing and implementing a transnational new product process;
- with international checks built into the process; and
- incorporating international commitment points in the process.

It also requires . . .

- using international project teams;
- doing market research and field trials in multiple countries;
- utilizing global criteria at gates; and
- establishing a global or regional structure to handle Go/Kill or gate decisions.

---

*5. **Leverage your core competencies.** Synergy with the base business and its strengths is vital to success; "step-out" projects tend to fail more often.*

"Attack from a position of strength" may be an old adage, but it certainly applies in new products. That is, leverage your in-house resources and skills, seeking synergies between your new product initiatives and your base business. Synergy is the common thread that binds the new business to the old. When translated into product innovation, synergy is the ability to leverage existing and in-house strengths, resources, and capabilities to advantage in the new product project. By contrast, "step-out" projects take the firm into territory that lies beyond the experience, expertise, and resource base of the business.

Leveraging core competencies or seeking synergies between new product programs and the base business has been the message from a number of studies on new product success and failure. Two types of synergy are important to product innovation:

▶ *Technological synergy:* the project's ability to build on in-house development technology, utilize inside engineering skills, and use existing manufacturing (or operations and delivery) resources and skills.

▶ *Marketing synergy:* the project/company fit in terms of sales force, distribution channels, customer service resources, advertising and promotion, and market intelligence skills and resources.

The impact of these two synergy dimensions operating together is shown in Figure 3.3, based on the NewProd studies.[12] Note that highly "step-out" projects that lack both marketing and technological synergy (in the lower-left cell) suffer a failure rate of 77 percent. By contrast, more synergistic projects have much higher success rates. (Note that some cells in the figure had too few cases to draw meaningful conclusions.) Ironically, the best place to operate seems to be projects with medium to high-technological synergy coupled with moderate marketing synergy a 71 to 84 percent success rate! Indeed, those projects that featured extremely high synergy in both technology and marketing dimensions (upper-right cell) were few in number (8.6 percent of cases) and had about average success rates (53 percent successful), raising questions about staying "too close to home."*

The reasons for the impact of synergy are clear:

1. *Resources are available and at marginal cost.* In short, if the product can be developed using existing and in-house technical skills. This

---

*These very-close-to-home projects most often were incremental products, modifications, and tweaks: highly synergistic, but providing little opportunity for product differentiation.

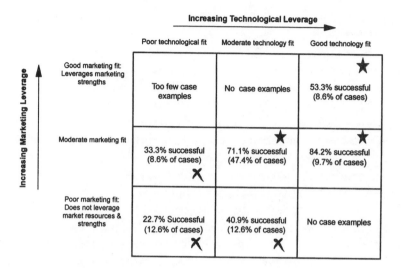

★ Stars indicate the best places to operate: strong leverage in term of technology; and moderate-to-strong leverage in terms of marketing competencies.

✗ Crosses indicate the worst place - low leverage both in marketing & technology.

Figure 3.3   Impact of Marketing & Technological Synergy—Ability to Leverage Core Competencies—on New Product Success Rates

Reprinted with permission from: R. G. Cooper & Kleinschmidt, E. J. *New Products: The Key Factors in Success.* Chicago: American Marketing Assoc., 1990, monograph.

is much less expensive (and less risky) than seeking outside technology and skills. Similarly, if the product can be sold to existing customers through an already-established company sales force or channel system, then this, too, is less expensive, less risky, and less time-consuming than seeking new distribution channels or building a new sales force.

2. *Experience.* The more often one does something, the better one becomes at doing it. If new product projects are closely related (synergistic) to current businesses, chances are there has been considerable experience with such projects in the past. The result is that it costs less (29 percent at each doubling of the number of new introductions, according to Booz-Allen & Hamilton),[13] and there will be fewer unpleasant surprises: uncertainty is less.

In designing new product strategies and selecting which new products to develop, never underestimate the role of synergy. Arenas and projects that lack any synergy invariably cost the business more to exploit. Further, unsynergistic projects usually take your firm into new and uncharted markets and technologies, often with unexpected pitfalls and barriers. There are simply too many unpleasant surprises in arenas that are new to the firm.

Key Points for Management

The ability to leverage core competencies or having strong synergy between the new product project and your base business is an important consideration in the selection of projects. Simply stated, such synergistic projects fare much better. So at minimum, build synergy criteria— marketing, technological, and operations—into your list of criteria for making Go/Kill and prioritization decisions. Projects where leveraging is possible should score more points.

I'm not saying "never do step-out projects!" Obviously, there are times when the nature of the opportunity is so great or the potential for competitive advantage so high that one must ignore traditional rules of leverage. All I'm saying is, be cautious of such step-out projects: they have a much higher failure rate and invariably will cost you twice as much and take twice as long as you expected. If you do venture into step-out projects, then at least consider partnering with someone who brings to the table those resources, expertise, and experience that you lack.

---

6. Market attractiveness is a key criterion for project selection and prioritization.

Market attractiveness is an important strategic variable. Porter's "five forces" model considers various elements of market attractiveness as a determinant of industry profitability.[14] Similarly, various strategic planning models for example, portfolio models, used to allocate resources among various existing business units, employ market attractiveness as a key dimension in the two-dimensional map or portfolio grid.[15]

In the case of new products, market attractiveness is also important. There are two dimensions of market attractiveness:

1. Market need, growth, and size: New products aimed at certain kinds of markets are more successful; and businesses whose new products are targeted at certain kinds of markets have a more successful innovation effort. These markets are ones . . .

   - that are large and growing (with more emphasis on growth than on size);

- where there is a strong customer need for such products, and where the purchase is an important one for the customer;
- which are in the earlier stages of the product life cycle (early growth and late growth stages); and
- where margins earned by existing players in the market are higher.

2. Competitive situation: Highly competitive markets yield more negative results for new products, namely, negative markets characterized by . . .

   - intense competition and where players compete on the basis of price;
   - competitors with high-quality and strongly competitive products;
   - and competitors whose sales force, channel system, and support service are strongly rated.

   Products aimed at such negative markets are only marginally less successful, however, according to both our NewProd studies and the Stanford Innovation Project.[16]

The message is this: products succeed in spite of the external environment they face. They succeed because they are superior and well defined; are executed in a quality fashion and driven by a multifunctional team; and have certain synergies with the business. While a positive external environment—having a large and growing market with weak competition—helps pave the way for a success, don't count on external conditions to make up for a multitude of internal sins and weaknesses. In short, if the product and project are weak, the external environment will not save the day! Nonetheless, because both elements of market attractiveness—market potential and competitive situation—do have an impact on the new product's fortunes, both should be considered as criteria for project selection and prioritization.

Key Points for Management

Market attractiveness—need level, size, and growth as well as the competitive situation—is only a moderate success factor. This is surprising, given all the attention "market attractiveness" receives in various strategy models. Clearly, while the external environment does enhance the odds of success, the dominant success factors have much more to do with how you organize, plan, resource, and execute projects.

Market attractiveness is a plus, however, and should not be ignored. I recommend that in your list of Go/Kill and prioritization criteria, market attractiveness be included, particularly those items that capture the market need, growth, and size. In Chapter 5, where I outline project selection and prioritization methods, I include some of the items listed above (the bullet points) as important gate criteria.

7. *Speed is everything! But not at the expense of quality of execution.*

Speed is the new competitive weapon. Speed to market in product development has payoffs in three ways, according to pundits:

1. *First into the market wins.*[17] This is a popular view, but there is conflicting evidence on this: as Crawford points out, there exist no hard data to show that "first in wins," except those where the second and third entries have comparable products.[18] (For more insights into the impact of order of entry, see endnote 19.)[19]

   Our own results show that being "first in" has a positive impact, but only marginally so:[20] indeed, being first in with a new product (versus second or third) yields a higher success rate and greater profits, but the differences are small (see Figure 3.4). Additionally, we find that speed and new product profitability are connected, but certainly not in a one-to-one fashion.

2. *Speed equals profits.* A spreadsheet analysis of the profitability impact of time-to-market often reveals startling effects. There are two reasons. First, money has a time value; thus, deferring the profits from a new product by even one year can hurt profitability severely. Second, many new products have a fixed window of opportunity (a finite and often short product life). For every month the launch is postponed, there is one less month's revenue over the life of the product.

One often-cited McKinsey report reveals the profound impact of time-to-market on the new product's profitability over its life—see Figure 3.5:

- A six-month Launch delay reduces profitability by one-third.
- High production costs (9 percent higher than expected) reduce profitability by 22 percent.

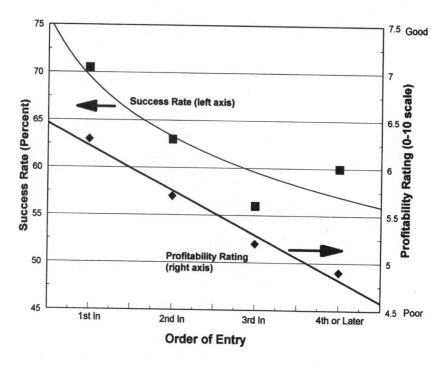

Figure 3.4   Impact of Order of Entry on Performance—Success Rates and Profitability

Source: NewProd studies, Cooper & Kleinschmidt, see endnote 20.

- Being 50 percent over budget in the development costs reduces profitability *only slightly* (by 3.5 percent).[21]

Another study suggests that a 20 percent reduction in time-to-market could increase the NPV of a new auto model by $350 million.[22]

Here again, the conclusions may be overstated. As Crawford notes, the McKinsey data were taken out of context. Moreover these percentages were for a very atypical and highly dynamic market situation (20 percent annual market growth rate; 12 percent annual price erosion; and a very short five-year product life). Even the report's author warns the reader of the dangers of an overemphasis on speed.[23] Further, our analysis of the profit impact of speed for *more typical market situations* reveals a *less dramatic effect of cycle time*. In numerous simulated examples, profitability (rate of return, IRR) decreases approximately with the square root of increasing development time (for example, increasing the development time fourfold cuts profitability approximately in half).

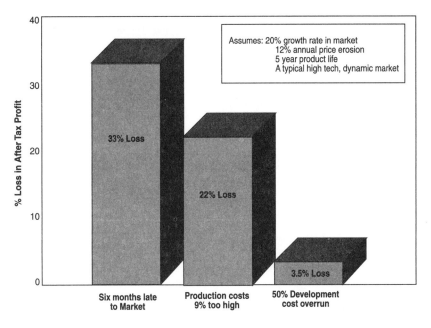

Figure 3.5 Sensitivity of Profits over Product Life
Source: McKinsey & Co. See endnote 21.

3. *Speed means faster response and fewer surprises.* The rapidly changing market and competitive conditions found in most markets gives the fast-response company the edge. For example, consider the advantage that fast-paced firms such as Toyota and Chrysler enjoy (three years to develop a new car) versus the traditional seven years taken by GM and Mercedes—a lot changes in the car market in seven years! Further, one report reveals that U.S. managers are looking at product lifetimes as short as two years in some industries;[24] this increasing product obsolescence means shorter windows of opportunity, hence the need for more rapid product innovation.[25] But such short life cycles are not universal—they're only true for a handful of very dynamic industries.

The goal of reducing the development cycle time is admirable. Most firms have reduced product development cycle times over the past five years, with the average reduction being about one-third.[26] But a word of caution here: speed *is only an interim objective* . . . a means to an end. The ultimate goal, of course, is a steady stream of successful new products. For example, the PDMA's best practices study found that the best firms actually took a little longer to develop new products than the average performer, which might be a reflection of the more challenging projects undertaken.[27] Further, many of the practices naively employed in order to reduce time-to-market ultimately cost the company money—they achieve the interim objective (bringing the product quickly to market) but fail at the ultimate objective (profitability). Some examples of poor practices:

- Cutting short the early phases of a new product project—the up-front-homework and the market studies—only to discover later that the product design does not meet customer needs, and the project itself is an ill-conceived one.
- Moving a product to market quickly by shortening the customer-test phase, only to incur product reliability problems after launch—resulting in lost customer confidence and substantial warranty and servicing costs.
- Focusing only on easy, quick-hits—line extensions and minor modifications—but paying the price later via a lack of significant new products and loss of longer-term competitive advantage.

Be careful in your quest for cycle-time reduction: too often the methods used to reduce development time yield precisely the opposite effect, and in many cases are very costly: they are at odds with sound management practice. Shortcuts are taken with the best intentions, but far too frequently result in disaster: serious errors of omission and commission, which not only add delays to the project, but often lead to higher incurred costs and even product failure.

Here are six *sensible* ways to reduce cycle time—ways that are totally consistent with sound management practice and are also derived from our lessons for success outlined above. In short, not only will these six methods increase the odds of winning, but they also reduce the time-to-market!

1. *Do it right the first time.* Emphasize quality of execution at every stage of the project. The best way to save time is by avoiding having to recycle back and do it a second time. Quality of execution pays off not only in terms of better results, but also by reducing delays (see success factor #5, previous chapter).
2. *Insist on up-front homework and demand sharp, early product definition.* Doing up-front homework and getting clear project definition, based on fact rather than hearsay and speculation, saves time

downstream: less recycling back to get the facts or to redefine the product requirements and sharper targets to work toward (see success factors #1 and #3, previous chapter). Recall that one of the greatest time wasters we uncovered in our NewProd project studies is the lack of sharp product definition—constantly changing product specs and moving goalposts.

3. *Build in the voice of the customer.* Far from adding time to the project, undertaking the necessary work with customers—from the inception stages right through to launch—actually improves time-to-market. These actions ensure that the product is right, that it meets customer needs, that it functions well in the field, and that the right Launch plan is in place. Deficiencies in any one of these areas spells much added time to the project (see success factor #2, previous chapter).

4. *Use parallel processing.* The relay race, sequential, or series approach to product development is antiquated and inappropriate. Given the time pressures of projects coupled with the need for a complete and quality process, a more appropriate scheme is a rugby game, or *parallel processing.* With parallel processing, activities are undertaken concurrently (rather than sequentially); thus more activities are undertaken in an elapsed period of time. The new product process must be multidisciplinary and cross-functional, with each part of the team—marketing, R&D, manufacturing, engineering—working together and undertaking its parallel or concurrent activity. Note that the play is a lot more complex using a parallel play or rugby scheme (versus a series approach); hence the need for a disciplined game plan.

5. *Prioritize and focus.* The best way to slow projects down is to dissipate your limited resources and people across too many projects. By concentrating resources on the truly meritorious projects, not only will the work be done better; it will be done faster. But focus means tough choices: it means killing other, perhaps worthwhile projects. And that requires good decision making and the right criteria for making Go/Kill decisions (see success factor #4, previous chapter).

6. *Organize around a multifunctional team with empowerment.* Multifunctional teams are essential to timely Development. "Rip apart a badly developed project and you will unfailingly find 75 percent of slippage attributable to: 'siloing', or sending memos up and down vertical organizational 'silos' or 'stovepipes' for decisions; and sequential problem solving," according to Peters.[28] Sadly, the

typical project resembles a relay race, with each function or department carrying the baton for its portion of the race, and then handing off to the next runner or department (see success factor #3, this chapter).

Key Points for Management

Speed in product development is important because it yields competitive advantage; it means less likelihood that the market has changed; and it means a quicker realization of profits. But there is also a dark side to speed:

- First, there is not a one-to-one link between speed and profits.
- Second, many of the actions people take in the interest of reducing cycle time have very negative effects, and in some cases increase time-to-market and reduce profitability.
- Finally, the quest for cycle time reduction may bias one's new product portfolio toward short-term, limited projects to the long-term detriment of the business.

I outlined six sensible ways above to achieve cycle time reduction—ways that not only speed new product to market, but also lead to higher profitability. Note from Figure 3.6 the *double positive impacts* of these six drivers on both cycle time reduction and profitability. Five of the six have to do with implementing a high-quality new product process, something I urge your leadership team to initiate. The sixth deals with organization—the use of true cross-functional teams—again something within the domain of the leadership team of the business.

Back to Basics

New product success is not chance or serendipity. It is the result of hard work, careful planning, and constant dedication. That's what makes winners in any game. This chapter has highlighted seven additional critical success factors that distinguish successful businesses and winning new products from the also-rans. These seven have less to do with the design of a new product process—those success factors were outlined in the previous chapter—but are nonetheless vital to success and have a direct bearing on how you manage your business's product innovation effort.

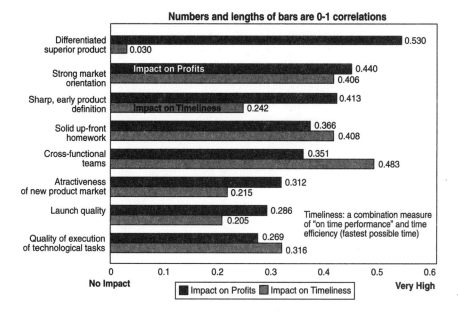

Figure 3.6 Success Factors & Their Impacts on Profitability & Timeliness
Source: NewProd studies, endnote 17.

Recall the key messages in this chapter:

1. You can't win the war without troops! The *resources must be in place.* Undertake a resource audit—both resource needs and resource availability—to see if your new product resources are adequate to achieve your goals and what the negative impact of resource deficiencies is on your business's new product results.

2. *Product advantage* is paramount, and every effort must emphasize gaining competitive advantage via the product. So build Go/Kill criteria into your decision gates that stress product advantage, and ensure that projects feature those actions I outlined above that logically lead to product advantage.

3. Don't forget the *soft side* of product development—the people issues. Move toward true cross-functional teams: empowered, but also accountable for results. Install a dedicated team leader for key projects, from beginning to end of projects; ensure that team members have the time freed up to stay focused and to work on their projects; keep the team small and provide the means for good team communication and interaction; and work on improving the climate for innovation in your business.

4. The *international dimension* remains an enigma for most businesses

when it comes to product development, so work on it! Try to move projects more toward the upper right of our international dimensions diagram (Figure 3.2). This means adopting a consistent new product process around the world—a transnational process, complete with international checks and commitments built in at various stages; international project teams; market research undertaken in multiple countries; global criteria for making Go/Kill and prioritization decisions; and a global gating organization.

5. Attack from a *position of strength* when selecting new product projects to invest in. Pastures may look greener on the other side of the fence, but in new products warfare, likely those pastures or arenas contain minefields. What's more, you'll probably find that your troops aren't even well suited to the terrain there. So understand your marketing, technological, and operations strengths, and try to select projects that leverage your strengths, expertise, resources, and experience.

6. Attacking an *attractive market* does not guarantee big rewards, but it sure helps. So build market attractiveness—market size, potential, growth, and the competitive situation—into your list of Go/Kill screening criteria. And score projects more points when they are targeted at such attractive markets.

7. *Emphasize speed,* but sensibly. Don't become a speed demon, where speed to market takes precedence over all other considerations. Speed yields competitive advantage, higher profitability, and fewer surprises at Launch. But there is also a dark side to speed. So build in best practices for effective cycle time reduction: quality of execution; up-front homework and sharp, early product definition; voice of the customer; parallel processing (new product rugby); focus; and cross-functional teams.

These seven items may seem fairly obvious and basic. Moreover, it is rather ironic that it has taken years of empirical research to prove the obvious—that these seven factors, and the six in the previous chapter—really do make the difference between winning and losing the new products war. On the other hand, as has been true in warfare over the centuries, it is the fundamentals and obvious factors that make all the difference, and *all too often people get these wrong.* So I urge you to stop looking for magic solutions, quick fixes, and flavors of the month: it's *back to basics* in order to win at new products warfare. And the seven factors in this chapter combined with the six in Chapter 2 are a good beginning list to focus on.

Time to Take Stock: A New Product Performance and Practices Audit

How well is your business performing in terms of the three cornerstones of new product performance? And how do you rate on the critical success factors outlined in this chapter and the previous chapter? The first place to begin is with an audit of your new product performance and practices.

In Chapter 1, I urged you to keep score—to start tracking your new product performance. Some businesses have gone far beyond that. Many of the companies who took part in our most recent benchmarking study wanted to know how well they were doing—both in terms of performance as well as best practices—versus the other businesses in the study, and especially versus the top performers. We now can provide this analysis for you via our *ProBE* service (see Appendix A). *ProBE* is a benchmarking tool that compares your business's performance and practices to other businesses', and pinpoints your relative strengths and weaknesses when it comes to product development—an excellent way to probe what needs fixing and overhauling in your business.

The Beginning of a Solution . . .

This chapter and Chapter 2 have outlined three cornerstones and 13 critical success factors—factors that distinguish successful new products, projects, and businesses from the losers.

I introduce these 13 success factors for two reasons. In the next chapter, we charge into overhauling your new product process, and in the chapters that follow, into more prescriptions and actions that your leadership team should take. Each of these actions is based on these success factors, and so it's important that you understand the foundation for these prescriptions. Throughout these chapters that follow, I attempt to build on the success factors, and also to logically build them into my prescriptions.

There is a second reason I spend so much time on the key cornerstones and success factors. Before you charge ahead, pause for a moment: remember, the beginning of a solution is understanding the problem. So, reflect on the three cornerstones of success and on the 13 success factors, and take stock of your own situation. Consider how well (or how badly) your business fares on each: your practices, methods, results. I urge you to undertake a new product audit before you charge into seeking solutions (see above "Time to Take Stock").

4

The *Stage-Gate*™ New Product Process

A process is a methodology that is developed to replace the old ways and to guide corporate activity year after year. It is not a special guest. It is not temporary. It is not to be tolerated for a while and then abandoned.
—**Thomas H. Berry, Managing the Total Quality Transformation[1]**

Stage-Gate™ Processes

A process for product innovation is one solution to what ails so many businesses' new product programs.[2] Facing increased pressure to reduce the cycle time yet improve their new product success rates, companies are increasingly looking to new product processes, or *Stage-Gate*™ methods, to manage, direct, and control their product innovation efforts. That is, they have developed a systematic process—a blueprint, template, or roadmap—for moving a new product project through the various stages and complex steps from idea to Launch. But most important, they have built into their roadmap the many *critical success factors* and *industry best practices* from Chapters 2 and 3 in order to heighten the effectiveness of their efforts. Consider these examples:[3]

> 3M has traditionally had an enviable new product track record. An innovative corporate culture and climate are often cited as 3M's secret to success. But for years 3M has also had in place various stage-and-gate systems for managing the innovation process. Thus creativity and discipline are blended to yield a successful new product program.

Procter & Gamble, always noted for its forward-thinking management methods, faced tougher times in its new product efforts in the 1980s. A senior management task force tried to find out why. One fact uncovered was that back in 1964, the company had implemented a new product gating system at a time when most people hadn't dreamed of the concept. The system worked well for 15 years, but fell from favor in the late 1970s with the advent of a new generation of managers. Beginning in the 1980s, new product performance in the company deteriorated. One recommendation of the task force: "Let's get back to basics and redesign and reimplement the stage-gate process." The company has. P&G relaunched a 1990s version of its game plan: a stage-and-gate model or SIMPL process for driving new products to market. And results are very positive.

Northern Telecom, a telecommunications equipment manufacturer, which has successfully penetrated the world market in the past few decades, implemented a *gating* process for new products in the early 1980s. The model cost approximately $1 million to design and implement, but paid for itself on the first major project. The documented results are impressive: shorter times-to-Launch, fewer mistakes, less recycling and rework in the process, and a more successful development effort.

Exxon Chemical began piloting a *Stage-Gate*™ process in its polymers business unit in the late 1980s. So successful was the process that Exxon Chemical has rolled the method out throughout its entire chemical business, and around the world. According to the father of Exxon's Product Innovation Process," the implementation of the PIP has probably had more impact on the way we do business than any other initiative at Exxon Chemical undertaken in the last decade."

Lego, the successful Danish toy manufacturer, replaces about one-third of its product line every year with new items—new castles, new towns, and so on. In order to accomplish this rapid introduction of new products consistently, successfully, and year after year, a process was needed. Since the late 1980s, Lego has been relying on a *Stage-Gate*™ new product process to ensure that everything comes together for these many and rapid launches each year.

Hewlett-Packard grows organically, largely because of a steady stream of brilliant new products. How? Some say it is because of the innovative culture and passion for innovation that was established right from the beginning by the company's two founders. Others say it is because of the dynamic nature of the industries that HP elects to target. Both reasons are right. But underlying successful new products at HP is a stage-and-gate process—their Phased Review process—which has been in place since the 1960s (although their 1990s Life Cycle version is quite different from the original model).

According to the PDMA's 1997 best practices study, "nearly 60% of the firms surveyed use some form of *Stage-Gate™* process (Cooper 1990). Over half of the firms which have adopted *Stage- Gate™* processes have moved from a basic process to more sophisticated versions with formal process ownership and facilitation (18.5% of the total) or third generation processes with more flexible gates and stage structures (Cooper 1994). Third-generation processes match the complexity and difficulty of the project."[4] The adopters of new product processes or *Stage-Gate™* methods are leading firms around the world, including Polaroid and Kodak; many firms in the chemical business, such as Exxon Chemical, Rohm and Haas, ICI, Mobil Chemical, Dow Chemical, Asahi Chemical, and various divisions at Du Pont, Air Products, and B. F. Goodrich; high-technology companies such as Hewlett-Packard, Northern Telecom, IBM, Lucent, Microsoft, Corning, and Emerson Electric; consumer goods firms, such as Procter & Gamble, SC Johnsons Wax, Reckitt & Colman, Carlsberg, and Guinness; and numerous service providers, such as NYNEX, U.S. West, American Express, VISA, and Royal Bank of Canada.

Stage-Gate™ methods work! According to the same PDMA best practices study cited above, "the best [companies] are more likely to use some type of formal NPD process than the rest. They are more likely to have moved from simpler *Stage-Gate™* processes to more sophisticated facilitated or third generation processes."[5] So, the challenge in this chapter is this: given the 13 critical success factors gleaned from new product success-and-failure experiences (previous two chapters), and given the various best practices identified, how can you translate these into an operational and effective new product methodology? For example, how do you build in quality of execution, or a strong market orientation, or better predevelopment homework? And what is your role as a member of the leadership team to ensure that such a *Stage-Gate™* process is implemented in your business, and really does get followed?

Key Points for Management

Do you have a systematic, formal new product process in your business? Many leading companies do and the results seem to be worth the effort. So, by this point, you're probably thinking that you should either . . .

- move to get a new product process designed and installed in your business; or if you already have a process . . .
- have your current process audited, and begin an overhaul of the process.

Before you proceed, here are some points to ponder—some of the goals that such a process must achieve. Does yours?

The Goals of an Overhauled New Product Process

Goal #1: Exemplary Quality of Execution . . . Second to None

The argument that the proponents of total quality management make goes something like this: "The definition of quality is precise: it means meeting all the requirements all the time.[6] It is based on the principle that all work is a process. It focuses on improving business processes to eliminate errors." The concept is perfectly logical and essentially simple. Most smart things are. And the same logic can be applied to new product development.

Product innovation is a process. It begins with an idea and culminates in a successful product Launch. But processes aren't new to the business environment. There are many examples of well-run processes in business: for example, manufacturing processes, information processes, and so on.

A quality-of-execution crisis exists, however, in the product innovation process. There exists the need for a more *systematic and quality approach* to the way firms conceive, develop, and launch new products. The way to deal with the quality problem is to visualize product innovation as a process, and to apply *process management* and *quality management techniques* to this process. Note that any process in business can be managed, and managed with a view to quality. Get the details of your processes right, and the result will be a high-quality output.

Quality of execution is the goal of the new product process. More specifically, the ideal process should:

1. *focus on completeness:* ensure that the key activities that are central to the success of a new product project are indeed carried out—no gaps, no omissions, a "complete" process.
2. *focus on quality:* ensure that the execution of these activities is proficient—that is, treat innovation as a process, emphasize DIRT-FooT (doing it right the first time), and build in quality controls and checks.
3. *focus on the important:* devote attention and resources to the pivotal and particularly weak steps in the new product process, notably the up-front and market-oriented activities.

Stage-Gate™ is simply a *process management tool* for product innovation. *Stage-Gate™* builds into the innovation process *high quality of execution* in much the same way that quality programs have been successfully implemented on the factory floor. How?

- by establishing quality-control checkpoints—the gates—where the quality of projects and the "goodness" of work underlying projects is scrutinized by senior management.
- by designating the leadership team as the main gatekeepers in the business—you are the quality controllers!
- by using clear and consistent metrics at gates—the Go/Kill criteria—so that projects are judged objectively and proficiently.
- by defining what activities, tasks, methods, and best practices should be built into the stages of the process to deliver a winning product.
- by specifying visible deliverables to gates, along with action standards—what the project team is expected to deliver to the gate review.
- by having an effective resource allocation method at gates, to ensure that resources—people, time, and money—are available to enable the project team to do a quality job.

The ultimate goal here is doing the right projects . . . and doing them right!

Goal #2: Sharper Focus, Better Project Prioritization

Most businesses' new product efforts suffer from a lack of focus: too many projects, and not enough resources. Earlier, adequate resources were identified as a principal driver of businesses' new product performance;

but a lack of resources plagues too many firms' development efforts. Sometimes this lack is simply that management hasn't devoted the needed people and money to the company's new product effort. But often, this resource problem stems from trying to do too many projects with a limited set of resources—that is, from a *lack of focus*, the result of inadequate project evaluations. The root cause of this lack of focus is management's failure to set priorities and make tough Go/Kill decisions. In short, the Go/Kill gates are weak.

The need is for a *new product funnel*, rather than *tunnel*. A *new product funnel* builds in tough Go/Kill decision points; the poor projects are weeded out; scarce resources are directed toward the truly meritorious projects; and more focus is the result. One funneling method is to *build the new product process around a set of gates* or Go/Kill decision points. These gates are the bail-out points where we ask, "Are we still in the game?" They are the *quality-control checkpoints* in the new product process, and check the quality, merit, and progress of the project.

Goal #3: A Strong Market Orientation

If positive new product performance is the goal, then a market orientation—executing the key marketing activities in a quality fashion—must be built into the new product process as a matter of routine rather than by exception. Marketing inputs must play a decisive role from beginning to end of the project. The following nine actions are *integral and vital plays* in the new product game plan:

- Preliminary market assessment
- Market research to determine user needs and wants
- Competitive analysis
- Value-in-use analysis
- Concept testing
- Customer reaction and feedback during Development
- User tests and field trials
- Test market or trial sell
- Market Launch based on a solid marketing plan

How do you ensure that your business's new product process is decidedly market-oriented?

▶ First, the key marketing tasks should be *designed into your new product process*. In many businesses' new product processes, they are not! If you already have a new product process, read through it, and see how many of the nine vital marketing actions are left out.

▶ Second, the leadership team—the gatekeepers—must mandate that such marketing actions be undertaken in projects. When they're not, stop the project! The problem is that, in the short term, marketing actions are treated as "optional" or *discretionary.* By contrast, technical activities, such as the physical development of the product, undertaking a trial production run, or doing lab tests to meet regulatory requirements, are normally not discretionary. Reconsider what's important!

▶ Finally, make the marketing resources available to project teams. You can't win games without players on the field!

Goal #4: Better Up-Front Homework and Sharp, Early and Stable Product Definition

New product success or failure is largely decided in the first few plays of the game—in those crucial steps and tasks that precede the actual Development of the product. The up-front homework defines the product and builds the business case for Development. The ideal new product process ensures that these early stages are carried out and that the product is fully defined before the project is allowed to become a full-fledged Development project.

The need for solid up-front homework parallels the case for a stronger market orientation (Goal #3). Once again the onus is on you, the leadership team, to be the enablers. Your task is to ensure that your new product process does indeed include solid homework and stable, fact-based product definition. For example, build in a product definition checkpoint in your process. And be prepared to halt projects if the homework and product definition aren't in place. Finally, you must make available the resources required to do the up-front work.

Goal #5: Fast-Paced Parallel Processing

New product teams face a dilemma. On the one hand, they are urged by senior management to compress the cycle time—to shorten the elapsed time from idea to Launch. On the other hand, they are urged to improve the effectiveness of product Development: cut down the failure rate—do it right! This desire to "do it right" suggests a more thorough, longer process.

Parallel processing is one solution to the need for a complete and quality process, yet one that meets the time pressures of today's fast-paced business world. Traditionally, new product projects have been managed via a *series approach*—one task strung out after another, in sequence. The analogy is that of a relay race, with each department running with the project for its 100 meter lap. Phrases such as "hand off," "passing the project on," "dropping the ball," and "throwing it over the wall" are common in this relay race approach to new products.

In marked contrast to the relay or sequential approach, with parallel processing many activities are undertaken *concurrently* rather than in series. The appropriate analogy is that of a rugby match rather than a relay race.[7] A team (not a single runner) appears on the field. A scrum or huddle ensues, after which the ball emerges. Players run down the field in parallel with much interaction, constantly passing the ball laterally. After 25 meters or so, the players converge for another scrum, huddle, or gate review, followed by another stage of activities.

With parallel processing, the game is far more intense than a relay race and more work gets done in an elapsed time period: three or four activities are done simultaneously and by different members on the project team. Second, there is less chance of an activity or task being overlooked or handled poorly because of lack of time: the activity is done in parallel, not in series, and hence does not extend the total elapsed project time. Moreover, the activities are designed to feed each other—the metaphor of the ball being passed back and forth across the field. And finally, the entire new product process becomes cross-functional and multidisciplinary: the whole team—marketing, R&D, engineering, manufacturing—is on the field together, participates actively in each play, and takes part in every gate review or scrum.

Goal #6: A True *Cross-Functional Team Approach*

The new product process is cross-functional: it requires the input and active participation of players from many different functions in the organization. The multifunctional nature of innovation coupled with the desire for parallel processing means that a *cross-functional team approach* is mandatory. Essential ingredients are:

- a cross-functional team with committed team players.
- a defined team captain or leader, accountable for the entire project.
- a leader with formal authority (co-opting authority from the functional heads).

▶ a fluid team structure, with new members added or dropped as work requirements demand.

▶ a small core group of responsible, committed and accountable team players from beginning to end.

Goal #7: Products with Competitive Advantage—Differentiated Products, Unique Benefits, Superior Value for the Customer

Don't forget to build in product superiority at every opportunity. This is one key to new product success, yet all too often, when redesigning their new product processes, firms fall into the trap of repeating current, often faulty, practices: there's no attempt to seek truly superior products. And so the results are predicable—more ho hum, tired products. Here's how to drive the quest for product advantage:

▶ Ensure that at least some of the criteria at every gate focus on product superiority. Questions such as "Does the product have at least one element of competitive advantage?", "Does it offer the user new or different benefits?", and "Is it excellent value for money for the user?" become vital questions to rate and rank would-be projects.

▶ Require that certain key actions designed to deliver product superiority be included in each stage of the process. Some of these have been mentioned above (Goals #3 and #4) and include: customer-focused ideation; user needs-and-wants market research studies; competitive product analysis; concept and protocept tests, preference tests and trial sells; and constant iterations with customers during Development via rapid-prototype-and-tests.

▶ Demand that project teams deliver evidence of product superiority to project Go/Kill reviews: make product superiority an important deliverable and issue at such meetings (rather than just dwelling on the financial calculations).

Goal #8: A Fast-Paced and Flexible Process

The new product process must be built for speed. This means eliminating all the time wasters and work that adds no value in your current new product process. It also means designing a flexible process, one that accommodates the risks and nature of different projects. Leading firms are now moving toward my *third-generation Stage-Gate™ process*,[8] which builds in flexibility, fluidity, fuzzy gates, focus, and facilitation. More on this next generation process later in the chapter.

Key Points for Management

You've just seen the eight goals of a well-crafted new product process. Recall from our benchmarking studies that merely having a formal, documented process leads to *no improvements in performance;* rather, it's the *nature* and *quality* of that process that makes all the difference.

Let's assume that you've decided either to develop a new product process or to overhaul your existing one, and so you've set up a task force to do so. Make sure that your task force understands clearly these eight goals. *Make these goals part of their mandate!* If they just go through the motions and merely document your current practice, you haven't gained a thing. Impress upon them that, whatever else they do, they must design a process that truly delivers on these eight goals.

The Structure of the *Stage-Gate™ Process*

These eight key goals, together with the 13 critical success factors from Chapters 2 and 3, have been fashioned into an effective new product process or *Stage-Gate™* model. I don't expect that senior management know all the details and intricacies of *Stage-Gate™;* but it's important that you know enough to decide whether your own process measures up, and where the gaps are. And if you do decide to lead here—to sponsor the design and implementation of a new product process in your business—then you should know a little about the concept and operations of a *Stage-Gate™* approach. Finally, since you are the gatekeepers, the expectation is that you have a solid understanding of your own process, gate deliverables, criteria, and so on. So get set for a quick introduction to *Stage-Gate™.*

The *Stage-Gate™* new product approach is a conceptual and operational model for moving a new product project from idea to Launch.[9] It is a blueprint for managing the new product process to improve effectiveness and efficiency. *Stage-Gate™* methods break the innovation process into a predetermined set of stages, each stage consisting of a set of prescribed, cross-functional, and parallel activities. The entrance to each stage is a gate: these gates control the process and serve as the quality-control and Go/Kill checkpoints. This stage-and-gate format leads to the name *"Stage- Gate"* process.*

The *Stage-Gate™* method is based on the experiences, suggestions, and observations of a large number of managers and firms and on my own and others' research in the field. Indeed my observations of what happened in over 60 case histories laid the foundations for the approach.[10] Since this *Stage-Gate™* method first appeared in print, it has been implemented in whole or in part in hundreds of leading firms worldwide, many of which have provided an excellent "laboratory setting" to further refine and improve the process. For example, stage-gaters have periodic benchmarking sessions among themselves, where they compare notes and learn from each other, and I am often asked to attend these sessions.

The Stages

The *Stage-Gate™* process breaks the new product project into discrete and identifiable stages, typically four, five, or six in number (Figure 4.1):[11]

- Each stage consists of a set of parallel activities undertaken by people from different functional areas within the firm. In most firms' *Stage-Gate™* methods, stages lay out a list of prescribed or highly recommended actions and best practices.
- Each stage is designed to gather information needed to advance the project to the next gate or decision point.
- Each stage is cross-functional, and no stage is owned by a functional area or department: there is no "R&D stage" or "marketing stage"!

For the first few stages, each stage costs more than the preceding one: the process is one of incremental commitment. For example, Stage 1 might cost $5,000, Stage 2 costs $50,000, Stage 3 costs $500,000, and so on. In order to manage risk, however, as the amounts at stake increase, then the uncertainties of the project must decrease. Note that risk is

---

*Although many other names are used besides stage-gate, including PDP (Product Delivery Process), PIP (Product Innovation Process), NPP (New Product Process), Gating System, and Product Launch System.

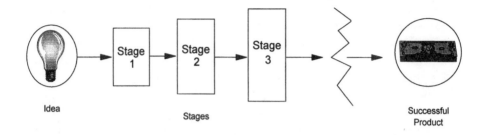

Each stage contains prescribed activities and best practices.

Figure 4.1 The *Stage-Gate*™ Method Breaks the New Product Process into a Series of Logical Stages

some combination of *amounts at stake* and *uncertainties*. Thus the process is deliberately designed to drive uncertainties down at each successive stage, so that by the time you have completed Stage 2 in the process, you are much wiser than you were at the completion of Stage 1. Each stage then can be viewed as a set of activities or tasks whose purpose is to gather information to drive down uncertainties. In this way, risk is managed.

An Overview of the Process

The general flow of the typical or a "generic" *Stage-Gate*™ process is shown in Figure 4.2. A quick review of the flow diagram shows that "Development" is the middle stage, and not surprisingly, "Full Production and Market Launch" is the final stage. The process is triggered by an idea (left circle), followed by two homework stages. Stage 1 is a fairly quick scoping to enable a narrowing of the field of projects, and the remaining projects enter Stage 2, the second homework stage, for a more detailed investigation. Following the "Development stage" is "Testing and Validation." Most important, a Post Implementation Review takes place at the very end (right circle). Let's walk through the stages in the process in Figure 4.2 quickly from left to right:

Stage 1—Preliminary Investigation: This is a quick investigation and scoping of a large number of potential projects, done relatively quickly and inexpensively, and based largely on "desk research." This stage provides inexpensive information to enable the field of projects to be narrowed before Stage 2.

Stage 2—Detailed Investigation (Build the Business Case): Stage 2 is a much

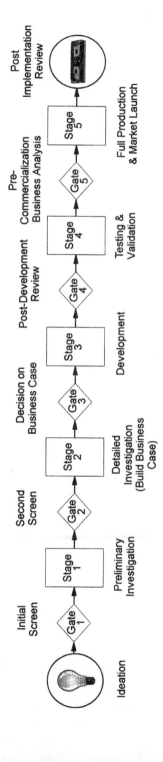

Figure 4.2 An Overview of a Typical Five-Stage, Five-Gate *Stage-Gate™* Process

Source: Cooper, endnote 3.

more detailed investigation, leading to a *business case*. This is where the bulk of the vital homework is done and most of the market studies are carried out. These result in a business case that includes the product definition, the project justification, and a project plan.

Stage 3—Development: Stage 3 is an expensive stage. Here, the actual design and development of the new product takes place, along with some product testing work. The deliverable at the end of Stage 3 is a "lab-tested product." Full production and marketing plans are also developed in this potentially lengthy stage.

Stage 4—Testing and Validation: The purpose of Stage 4 is to validate all commercial facets of the product and project—to verify the proposed new product, its marketing and production. This stage includes tests or trials in the marketplace, lab, and plant.

Stage 5—Full Production and Market Launch: This is the full commercialization stage, and marks the beginning of full production, marketing, and selling. Here the marketing, production/operations, distribution, Quality Assurance (QA), and post-Launch monitoring plans are executed.

The process concludes with a Post Implementation Review held about six to 18 months after a successful launch. The review closes the loop, terminates the new product project, and provides essential organizational learning.

There are two additional stages not formally designated in the above model. One of these is *idea generation:* it is shown on the flow model, but isn't numbered as a stage per se. Idea generation is a critical activity, but one that occurs prior to beginning the new product process: ideas are the inputs or triggers of the new product process.

The other nondesignated stage its *strategy formulation,* also an essential activity. This strategy formulation stage is left out of the *Stage-Gate™* model for now, not because it is unimportant, but because it is a strategic activity as opposed to process or tactics. Thus, strategy formulation is best superimposed over (or atop) the process model. It is a prerequisite to the *Stage-Gate™* model, and is the topic of Chapter 7.

The Gates

Preceding each stage is a gate or a Go/Kill decision point (see following page). The gates are the scrums or huddles on the rugby or football field. They are the points during the game where the team converges and where all new information is brought together. Gates serve as qual-

Some Gating Definitions

Gates
These are project review and decision meetings. They are the Go/Kill decision points in the *Stage-Gate™* new product process. Here, projects are evaluated by management, resources are allocated to projects, and poor projects are killed before additional resources are wasted.

Gatekeepers
Gatekeepers are a management team of decision makers and resource owners responsible for facilitating the rapid commercialization of selected projects. In a five-stage, five-gate process, typically it is you, the leadership team of the business, who are the gatekeepers from Gate 2 or 3 on.

Gatekeeping
Gatekeeping is management practices, behaviors, rules, and procedures that govern decision making and project facilitation designed to enable project teams to move good projects forward to rapid and effective commercialization. Note the emphasis on *enabling* rather than simply judging here.

These definitions are from Dr. Larry Gastwirt of Vantage Consulting, who undertook a study into effective gatekeeping within Exxon Chemical. Dr. Gastwirt, when he worked at Exxon, was the "father" of Exxon Chemical's PIP or Product Innovation Process, a *Stage-Gate™* process.

ity-control checkpoints, as Go/Kill and prioritization decision points, and as points where the path forward for the next play or stage of the process is decided.

Gates are usually manned by senior managers from different functions, who own the resources required by the project leader and team. The first few gates involve relatively few resources, and usually the gatekeepers are middle-level managers from R&D, marketing, engineering, and perhaps sales and operations. By Gate 3, which opens the door to a full-fledged development program, resource commitments are significant. Typically, from Gate 3 on, the leadership team of the business are the gatekeepers for all significant projects.

Gates have a common structure (see Figure 4.3). Gates consist of three main elements:

1. A set of required *deliverables:* what the project leader and team must bring to the decision point (for example, the results of a set of

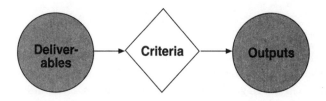

Deliverables: a prescribed list of items - results of completed actions - that the Project Leader must present to the gate

Criteria: a set of hurdles, criteria or questions that the project is judged on - to make Go/Kill & prioritization decisions

Outputs: a decision: Go/Kill/Hold/Recycle
an approved Action Plan: timeline, resources, deliverables for next gate

Figure 4.3   Gates Have a Common Format

completed activities). These deliverables are visible, are based on a standard menu for each gate, and are decided at the output of the previous gate. Management's expectations for project teams are thus made very clear.

2. *Criteria* against which the project is judged: these can include must-meet or knockout questions (a checklist) designed to weed out misfit projects quickly, for example:

   - Does the proposed project fit our business's strategy?
   - Does it meet our SHEL (safety, health, environmental, and legal) policies?

   There are also should-meet criteria or desirable factors, which are scored and added (a point count), which are used to prioritize projects, for example:

   - level of sustainable competitive advantage;
   - ability to leverage core competencies; and
   - market growth rate.

3. Defined *outputs:* for example, a decision (*Go/Kill/Hold/Recycle*), an approved action plan for the next *stage* (complete with people required, estimated money and person-days budget, and time schedule), a list of deliverables, and date for the next gate.

Key Points for Management

Do you know where your projects are? One of the first payoffs of implementing a *Stage-Gate™* process is being able to locate projects at one of five stages in the process. That is, you can map out your portfolio of projects, placing projects in each of five stages. Often there are surprises: Projects thought to be in the final stages are suddenly discovered to be missing activities that ought to have been done in the earlier stages. And so it's not clear where the project is!

If you currently have a new product process, take a critical look at it. Answer the following questions:

▶ Are your stages clearly defined?
▶ Are your projects clearly located within the stages (you can identify which stage each of your projects are in)?
▶ Are gates clearly defined, complete with . . .

- a standard menu of deliverables for each gate (you can produce the list)?
- visible criteria for making Go/Kill and prioritization decisions—either must-meet or should-meet, or both (again, you can produce the list)?
- defined gate outputs?

If not, maybe your process is an *imaginary process*, and lacks substance. Perhaps it's time to make your process a little more concrete and real.

The *Stage-Gate™* Process from Beginning to End

Let's take a closer look at the *Stage-Gate™* process and gain a solid idea of what's involved at each stage and gate. The next chapter lowers the microscope on the gates, which is where senior management plays a critical role. But for now, let's just go through the model, which you can follow stage-by-stage in Figure 4.2.[12]

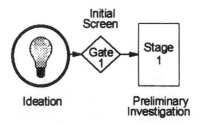

Idea Generation (or Ideation)

Ideas are the feedstock or trigger to the process, and they make or break the process. Don't expect a superb new product process to overcome a deficiency in good new product ideas. The need for great ideas coupled with high attrition rate of ideas means that the idea generation stage is pivotal: you need great ideas and lots of them. Many companies consider ideation so important that they handle this as a formal stage in the process, and build in a *defined, proactive idea generation and capture system.*

Four components of an idea generation and capture system that you can implement are these:

1. *Establish a focal point:* The problem is that idea generation is everyone's job and no one's responsibility. There's no one charged with making ideas happen, and there's no one to send good ideas to for action. The first step is to assign one person the responsibility of stimulating, generating, and handling new product ideas—a focal point or lightning rod for ideas.
2. *Identify the sources:* Where do good ideas come from? And where should they be coming from? The second step is to make a list of possible sources of new product ideas.
3. *Grease the path:* The next step is to stimulate and facilitate the flow of ideas from these sources. For example, suppose you've identified your sales force as a potential but underutilized source of ideas. Greasing the path might involve a sales force idea contest; featuring idea generation at your next annual sales force meeting; an easy-to-use idea kit so salespeople can submit their ideas quickly; and so on. Table 4.1 lists some ways to grease the path and get good new product ideas.
4. *Finally, set up an idea capture and handling system,* complete with IT support. The system in Figure 4.4 is a good example. Here . . .

   - Idea submissions should be easy to prepare, for example, and can be submitted via e-mail—a simple one-page form.
   - In some companies, ideas are public (for example, on *Lotus Notes* or *Intranet*) so that others can see them and make comments and suggestions.
   - Set up an idea screening group—the Gate 1 gatekeepers—to meet monthly to review ideas. Timely decisions are important.
   - Make sure this Gate 1 group uses a consistent list of published criteria, so that decisions are fair, and feedback is pro-

Table 4.1   Twenty-One Ways to Grease the Path and Get Great New Product Ideas

1. Run pizza-video parties, as Kodak does—informal sessions where groups of customers meet with company engineers and designers to discuss problems and needs and brainstorm potential solutions.
2. Allow time off—scouting time—for your technical people to putter on their own pet projects. 3M allows 15 percent time off; Rohm and Haas allows 10 percent.
3. Make a customer brainstorming session a standard feature of your plant tours.
4. Run focus groups with your customers—let them "play with products" and identify problems and desires.
5. Set up a customer panel that meets regularly to discuss needs, wants, and problems that may lead to new product ideas.
6. Survey your customers: find out what they like and dislike in your and competitors' products.
7. Use Product Value Analysis, as pioneered by Ron Sears—customers interacting with facets of your product, and then expressing their views, concerns, and difficulties.[13]
8. Undertake "fly-on-the-wall" or "camping out" research with customers, as does Fluke and HP (for example, anthropological research).
9. Observe your customers using (or misusing and abusing) your products.
10. Do what MIT's Eric Von Hippel suggests: identify your lead users—your innovative customers—and work closely with them.[14]
11. Use iterative rounds: a group of customers in one room, focusing on identifying problems; and a group of your technical people in the next room, listening and brainstorming solutions. The proposed solutions are then tested immediately on the group of customers.
12. Hire sales and technical people who can recognize potential new products. Train, encourage, and motivate them to do so.
13. Routinely survey your competition. Analyze their products, strategies, and business successes.
14. Set up a key word search that routinely scans trade publications in multiple countries for new product announcements, news, and so on.
15. Insist that your technical people—scientists, engineers, designers—visit customers with salespeople at least once per month (and not just on a trouble-shooting visit).
16. Treat trade shows as intelligence missions, where you view all that is new in your industry, under one roof.
17. Have your technical and marketing people visit your suppliers' labs and spend time with their technical people—find out what's new with them.
18. Set up an idea suggestion scheme or contest in your business. Promote it widely, and offer prizes and awards for good ideas.

continued

Table 4.1 Twenty-One Ways to Grease the Path and Get Great New Product Ideas (*continued*)

---

19. Run some group creativity sessions—brainstorming or synectics—in your business.
20. Set up an idea vault, and make it open and easily accessed. Allow employees to review the ideas and add constructively to them.
21. Set up a liaison with key researchers at universities. Consider supporting the research of some.

---

vided to the submitter (with reasons why his or her idea was rejected or accepted).

- Feedback to the submitter must be timely and in writing—a good reason to use gate criteria and a scoring sheet.
- Go ideas move to Stage 1, so empower the Gate 1 gatekeepers to be able to allocate resources and people at the gate meeting.
- Establish an idea vault for Kill and Hold ideas (again, group software makes it possible for this vault to be public, so that others in your business can augment ideas in the vault).
- Consider some token awards or recognition to successful idea submitters, whose ideas progress past Gate 1.

Gate 1: Initial Screen

Initial screening is the first decision to commit resources to the project: the project is born at this point. If the decision is Go, the project

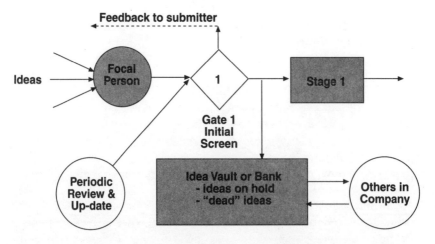

Figure 4.4 An Example of a Systematic Idea Capture and Handling Process

moves into the preliminary investigation stage. Thus, Gate 1 signals a preliminary but tentative commitment to the project: a flickering green light.

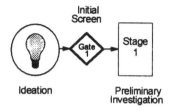

Gate 1 is a "gentle screen" and amounts to subjecting the project to a handful of key must-meet and should-meet criteria. These criteria often deal with strategic alignment, project feasibility, magnitude of opportunity and market attractiveness, competitive advantage, synergy with the business's resources, and fit with company policies. Financial criteria are typically not part of this first screen. A checklist for the must-meet criteria and a scoring model (weighted rating scales) for the should-meet criteria can be used to help focus the discussion and rank projects in this early screen.

Exxon Chemical has implemented its PIP (Product Innovation Process) whose initial gate has a handful of key Yes/No criteria:

- Strategic fit—Does the proposal fit within a market or technology area defined by the business as an area of strategic focus?
- Market attractiveness—Are the market size, growth, and opportunities attractive?
- Technical feasibility—Is there a reasonable likelihood that the product can be developed and produced?
- Killer variables—Do no known killer variables exist (for example, obsolescence, environmental issues, legislative actions)?

At Exxon Chemical, the gatekeepers include both technical and business (marketing) people. At this "Start Gate" meeting, project ideas are reviewed against these four criteria using a paper-and-pencil approach: this list of must-meet criteria is scored (Yes/No), and the answers to all questions must be Yes; a single No kills the project.

Stage 1: Preliminary Investigation

This first and inexpensive stage has the objective of determining the project's technical and marketplace merits. Stage 1 is a quick scoping of the project, often done in less than one calendar month's elapsed time and involving for 10 to 20 person-days' work effort. Key activities in Stage 1 include:

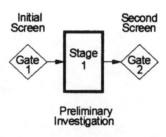

1. *Preliminary market assessment:* a quick scoping of the marketplace and a relatively inexpensive step very early in the life of a project, designed to assess market existence, probable market size, and market acceptance, and also to flesh out the idea into a defined concept. This is largely *detective work,* and might include desk research; a library and key word search through various trade magazines, commercial databases, and reports; utilizing in-house information and people; contacts with a few lead users; a few focus groups on users/customers; and even a quick concept test with a handful of potential users.
2. *Preliminary technical assessment:* a quick technical appraisal to propose a technical solution, map out a probable route, and assess technical costs, times, and risks. This work is largely conceptual: technical literature search; utilizing in-house technical expertise; brainstorming and creative problem-solving sessions; reviewing competitive product solutions; drawing on technical gurus outside the firm.
3. *Preliminary business assessment:* a quick financial assessment (for example, calculate the payback period) based on very rough estimates of sales, costs, and investment required; a cursory legal assessment; and a quick risk assessment.

Stage 1 thus provides for the gathering of both market and technical information—at low cost and in a short time—to enable a cursory and first-pass financial analysis as input to Gate 2. Because of the limited effort, and depending on the size of the project, very often Stage 1 can be handled by a team of just a few people (perhaps from marketing and from a technical group) in less than one month.

Gate 2: Second Screen

The project is subjected to a second and somewhat more rigorous screen at Gate 2. This gate is essentially a repeat of Gate 1: the project is reevaluated in the light of the new information obtained in Stage 1. If the decision is Go at this point, the project moves into a heavier spending stage.

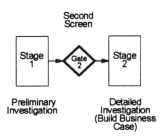

At Gate 2, the project is again subjected to the original set of must-meet and should-meet criteria used at Gate 1. Here additional criteria may be considered, dealing with sales force and customer response to the proposed product, potential legal, technical, and regulatory "killer variables"—all the result of new data gathered during Stage 1. Again, a checklist and scoring model facilitate this gate decision. The financial return is assessed at Gate 2, but only via a quick and simple financial calculation.

Reckitt & Colman, makers of well-known consumer brands such as Lysol, Easy Off and Air Wick, uses a well-crafted four-stage, four-gate Product Development Process. Gate 2 follows the preliminary investigation, called the "Concept Stage," and opens the door to a more detailed investigation, the "Feasibility Stage." The spirit of Gate 2 is: "does the initial evidence suggest the concept can win in the marketplace?" Gate 2 features a combination of must-meet and should-meet criteria. The must-meet items must yield Yes answers; the should-meet items are rated on scales. R&C's Gate 2 questions are shown in Table 4.2. At successive gates, many of the should-meet point count items become must-meet.

Hoechst's scoring model, used at Gates 2 and 3, is another example of well-crafted gate questions. It is illustrated in Appendix B and described in Chapter 6, as it sees double duty—as both a gate Go/Kill decision tool and also as a portfolio management model.

Table 4.2   Typical Gate 2 Questions (Reckitt & Colman)

1. Strategy and Priorities	
a) Does the project fit the corporate strategy?	M
b) Does the project fit the category strategy?	M
c) Does the project fit the operating unit strategy?	M
2. The Consumer	
a) Is there consumer appeal (that is, clear consumer need and expectation of consumer benefit)?	S
b) Is the market/category of an attractive size and with growth potential?	M
c) Does the concept have competitive advantage?	M
d) Is there a clear and viable marketing proposition?	S
3. The Trade	
a) Are there existing company trade channels?	M
b) Does the product have trade appeal and fit?	S
4. Technical	
a) Is manufacturing or procurement feasible?	S
b) Are there any serious issues—legal?	M
c) Issues—health and safety?	M
d) Issues—environmental?	S
5. Financial	
a) Does the project have a national potential?	M
b) Are financial projections in line with financial criteria?	S
6. Other	
a) Does the project have international potential?	S

M = must-meet   S = should-meet (scored on a scale)

Stage 2: Detailed Investigation (Build the Business Case)

The business case opens the door to product development. Stage 2 is where the business case is constructed: this stage is a detailed investigation stage that clearly defines the product and verifies the attractiveness of the project prior to heavy spending. It is also the *critical homework stage*—the one found to be so often weakly handled. Exhibit 4.5 maps out the major activities and events in this pivotal stage. Here are the key actions:

1. *User needs-and-wants studies* help flesh out the idea into a "winning" new product definition. This is market research that must entail in-depth surveys or face-to-face interviews with prospective customers and users to determine customer needs, wants, and preferences; likes, dislikes, and order-winning criteria; product performance requirements; and a definition of the customer's wish list.

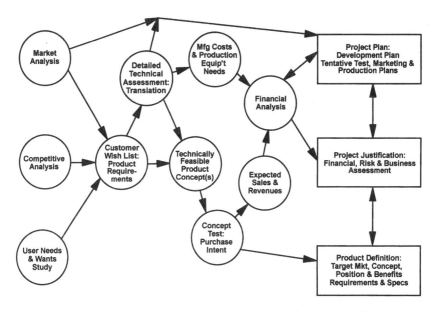

Figure 4.5   The Key Activities in Stage 2 in Building the Business Case

Hewlett-Packard used extensive market research (including consumer choice modeling studies) to pinpoint desired features and attributes that customers desired in a hand-held calculator. What came out of the study was the desire to see results graphically, which led to HP's graphics display calculator (where the graph or equation is shown visually on an LED display). The product has been a great winner for HP.

The examples cited earlier, namely, for Fluke's Process Calibrator, *Transitions III*, and ECC's Opacitex clay, also are excellent illustrations of the type of Stage 2 *user needs-and-wants studies* that you should demand.

2. *Value-in-use studies* provide an assessment of the customer's economics—what economic value the product will bring to the customer (this often involves an in-depth look at the customer's use system, the current solution, and various cost drivers).

3. *Competitive analysis* is also a part of this stage. Here the project team should investigate direct and indirect competitors: their products, to uncover their strengths and weaknesses; their business performance, to gain insights into how well each is doing; and their strategies and bases of competition, to understand how each competes, and what works and what doesn't.

4. *Concept testing* is needed here. This means testing the proposed product in concept or *protocept* form to gauge customer interest, liking, and purchase intent (and an estimate of expected sales and price sensitivity). Note that the product is not yet developed, but a model or representation of the product is displayed to prospective users to assess response.

> In Fluke's new product process, potential customers "see" the instrument before it even exists. The description and specifications of the proposed product are developed, and a dummy brochure is produced—a brochure that is very close to the final, four colors and all. The argument is that it's much cheaper to develop a brochure than to develop a product! Prospective users are shown the proposed product (in concept form in the brochure), asked to critique it, and then to indicate their liking and purchase intent. In this way, Fluke tests the proposed product even before Development begins!

This concept test is vital because it helps spot product deficiencies when they can still be corrected, and also gauges purchase intent, a key input into the determination of expected sales volumes. Price sensitivities can also be measured, although with some caution.

5. *Detailed technical assessment* in Stage 2 focuses on the technical feasibility of the project. Customer needs and "wish lists" are translated into a technically and economically feasible solution; the likely technical solution is identified; technical feasibility is demonstrated; and technical risks along with safety, health, legal, and regulatory issues are assessed and dealt with.

   This translation usually involves some preliminary design or physical technical work (such as laboratory work, modeling, or the development of a crude working model or protocept). But Stage 2 is not a full-fledged Development project! A good rule of thumb is: "spend no more than 10 percent of technical Development costs on technical feasibility work in Stage 2." The idea is to take the technical work far enough so that technical feasibility is demonstrated, but don't develop the product—that happens in the next stage.

6. *A manufacturing (or operations) appraisal* is part of building the business case, where issues of manufacturability, costs to manufacture, and investments required are investigated. If appropriate, detailed legal, patent, and regulatory assessment work is undertaken in order to remove risks and to map out the required action.

7. Finally, *a detailed financial analysis is* conducted as part of the justification facet of the business case. This financial analysis typically involves a discounted cash flow approach (NPV and IRR or ROI percent), complete with sensitivity analysis to look at possible downside risks. Most businesses agree on a standard, compiled spreadsheet and use that for all Gate 3, 4, and 5 meetings. Recent evidence has begun to cast doubt on the validity of NPV as an appropriate financial gauge of the value of the project, however. More on this topic in next chapter on gates and gatekeeping, where better methods than traditional discounted cash flow and NPV methods are proposed.

The result of Stage 2 is a *business case* for the project. The business case comprises three crucial elements: the "what and for whom"; the "why"; and the "how, when, how much, and by whom."

The Business Case:
1. *What is the product and who will it be sold to?*

    The *product definition* is developed and agreed to. Recall from Chapter 2 the importance placed on sharp, early product definition prior to Development. Note that this definition goes *well beyond a technical definition* (for example, product specifications); it includes:

    ◗ specification of the target market: exactly who the intended users are.
    ◗ description of the product concept and the benefits to be delivered.
    ◗ delineation of the positioning strategy (including the price point).
    ◗ a list of the product's features, attributes, requirements, and high-level specs (prioritized: "must have" and "would like to have").

2. *Why invest in this project?*

    A *thorough project justification* is developed. This includes the strategic rationale for the project, the financial analysis, and a business risk assessment. The financial sensitivity analysis provides useful inputs to the risk assessment, by addressing a set of "what if" questions.

3. *How will it be undertaken, when, by whom, and how much will it cost?*

A *project plan* is developed. The general rule is that, at each gate, senior management wants to see a detailed plan of action for the next stage—in this case, a detailed Development plan—and also a tentative or throw-away plan through to Launch, with extraordinary expenditure items highlighted.

Stage 2 involves considerably more effort than Stage 1, and requires the inputs from a variety of sources. Stage 2 is best handled by a team consisting of cross-functional members: the core group of the eventual project team.

Gate 3: Decision on the Business Case

Gate 3 is often called the "money gate." This is the final gate prior to the Development stage, the last point at which the project can be killed before entering heavy spending. Once past Gate 3, financial commitments are substantial. In effect, Gate 3 means "go to a heavy spend." Gate 3 also yields a sign-off on product definition. Because of its importance, the Gate 3 gatekeepers are usually the leadership team of the business.

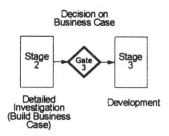

The qualitative side of this evaluation involves a review of each of the activities in Stage 2. It checks that the activities are undertaken, the quality of execution is sound, and the results are positive. Recall that gates have a predefined list of deliverables, and as a gate quality controller, your role is to review these deliverables to ascertain that they are of high quality. Table 4.3 provides a sample and fairly generic list of deliverables for Gate 3 at WR Grace, a major chemical and materials company. Every one of your gates should have a similarly mapped-out list.

Next, Gate 3 subjects the project once again to the set of must-meet and should-meet criteria used at Gate 2, but they are more rigorously applied at Gate 3. Finally, because a heavy spending commitment is the

Table 4.3 Sample Deliverables to Gate 3 (the "Go-to-Development" Gate)

A WR Grace Division

- Strategic fit confirmed
- Detailed market assessment
- Detailed technical/manufacturing assessment
- Resource constraints (capital, people)
- Detailed financial assessment
- Detailed legal/regulatory assessment
- Potential killer variables addressed
- Critical success factors are understood and feasible to achieve
- Recommendations to proceed, hold, or kill
- Detailed plan for Stage 3 (Development)
- High-level plan for remaining stages

result of a Go decision at Gate 3, the results of the financial analysis are an important part of this gate decision.

If the decision is Go, Gate 3 sees commitment to the product definition and agreement on the project plan that charts the path forward: the Development plan and the preliminary operations and marketing plans are reviewed and approved at this gate. The full project team—an empowered, cross-functional team headed by a leader with authority—is designated. The resources—both people and money—are committed. And a list of deliverables for the next gate is agreed to.

Stage 3: Development

Stage 3 witnesses the implementation of the Development plan and the physical development of the product. Some in-house or lab testing usually occurs in this stage as well. The main deliverable at the end of Stage 3 is a prototype product—one that has been lab- or in-house-tested, and also has undergone some preliminary customer tests (feedback from customers has been received).

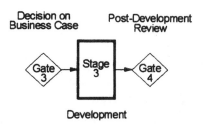

The Development plan, which you, the leadership team, sign off at Gate 3, is the roadmap for Stage 3. This Development plan consists of:

- a chronological listing of activities, actions, and tasks;
- a timeline or time schedule, showing beginning and end points of these actions;
- resources required for each action or task, notably personnel, person-days and money; and
- milestones to be achieved throughout the Development phase.

The timeline is a critical element of the plan. The plan is developed, complete with the tasks to be done and the deadline dates. It must be aggressive, causing team members to stretch a bit. But it must also be realistic. Further, *deadlines must be regarded as sacred* if speed is the objective. By sacred deadlines, I mean that a predetermined date is adhered to as a guideline for planning, with no excuses. Delays are dealt with via extra input of effort and resources, *not postponement*.

The emphasis in Stage 3 is on technical work. That is, technical work proceeds to develop rapid prototypes and then the final prototype. Some lab or engineering and in-house testing takes place here as well.

Marketing and manufacturing activities also proceed in parallel. For example, market analysis and customer feedback work continue concurrently with the technical development, with constant customer opinion sought on the product as it takes shape during Development. These activities are back-and-forth or iterative, with each development result—for example, rapid prototype, working model, first prototype, and so on—taken to the customer for assessment and feedback.

Meanwhile, detailed test plans, market launch plans, and production or operations plans, including production facilities requirements, are developed. An updated financial analysis is prepared, while regulatory, legal, and patent issues are resolved.

For lengthy projects, numerous milestones and periodic project reviews are built into the Development plan. These are not gates per se: Go/Kill decisions are not made here; rather these milestones provide for project control and management: they are checkpoints along the way where the team checks to make sure that the project is on schedule and on budget. One rule of thumb is that if several milestones in a row are missed, the project is flagged, and the project leader must call for a full review of the project (in my model in Figure 4.2, the project cycles back Gate 3, so that you gatekeepers can reconsider the wisdom of continuing with this project, now in trouble). In this way, milestone points can be used to *blow the whistle* on projects that are heading off course, before the problem becomes too serious.

Gate 4: Post-Development Review

The post-Development review is a check on the progress and the continued attractiveness of the product and project. Development work is reviewed and checked, ensuring that the work has been completed in a quality fashion, and that the developed product is indeed consistent with the original definition specified at Gate 3. This gate also revisits the economic issues via a revised financial analysis based on new and more accurate data.

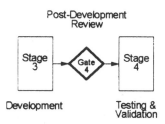

By Gate 4, the decision emphasis has shifted from the main question at the earlier gates, namely, "Should you invest in this project?" to "How well is the project unfolding—is it on track?" The Go/Kill criteria at Gates 4 and 5 reflect this shift. Certainly, the Gate 3 criteria that deal with strategic fit and financial performance are revisited, but now most of the gate questions focus on the successful completion of tasks, and the fact that positive results are being achieved—that the deliverables are in place and positive.

Gate 4 sees the test or validation plans for the next stage approved for immediate implementation, and the detailed marketing and operations plans reviewed for probable future execution. Capital expenditure decisions are often approved at Gate 4 as well.

Stage 4: Testing and Validation

This stage tests and validates the entire commercial viability of the project: the product itself, the production process, customer acceptance, and the economics of the project. A number of activities are undertaken at Stage 4:

1. *In-house product tests:* extended lab tests to check on product quality and product performance under controlled or lab conditions.
2. *User tests or field trials of the product:* to verify that the product functions under actual use conditions, and also to gauge potential

customers' responses to the product—to confirm purchase intent and market acceptance.

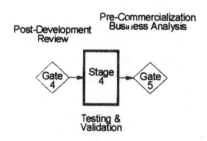

3. *Trial, limited, or pilot production:* to test, debug, and prove the production process, and to determine more precise production costs and throughputs.
4. *Pretest market, test market, or trial sell:** a mini launch of the product in a limited geographic area or single sales territory. This is a test of all elements of the marketing mix, including the product itself, and gauges customer response, measures the effectiveness of the Launch plan, and determines expected market share and revenues.
5. *Revised financial analysis:* to check on the continued economic viability of the project, based on new and more accurate revenue and cost data.

During the development of a new telephone handset, a major telephone manufacturer assembled 100 prototype units. Fifty of these were used for in-house reliability tests (lab tests). The other 50 were installed in customers' homes. The customer tests proved crucial to the product's eventual success, when a potentially disastrous flaw in the product's design was uncovered: in the wall-phone design, the receiver fell off the hook when a nearby door was slammed hard enough to jiggle the wall. The lab, of course, had solid concrete walls, and the problem went undetected until the customer test. A minor design modification overcame the problem before thousands of phones with faulty receivers found their way into households.

---

*A test market or trial sell is both expensive and time-consuming, yields information that can be sometimes obtained via other methods, and hence is not always appropriate for every project.

Ironically, the same company was not quite so lucky in a subsequent product development. In the interest of saving some time, the field trials were cut short. And it wasn't until the product was commercialized that the design flaw was discovered: the fact that the phone's circuitry picked up local AM radio signals, something that was not found in the lab, but was unfortunately discovered in thousands of households following Launch!

Gate 5: Precommercialization Business Analysis

This gate opens the door to full commercialization: market Launch and full production or operations starts up. It is the final point at which the project can still be killed. Although some managements consider this gate largely a formality, note that this gate is important because it signifies that the leadership team of the business is 100 percent aligned and in support of the commercial Launch of the product.

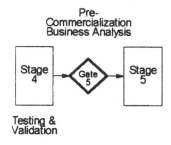

This gate scrutinizes the quality of the activities at the testing and validation stage and their results. Criteria for passing the gate focus largely on expected financial return and appropriateness of the launch and operations start-up plans. The operations and marketing plans are reviewed and approved for implementation in Stage 5.

Additionally some businesses' senior managements desire post-Launch plans in place and approved here. The post-Launch plan can be short term, dealing largely with monitoring the launch (what performance metrics will be measured and how?), and making needed fixes along the way. The post-Launch plan can also be longer-term, often called the Life Cycle Plan. This answers the question: what is the long-term future for this product—what new variants, improvements and even replacement products are envisioned? Ideally some of these longer-term issues in the Life Cycle Plan have been part of the discussion at earlier gates (such as at Gate 3, where the strategic rationale was reviewed in the business case), but here at Gate 5, the specifics are provided.

Stage 5: Full Production and Market Launch

This final stage involves implementation of both the marketing Launch plan and the production or operations plan. Other supporting plans, such as the distribution/logistics plan and the quality assurance plans, are also executed. The post-Launch monitoring plan kicks in early in the Launch stage, where the project's performance on key metrics takes place, and the project team responds with necessary action. Finally, some elements of the longer term Life Cycle Plan begin to be implemented—for example, needed improvements and new variants of the product.

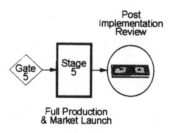

Post Implementation Review

Gate 5 — Stage 5

Full Production & Market Launch

No project ever runs perfectly during the Launch phase. But given a well-thought-out plan of action backed by appropriate resources, and of course, barring any unforeseen events, it should be clear sailing for the new product . . . another new product success!

Post Implementation Review

At some point following commercialization (often six to 18 months after), the new product project must be terminated. The project team is disbanded, and the product becomes a "regular product" in the firm's product line. This is also the point where the project and product's performance is reviewed. The latest data on revenues, costs, expenditures, profits, and timing are compared to projections to gauge performance. Gaps or variances between actual performance and projected performance are identified, and reasons for these gaps are explored. Finally a postaudit is carried out: a critical assessment of the project's strengths and weaknesses, what you can learn from this project, and how your business can do the next one better. This review marks the end of the project. Note that the project team and leader remain accountable for the success of the project through this post-Launch period, right up to the point of the post implementation review.

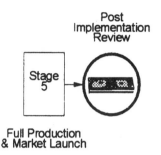

This is a critical review point in the project, but often does not take place. Rather, the project team members go their own way, while the product itself drifts into the history books. This is wrong! First, there is lost accountability. Insist that the project team report back to you, the Gate 3, 4, and 5 gatekeepers, with a full account of what they achieved versus what they promised. Second, no one knows whether the project was really a success! Finally, there is no organizational learning. Make sure that this final review occurs.

Some businesses split this post implementation review into two reviews. The first is held relatively soon after launch to bring the gatekeepers up-to-date on results thus far, and to seek approval and resources needed for course corrections. Then the final review takes place, much as described above, after the business results are known.

Built-in Success Factors

The logic of a well-designed new product process, such as the *Stage-Gate™* process in Figure 4.2, is appealing because it incorporates many of the factors and lessons vital to success and speed that I highlighted in previous chapters:

1. The process places much more emphasis on the homework or pre-Development activities. Stages 1 and 2—the preliminary investigation and the detailed investigation stages—are essential steps before the door to Development is opened at Gate 3.
2. The process is multidisciplinary and cross-functional. It is built around an empowered, cross-functional team. Each stage consists of technical, marketing, production/operations, and even

financial activities, necessitating the active involvement of people from all of these areas. The gates are cross-functional too: gates are manned by gatekeepers from different functions or departments in the firm, namely, the managers who own the resources needed for the next stage. Alignment among senior managers and across functions is assured.

3. Parallel processing, via a rugby game approach, speeds up the process. Activities in each stage are undertaken concurrently, rather than sequentially, with much interaction between players and actions within each stage. Compared to the series or relay race approach, many more activities are done in a given time period, and time compression is the result. One caveat: projects must be resourced properly in order that this rugby approach work.

4. A strong market orientation is a feature of the process. Marketing inputs begin in Stage 1, and remain an important facet of every stage from beginning to end of the process. Stage 2 sees extensive marketing research and customer information as vital inputs to the design of the product and justification of the project. Even during the lengthy Development stage, there is constant customer input and feedback as the product starts to take shape. As a gatekeeper, it is your job to ensure that projects not pass through gates *until the marketing actions have been completed* in a quality way.

5. A product definition step is built into the process at Stage 2, the detailed investigation. It is here that the project and product are both defined and justified. This product definition is a key deliverable to Gate 3; without it, the project cannot proceed to Development.

6. A parallel theme is an emphasis on delivering a superior, differentiated product—one that offers customers unique benefits and superior value for money. The actions in Stage 2, with an emphasis on user needs-and-wants studies (recall the Fluke, *Transitions III* and ECC Opacitex examples) along with customer feedback throughout the process doesn't guarantee product superiority, but they certainly improve the odds. And gate criteria that demand product superiority help deprioritize mediocre, ho-hum product projects, and reallocate resources to projects that promise to deliver products that delight the customer.

7. There is more focus. The process builds in decision points in the form of gates. These gates weed out poor projects early in the

process and help focus scarce resources on the truly deserving projects. And so the good projects are accelerated to market. Via defined gate criteria, gates also ensure that you do *the right projects*—ones that are strategically aligned and important, that leverage your core competencies, that target more attractive markets, and that promise to deliver unique, superior products.

8. There is a strong focus on quality of execution throughout. The recommended activities within each stage lay out a roadmap for the project leader and team—there is less chance of critical errors of omission. The gates provide the critical quality-control checks in the process: unless the project meets certain quality standards, it fails to pass the gate.

9. The international dimension can easily be accommodated by the process, should you choose to do so. The *Stage-Gate™* process in some multinational companies is a transnational and universal one, used around the world by all business units. Stage activities include international checks, international involvement, and marketing and market research actions in multiple countries. Gate criteria can be designed to favor global and glocal projects versus strictly domestic ones. And project teams and gate meetings are also international.

10. Finally, the process is flexible and designed for speed, but without loss of discipline. Long lead time activities can be moved forward; gates can be combined and stages collapsed; and lower-risk projects can be fast-tracked. But these detours are conscious ones, decided at the previous gate, with full knowledge of the risks involved and approved by you, the gatekeepers.

Key Points for Management

Take a critical look at your own new product process in your business. Then take this 10-question test: Yes   No

1. Does my process emphasize the up-front homework before serious Development begins? Is "good" homework done in every major project?   ☐   ☐
2. Is my process multidisciplinary and cross-functional, building on empowered, cross-functional project teams?   ☐   ☐

3. Does my process feature parallel processing—a rugby game approach where activities are undertaken concurrently, rather than sequentially—to speed up projects? ☐ ☐

4. Is a strong market orientation a feature of the process— solid market studies, excellent customer information, products designed with good customer input? ☐ ☐

5. Is a product definition step built into the process before Development begins, where senior management and the project team signs off? ☐ ☐

6. Is there an emphasis on delivering a superior, differentiated product—one that offers customers unique benefits and superior value for money? Does my process build in criteria and activities to deliver this? ☐ ☐

7. Does my process achieve focus via tough Go/Kill decision points or gates, which weed out poor projects and allocate resources to the truly deserving projects? ☐ ☐

8. Is there a strong emphasis on quality of execution throughout? ☐ ☐

9. Does my process build in the international dimension— international involvement and checks, multicountry market research, international project teams, and gatekeeping? ☐ ☐

10. Is my process flexible and designed for speed but without loss of discipline? ☐ ☐

Score yourself and your new product method—one point for each Yes answer.

0–5 points:	You have major problems, and are probably underperforming considerably. Time for radical action.
6–8 points:	Fair, but needs improving. Identify the weaknesses and begin the overhaul.
9–10 points:	Good. Performance should be excellent. Fix the last item, and carry on.

Beyond *Stage-Gate™*: The Third-Generation *Stage-Gate* Process

What is beyond the *Stage-Gate™* process I described above? Those companies that have successfully installed a *Stage-Gate™* process (what I call a "second-generation process") are now moving toward my *third-generation version* of the process, according to the latest PDMA survey of best practices.[15] Here's the evolution:

First-generation processes were the phased review processes that appeared in the 1960s. They were largely engineering-driven, and featured laborious check-offs at each review point to ensure the successful completion of a number of key tasks. The method was more a *measurement and control* methodology, designed to ensure that the project was proceeding as it should and that every facet of it was completed, and on time. But the process was very technically focused. It applied strictly to the physical design and development of the product (for example, it was not cross-functional and excluded marketing and manufacturing people). It did not specify what actions should be taken in each stage, nor were best practices a part of the process. And the process was accused by some of being very time-consuming . . . very laborious check-offs.

Today's second-generation *Stage-Gate™* processes, as described in the chapter, evolved from the phased review process of the 1960s. They too consist of identifiable and discrete stages preceded by review points or gates. But that is where the similarities end. *Stage-Gate™* overcomes many of the objections found with first-generation processes. *Stage-Gate™* is cross-functional, with no department owning any stage—marketing and manufacturing are now integral parts of the process. The gates are also cross-functional, so that there is alignment of senior people on project priorities. The process is more holistic. It emphasizes the front-end more so (up-front homework and a stronger customer input). It specifies stage activities and best practices. And it builds in parallel processing.

Stage-Gate™ processes are *evergreen processes*, however, and are constantly evolving and improving. Experienced stage-gaters have improved their processes to emphasize *efficiency—speeding up* an already effective second-generation process, and *more efficiently allocating development resources.* According to the latest PDMA survey, almost one-half of companies that have adopted *Stage-Gate™* processes have evolved it to include some of the elements of my third-generation process.[16]

The third-generation process is a natural evolution, once the second-generation or *Stage-Gate™* process has been successfully installed in your business. It features six fundamental Fs:

1. Flexibility
2. Fuzzy (conditional) gates
3. Fluidity
4. Focus (project prioritization and portfolio management)
5. Facilitation
6. Forever green—always regenerating and improving

1. *Flexibility:* The process is not a straitjacket or hard-and-fast set of rules. Rather, each project can be routed through the process according to its specific risk level and needs. Stages can be omitted and gates combined, provided the decision is made consciously, at gates, and with a full understanding of the risks involved (see success factor #6 in Chapter 2). The new product process is essentially a *risk-management process,* and thus the risk level, the uncertainty, and the need for information dictate what steps and stages need to be done, and which can be left out. Typically, lower-risk projects omit some stages, activities, and gates, with this routing decision made at the previous gate.

   In the Royal Bank of Canada, one of North America's largest banks, the Business Banking unit uses a five-stage, five-gate new product process called RPR (right products right), not unlike the process shown in Figure 4.2. Senior management uses a *triage approach* and has defined three categories of projects, based on project scope, investment, and risk level. These are:

   - *system change requests,* which are relatively minor product changes and improvements, often in response to a request from a major corporate client. These go through a two-stage, two-gate version of the model.
   - *fast-track projects,* which are medium-cost projects and feature some risk (less than $500,000 development cost, but impact on multiple customers). These moderate-risk projects are tracked through a four-stage version of the model, which collapses the two homework stages into a single stage.
   - *major projects,* over $500,000, are considered higher risk, and pass through the full five-stage model.

2. *Fuzzy gates:* Here I mean "fuzzy" in the sense of fuzzy logic—a newer form of mathematics—where instead of just being binary (open or closed), gates can have various states in between. Thus,

Go decisions can be *conditional on some future event occurring,* and the decision can be made in the absence of perfect information, conditional on positive results delivered later.

Consider Rohm and Haas's gating process. If a project is reviewed at a gate and found to be missing one key deliverable (for example, the results of a legal or regulatory investigation), with today's process, the decision is to *hold the project,* waiting the results of this study. In the faster-paced third-generation *Stage-Gate™* process, the gate decision becomes a "conditional Go." The team moves ahead to the next stage, but is required to report back to the head gatekeeper the results of the missing study. If she is comfortable with the results, the *conditional Go* decision becomes a *full Go;* if not; the head gatekeeper calls for a full gate meeting and the project is reviewed again, possibly to be killed or rethought. The point is that the project moves ahead, and is not held up awaiting one piece of information; but there is *also a check* to ensure that the future information is forthcoming and that results are positive.

3. *Fluidity:* The process is fluid and adaptable. Activities are not married to specific stages, as they are today. Rather, there is overlapping of stages: some activities, normally done in the next stage, will begin before the previous stage is completed; long lead-time activities can be brought forward from one stage to an earlier one; and the demarcation between stages is more fluid. For example, in the case of overlapping stages, a project can be in two stages at the same time; that is, one stage can begin before the preceding one is complete.

Here's the rule at GTE's Network System Division in Boston: "Long lead-time activities can be brought forward from one stage to a previous one. For example, ordering materials or equipment with very long lead-times may best be done in an earlier stage even though the project may yet be canceled. The risks of placing the order earlier must be weighed against the extra cost of postponement of the launch (a quantitative assessment)."

4. *Focus:* The process is focused, much like a funnel, where poor projects are weeded out at each gate, and resources are reallocated to the best projects. This means tough Go/Kill decision points or

gates, coupled with effective *portfolio management*, where gates consider more than just the merits of the one project under review. Because focus, gates and portfolio management are such vital topics, I devote two chapters to these: Chapters 5 and 6.

5. *Facilitation:* The next F is facilitation, and I add this as a new element since the original *Third-Generation* article was written.[17] To my knowledge, there has *never been a successful installation of a* Stage-Gate™ *process* without a process manager or facilitator in place! And for larger companies, this is a full-time position. The role of this process facilitator—often called the key master, process manager, gate meister, or process keeper—is to make sure that the *Stage-Gate™* process works, efficiently and effectively. The process keeper facilitates every important gate meeting, acting as a referee, ensuring that gatekeepers follow the rules of the game (next chapter), and that a decision is made. She coaches the project teams, helping them overcome difficulties and roadblocks, and making sure that all the key deliverables are in place. The process keeper updates the process, and provides for continual process improvement; she trains new employees on how to use the system; and, most important, she is the scorekeeper in the game (see "Metrics" below).

No complex process, no matter how good, ever implemented itself. Experienced stage-gaters readily admit that the key to success here is not just in the design of the process, but in its implementation; and that if *Stage-Gate™* processes fail, it is because of faulty implementation rather than faulty design. So provide for facilitation: install a full-time "keeper of the process" in your business.

6. *Forever green: Stage-Gate™* processes are evergreen. They are being constantly renewed, redesigned, and improved, as user-companies gain experience with this approach. Some of the general improvements that businesses have made are the five Fs listed above. Other companies have adjusted their *Stage-Gate™* processes to suit their specific needs. Some examples:

- Corning Glass now *stage-gates* just about every discretionary expenditure—from technology developments through to plant expansions. That is, they have taken their original gating system far beyond new products.
- Rohm and Haas has expanded their *Stage-Gate™* process to accommodate science or exploratory research projects; Mobil Chemical has a custom-tailored *Stage-Gate™* process to cope with the development of technology platforms.

▶ The Royal Bank of Canada has adjusted the frontend of their *Right Products Right™* (a *Stage-Gate™* process) to provide a funnel to "suck in" and deal with third-party new products (products developed by other banks and/or software suppliers, which might be available for license, JV, or sale). And so on.

The point is that you should be constantly reviewing and re-energizing your new product process. And if you haven't updated your current process in the past two years, chances are it's becoming out-of-date . . . time for an audit and an overhaul!

Before moving too quickly to a 6F third-generation process, a word of caution: knowledgeable stage-gaters argue strongly that you should strive first for a basic and effective new product process, perhaps incorporating only some of the elements of my third-generation process (for example, facilitation and some facets of flexibility). Once this process is up and running well, then seek the full-fledged, fast-paced third-generation process. Advancing immediately to a full 6F process has its downside unless your process is in good shape to begin with: you should walk before you run here.

Metrics—How Well Are You Doing?

Is it too early to start thinking about new product metrics? Certainly not! I strongly subscribe to the view that "you cannot manage what you cannot measure," and "what gets measured gets done." Some firms have made the mistake of not implementing measurement of their new product process until too late in the war.

At a *Stage-Gate™* benchmarking session in Atlanta attended by leading firms, metrics and measures was a hot topic. Each company identified the metrics that it used to capture how well it was doing at new products. The conclusions:

First, there is no universal view on what should be measured. These different companies—all leaders—gauged a variety of different things. However, there were certain metrics that the majority of businesses used (shown in Tables 4.4 and 4.5).

Next, virtually every business began with a much longer list of metrics than it now uses. The message seems to be: error on the side of too many metrics at the beginning, and over time, you'll decide which ones are the most useful to your management group.

Table 4.4 Post-Process Metrics: How Well Are You Doing at New Products?

Short term (measured immediately):

Timeliness:
- cycle time (months)—from Gate 3 to Launch (not too useful; must be a relative measure).
- on-time launch (actual versus scheduled launch date; difference in months).
- actual time relative to fastest possible cycle time for that project.

Development & capital costs:
- staying within budget (variance).

Longer term (measured much later; for example, two years into launch, based on latest expected results):

Financial:
- profitability (NPV, IRR, payback period, break-even time).
  —versus objectives set at Gates 3 and 5.
  —versus your hurdle rate.
- sales (units, dollars, market share).
- manufacturing costs.
  (both items versus objectives).

Success rates:
- percent of products launched that became commercial successes.
  (must define "commercial success").
- percent of Development projects that became commercial successes.
- attrition curves (projects versus time)—Figure 1.5.

Percentage of your sales coming from new products
  (must define "new product").
  (also must define time horizon: for example, launched in past three years).

Percent of growth (or profits) generated by new products (similar to above)

The kinds of metrics various firms use fall into one of two broad categories:

1. *Post-process metrics:* These answer the question: "How well are you doing at new product development?" They are "post-process" in the sense that they can only be measured after the product is

Table 4.5   In-Process Metrics

Some in-process metrics are opinion or subjective:
Quality of gate meetings (& deliverables):
- rating cards filled out at gate meetings (for example, as used by Polaroid).

Degree of "deviation from NP Process rules":
- degree of change in product specs after Gate 3.
- number of design change requests.
- number of cancelled gate meetings due to "no-shows" by gatekeepers.

Proportion of projects are "really in" the NP process:
- a judgment call by the new product process manager.

Some in-process metrics are objective:
Timeliness of projects reaching gates:
- percent of projects at each gate that are on time (that is, when scheduled).
- mean variance—actual arrival at gates versus scheduled time (months or percentages).

On-budget performance:
- percent of projects that are on-budget in each stage.
- mean variance in budgets, by stage (as a percentage).

---

launched. These include both short-term metrics (measurable immediately after launch: for example, "the proportion of products launched on time") as well as longer-term metrics (that might take several years after launch to determine: for example, "the proportion of launches that became commercial winners"). Table 4.4 provides some commonly used post-process metrics.

Data on these post-process metrics are gathered on individual projects but are most often reported in aggregate: for example, percentage of sales achieved by new products launched in the past three years; or the average variance in on-time performance.

These are very important metrics. The trouble is, if these are the only metrics you employ, you might be waiting three or four years to find out how well you are doing—and that's too long to wait in order to take corrective action. So most companies use *in-process* metrics too.

2. *In-process metrics:* These answer the question: "Is our process

working . . . really?" These in-process metrics can be measured almost immediately, and capture how well new product projects are unfolding—for example, whether they are on time at gates, and whether deliverables to gates are in good shape. Obviously, achieving high scores on these metrics is not the ultimate goal; but they are immediately measurable (that is, you don't have to wait three years to find out the results). Think of these as *intermediate metrics* and early warning signals about ultimate results. Table 4.5 provides some good examples of in-process metrics.

Dow Corning uses its "red-green" chart as a visual metric to spot projects in trouble, or gates and stages in trouble (Figure 4.6). Here the various gates in their *Stage-Gate*™ process are shown across the top of the grid, while the projects are listed down the side. Inside each box is the expected date for the gate meeting—when the project should have reached that review point. The actual date—when it really arrived—is also shown. When a project is "on time," color the box green; when it is late, color the box red.

Reading across the rows, one can spot projects that are clearly in trouble—missing key gate review dates. Reading down the columns shows the gates that are missed, suggesting that the previous stage is very much in trouble. For example, in the grid in Figure 4.6, projects B and C are clearly off course; while Stage 2, the feasibility stage, appears to be the most problematic stage in the process.

Toward an Effective New Product Process

Many investigations, including our benchmarking and NewProd studies, have provided clues and insights into how to mount a successful product innovation effort. This chapter has translated these insights and lessons into a carefully crafted new product process that provides a roadmap and discipline, focuses on quality of execution, builds in upfront homework, is strongly market-oriented, and is backed by appropriate resources.

The benefits of the *Stage-Gate*™ process are evident. The model puts discipline into a process that, in too many firms, is ad hoc and seriously deficient. The process is visible, relatively simple, and easy to understand and communicate: as one senior executive exclaimed, "At least we're all reading from the same page of the same book." The require-

	Gate 2	Gate 3	Gate 4	Gate 5	Post Launch Review
Project A	Aug 1/97 Sept 1/97	Dec 1/97 Feb 1/98	Sept 1/98 Sept 1/98	Dec 1/98	—
Project B	Jul 1/97 Sept 1/97	Aug 1/97 Nov 1/97	Dec 1/97 Feb 1/98	Mar 1/98 Jun 1/98	Jun 1/99
Project C	Feb 1/97 Apr 1/97	Jun 1/97 Aug 1/97	Dec 1/98 Feb 1/98	June 1/98 Jul 1/98	Jul 1/99
Project D	Jun 1/97 Jun 1/97	Jul 1/97 Nov 1/97	Feb 1/98 Mar 1/98	Jul 1/98 Aug 1/98	Aug 1/99
Project E	Sept 1/97 Sept 1/97	Nov 1/97 Dec 1/97	Aug 1/98 Sept 1/98	Dec 1/98	—
Project F	Nov 1/97 Dec 1/97	Mar 1/98 May 1/98	Dec 1/98	—	—

▓ denotes late to the gate by more than 1 month ☐ denotes on time at gate

Figure 4.6 "Red-Green" Monitoring Chart

ments are clear: for example, what is expected of a project team at each stage and gate is spelled out. The process provides a roadmap to facilitate the project, and it better defines the project leader's objectives and tasks: the deliverables for each gate become the objectives of the team and leader.

But the design and implementation of a *Stage-Gate™* process is more complex than simply photocopying a flow model from Figure 4.2 of this book and displaying it on the office bulletin board. The next two chapters provide the insights that you and your business's leadership team need in order to reap the benefits of a *Stage-Gate™* process. Chapter 5 focuses on the gates and gatekeeping, one of your critical roles in the process. And Chapter 6 delves into the broader topic of portfolio management, project prioritization, and resource allocation—another key task of the leadership team.

5

Effective Gates
and Gatekeeping—
Picking the Winners

If a man look sharply and attentively, he shall see Fortune;
for though she is blind, she is not invisible.
—**Francis Bacon, Of Fortune, 1623.**

Focusing Resources on the Right Projects

New product resources are too valuable and scarce to waste on the wrong projects. But most new product projects are losers. Either they fail commercially in the marketplace, or they are cancelled prior to product Launch. Project selection—the ability to pick the right projects for investment—therefore becomes a critically important task for the leadership team of the business.[1] There are two major challenges here:

1. First, if your business is typical, the majority of projects in your portfolio are at best marginal ones and at worst unfit for commercialization. While some duds are the result of poor project management, others are simply bad projects to begin with—they should have been killed much earlier. The ability to spot these losers early in the process (and before too many resources have been spent on them) is one key to improved new product profitability.
2. Second, there are far more new product opportunities than there exist resources to commercialize them. So tough choices must be made! One trap that many businesses fall prey to is trying to do too many projects and not having enough resources to do them well! *Pipeline gridlock* is the result . . . projects taking too long; too

many projects in a waiting queue; and too many projects under-resourced. This pipeline gridlock stems from a downsized corporate environment (trying to do more with less), a lack of commitment of the needed resources to product innovation, and lack of focus due to poor gates.

The gates must work! As go the gates, so goes the process. Gates are the quality-control checkpoints in the process, where poor quality or bad projects are halted. Gates are where resources are allocated to projects—where the pivotal Go/Kill and prioritization decisions are made. And gates provide focus—focusing resources on the right projects. So if the gates don't work, your new product process will very quickly fall into a state of disrepair.

Pipeline gridlock and the inability to make tough choices plague even the best product developers:

One of the first tasks of a newly appointed business unit manager at Du Pont was to assess his portfolio of new product projects. He asked each senior scientist to submit a list of the new product projects each was working on, indicating how much time was allocated to each project and how long each had been on the books.

To his chagrin, not one person submitted a list shorter than two pages long. The typical reply was: "I'm working on 12 projects; they're all critical; I spend a few days per quarter on each; and they've been on the books for eight years!"

Undaunted, the business unit manager went to round two: "Please submit a list of the *three* projects that you're working on." The request had barely been circulated when he began to receive angry phone calls and visits from the scientists: "How dare you cut me down to three projects! All 12 of my projects are of critical importance to the company!"

What the business unit manager discovered the hard way was that people could not, would not, and *did not know* how to make tough choices. They lacked the will; they lacked the criteria; and they lacked the methods. And so priorities had never been set, and no focus ever achieved in the business unit.

A Weak Area

Our benchmarking studies reveal that project prioritization is among the weakest areas of all the ones studied: a proficiency score of only 49 points out of 100. In too many businesses, project evaluations are weak, deficient, or even nonexistent. The research reveals that there are no serious gates or Go/Kill points, no consistently applied criteria for making decisions, and a strong reluctance to stop substandard projects—projects take on a life of their own. The result is tunnels, not funnels; and available resources are thinly spread, while the good projects are starved for resources.[2] In our NewProd projects studies, initial screening is identified as one of the most poorly handled activities of the entire new product process—screening was rated as "adequate" in only 12 percent of the cases![3] Further, 37 percent of projects do not undergo a business or financial analysis prior to the Development phase, and 65 percent of projects do not include a precommercialization business analysis.

Even when undertaken, project evaluation is not as easy as it seems. Many businesses have a mediocre track record in picking winners. For example, for every four projects selected for Development, only one becomes a commercial success.[4] Management appears to be in error about 75 percent of the time: you'd be better off tossing a coin!

This failure at the gates—the inability on the part of many leadership teams to make tough choices and focus resources on the right projects—is the root cause for a host of new product problems:

- it means longer times to market, as too many projects wait in queues;
- it results in poor quality of execution—there just isn't the time or people to do a quality job;
- the up-front homework doesn't get done;
- the right kind of market input is missing;
- product definitions are unstable and often fuzzy; and
- launches are mediocre, as launch resources are spread too thinly;

which all lead to higher failure rates, longer cycle times, and lower profits.

Tough Choices

Project selection is about tough choices: its purpose is to concentrate scarce resources on the truly meritorious projects. The result is better focus, improved prioritization of projects, and ultimately faster development for the chosen projects.

In an ideal new product process, management would be able to identify the probable winners early in the game, and focus resources on those projects. Failure rates would be kept low, misallocated resources kept to a minimum, and the return maximized. This chapter is about gates: it tackles the difficult question of how to select winning new product projects. In it, we look at various approaches to project evaluation, with a particular emphasis on the earlier gates in the new product process.

Key Points for Management

As go the gates, so goes the process! The gates must work. And you, the leadership team, are the principal gatekeepers.

The gates are the quality-control checkpoints in the process, where you make tough decisions: culling out poor projects and focusing resources on the right ones.

Weak, inconsistent gates are prevalent in many businesses, however, which results in a plethora of other problems: poor homework and minimal customer input; unstable product definitions; long times-to-market; and higher failure rates.

If there is one area in new products warfare where you, the leadership team, must be 100 percent engaged and lead, it is here . . . at the gates.

Three Approaches to Project Selection: A Quick Look

The three main approaches to project evaluation and selection at gates include:

1. benefit measurement techniques;
2. economic models; and
3. portfolio selection/management methods.[5]

1. Benefit Measurement Techniques

Benefit measurement techniques require a well-informed management group to assess the project on a variety of characteristics.[6] Such methods typically avoid conventional economic data, such as projected sales, profit margins, and costs, but rely more on *subjective assessments* of *strategic variables* such as fit with corporate objectives, competitive advantage, and market attractiveness. Included in this category are *checklists* and their extension, *scoring models*. In the latter, ratings of project attributes are weighted and combined to yield a project score. I take a much closer look at these useful methods later in the chapter.

Benefit measurement techniques recognize the lack of concrete financial data at earlier stages of the project and the fact that financial analysis is likely to yield unreliable results. So they rely on subjective inputs of characteristics that are likely to be known. As such, these techniques are most useful at the earlier gates, for example, the initial idea screen and even the Go-to-Development decision point. But benefit measurement methods suffer from the fact that they treat each project in isolation, and do not take into consideration the impact of the project on the overall resource allocation question.

2. Financial or Economic Models

Economic models treat project evaluation much like a conventional investment decision. Computation approaches, such as payback period, break-even analysis, return on investment, and discounted cash flow (DCF including NPV and IRR) methods are used. To accommodate the uncertainty of data, probability-based techniques, such as decision tree analysis and Monte Carlo simulation, are proposed.

Although I recommend the use of certain of these financial methods—namely, payback, DCF, decision trees, and sensitivity analysis at some gates—recognize their weaknesses too! Their main deficiency is *simply the lack of solid, reliable financial data.* Another weakness is that, like benefit measurement models, economic models treat each project in isolation—for example, a return or payback is calculated for this one project, which is then compared to some magical hurdle rate. The approach does not deal with the overall resource allocation problem.

3. Portfolio Methods

Portfolio methods consider the entire set of projects, rather than each one in isolation. The original portfolio selection models were highly mathematical, and employed techniques such as linear, dynamic, and integer programming. The objective is to develop a portfolio of new and existing projects to maximize some objective function (for example, the expected profits), subject to a set of resource constraints. Anyone familiar with these programming techniques will immediately recognize the intellectual challenge that the mathematician and management scientist would have solving this portfolio problem. But, alas, in spite of the plethora of articles written, such techniques have not met with success: they simply require far too much data, including financial data on all projects (both potential projects as well as those in the pipeline), timing information, resource needs and availabilities, and probabilities of success.[7]

The portfolio issue remains an important one, however, and has led one popular book to predict that "R&D portfolio analysis and planning will grow in the 1990s to become the powerful tool that business portfolio planning became in the 1970s and 1980s."[8] The past few years have witnessed simplifications and improvements in the portfolio approaches described above that have made them more understandable and useful. These include methods to maximize the total value of the portfolio (such as Productivity Index or the Expected Commercial Value methods); methods to yield the right balance of projects (such as portfolio maps and bubble diagrams); and methods designed to yield a strategically aligned portfolio (as the Strategic Buckets method). Note that portfolio methods are not project evaluation tools per se (that is, they are not Go/Kill decision models). Rather, they are prioritization and resource allocation methods, and hence can be used *in conjunction* with some of the other methods above, such as benefit measurement or economic models. Because portfolio management is such an important topic, I devote the entire next chapter to it.

Popularity, Strengths, and Weaknesses of Project Selection Methods

Which methods are most popular as new product project selection tools? Our recent study on project selection, prioritization, and portfolio methods reveals decided preferences for certain approaches (although popularity does not necessary correlate with delivering superior results).[9] The breakdown on usage of various techniques is shown in Figures 5.1 and 5.2: for data on which methods dominate the project selection decision, and insights into which methods work best, see below "Recent Research."

Recent Research on Project Selection Methods

One of our most recent studies is on the project selection and portfolio management methods that companies employ, their strengths and weaknesses, and the performance results they achieve. That is, the methods used have been linked to performance results. Some of the discussion on project selection methods in practice in this chapter is taken from this research. The study was undertaken cooperatively with the IRI (Industrial Research Institute, Washington, D.C.). For more information, see note 9.

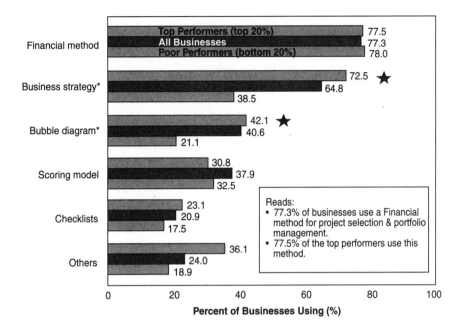

Top performers use Strategic approaches & Bubble Diagrams more so than do poorer performers.

Figure 5.1 Popularity of Project Selection & Portfolio Methods

Reprinted with permission from: R. G. Cooper, Edgett, S. J. and Kleinschmidt, E. J., "R & D portfolio management best practices study: methods used & performance results achieved," *Research-Technology Management,* July–August 1998, © Industrial Research Institute, Inc.

- *Financial or economic methods:* These are extremely popular project selection approaches. But don't be fooled: the businesses with the poorest performing portfolios rely almost exclusively on financial selection approaches, according to our recent research. A total of 77.3 percent of businesses surveyed use such an approach in project selection, with 40.4 percent of businesses citing this as their dominant project selection and portfolio management method.

- The *business's strategy* as the basis for allocating money across different types of projects: For instance, having decided the business's strategy, money is allocated across different types of projects and into different envelopes or buckets. Projects are then ranked or rated within buckets. A total of 64.8 percent of businesses use this approach; for 26.6 percent of businesses, this is the dominant method.

- *Bubble diagrams or portfolio maps:* Here, projects are plotted on an X–Y plot, much like bubbles or balloons. Projects are categorized

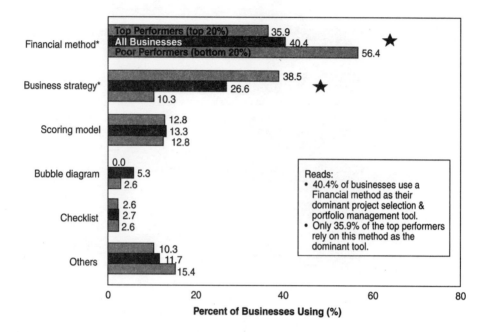

Poor performers rely more on financial methods. Top performers use Strategic approaches more.

Figure 5.2   Dominant Project Selection & Portfolio Method Employed
Reprinted with permission from: R. G. Cooper, Edgett, S. J. and Kleinschmidt, E. J., "R & D portfolio management best practices study: methods used & performance results achieved," *Research-Technology Management*, July–August 1998, © Industrial Research Institute, Inc.

according to the zone or quadrant they are in (for example, Pearls, Oysters, White Elephants, and Bread-and-Butter projects). A total of 40.6 percent of businesses use portfolio maps; only 8.3 percent of businesses use this as their dominant project selection method.

▶ *Scoring models:* projects are rated or scored on a number of criteria (for example, low-medium-high; or 1–5 or 0–10 scales). The ratings on each scale are then added to yield a project score, which becomes the criterion used to make project selection or ranking decisions. A total of 37.9 percent of businesses use scoring models; in 18.3 percent, this is the dominant decision method.

▶ *Checklists:* Projects are evaluated on a set of Yes/No questions. Each project must achieve either all Yes answers, or a certain number of Yes answers to proceed. The number of Yes's is used to make Go/Kill and/or prioritization decisions. Only 17.5 percent of businesses use checklists; and in only 2.7 percent is this the dominant method.

Traditional Portfolio Models: Great in Theory, But . . .

Although conceptually appealing, and perhaps the most rigorous, mathematically based portfolio models see more visibility in textbooks and journal articles than in corporate offices. Studies done in North America and Europe show that managers have a great aversion to these mathematical techniques, and for good reason.[10] The major obstacle is the amount of data required on the financial results, resource needs timing, and probabilities of completion and success for all projects. Mathematical portfolio approaches also provide an inadequate treatment of risk and uncertainty; they are unable to handle multiple and interrelated criteria; and they fail to recognize interrelationships with respect to payoffs of combined utilization of resources. Finally, managers perceive such techniques to be too difficult to understand and use.

Bubble Diagrams as Project Selection and Portfolio Models

The appeal of a portfolio approach lingers on, however, in the form of simplified versions that have been more recently packaged and promoted to industry. Certain variants of the technique still suffer from many of the same problems that traditional portfolio methods do—namely, the considerable data requirements, both financial and probability. But the simplified portfolio methods are much easier to understand and use; they don't require computer-based programming methods; and, most important, they present results in the form of visually appealing portfolio maps.

Our recent research reveals that bubble diagrams or portfolio maps, although recommended extensively by pundits and in the literature, see little use as the dominant decision method (see Figure 5.2). They have both strengths and weaknesses, with strategic alignment and decision effectiveness at the top of the list of strengths (based on performance results achieved by businesses using this method). Weaknesses include a failure to deal with project numbers versus resources and spending breakdowns that reflect strategic priorities. Bubble diagrams are also more laborious to use than other models.

Economic or Financial Analysis—Use with Care

Economic models are the most popular project selection tools (Figure 5.1). They are familiar to managers, and they are accepted for other types of investment analysis in the business—for example, for capital expenditure decisions. But they do have limitations. The toughest project selection decisions lie in the first few gates of the process when relatively little is known about the project. And it is here that traditional economic approaches suffer the most, because they require considerable financial data that are quite accurate. Someone must make estimates of expected sales in year 1, year 2, and so on; and estimates are required for selling prices, production costs, marketing expenses, and investment outlays. Often these variables are difficult to estimate, especially in the early stages of a project. And even when estimates are made, they tend to be inaccurate. More's study on firms' abilities to estimate expected new product sales confirms that estimates were in error not by 10 percent or 20 percent, but by orders of magnitude! So, economic models are usually considered most relevant for "known" projects (such as line extensions or product modifications—projects that are close to home and for which relatively good financial data is available), or at later stages of the new product process (for example, for Gate 3 and later).

Our project selection research shows that financial methods have little to commend them. They suffer a multitude of weaknesses, yet ironically are the most popular of all methods, both overall and as the most dominant method (Figures 5.1 and 5.2). In particular, financial methods are ineffective decision tools, according to performance results achieved (that is, they yield the *wrong* decisions); they are not fully understood by management; and they fail to deal with important portfolio issues, such as portfolio balance, gridlock and timeliness, and having the right number of projects for the available resources.[11]

There are more problems. Applying a financial screen to a high-risk or step-out project—perhaps your next major breakthrough product—will tend to kill it. The problem is not the project, which may well be a viable one; the problem is the application of the wrong evaluation technique. Here's why:

▶ A financial analysis that is done prematurely on a project will reject all but the sure bets. On higher-risk projects, a probability-adjusted financial analysis in effect multiplies a string of probabilities together. Not surprisingly, the resulting expected financial reward is quite small. Alternately, worst-case financial scenarios for higher-risk projects tend to come out very negative.

Procter & Gamble's two-in-one conditioner and shampoo technology platform is a technological breakthrough. It has spawned winning products such as *Pert* and *Pantene*. According to senior management, this program would *not have passed* the tough financial criteria applied to today's projects, simply because it was such an uncertain and high-risk project.

▶ Traditional DCF methods are *theoretically unsound* for determining the financial value of new product projects. The argument is that they tend to understate the value of higher-risk projects substantially because they *fail to recognize the options nature of the investment decision* (see below, "The Dark Side"). Later in the chapter, I'll introduce more appropriate methods to deal with this criticism.

The Dark Side of NPV:
Options Pricing Theory versus NPV

In recent years, some financial experts have recognized that the assumptions underlying traditional discounted cash flow (DCF) analysis (including NPV and IRR) are invalid in the case of new product investments. The net result is that NPV analysis *unfairly penalizes* certain types of projects, and by a considerable amount. Here's why:

In DCF analysis, the assumption is that the project is an "all-or-nothing" investment—a single and irreversible investment expenditure decision. In reality, however, investments in new product projects are made in increments: that is, management has a series of Go/Kill options along the way. As new information becomes available, the decision is made to invest more, or to halt the project. These Go/Kill options, of course, reduce the risk of the project (versus an "all-or-nothing" approach). When DCF is used, this lost option value is an opportunity cost that should be incorporated when the investment is analyzed.[12] But traditional spreadsheets used to generate NPVs do not!

By contrast, options pricing theory recognizes that management can kill the projects after each incremental investment is made—that management has options along the way. OPT is thus claimed to be the correct evaluation method, and a number of pundits have argued that NPV or DCF is "misused." Senior management at Eastman Kodak go further and state that "the use of options pricing theory (OPT) concepts brings valuable insights into the R&D valuation process" and that "an options approach often yields a substantially higher valuation than a DCF approach."[13] I have done a number of financial simulations, and conclude that the Kodak view is correct: when the project is a high-risk one—that is, when the probability of technical or commercial success is low, and the costs to undertake the project are high—then DCF and NPV *considerably understate the true value* of the project. This means that you will tend to kill otherwise valuable projects if you use the traditional NPV!

Financial analysis involving economic models is a powerful and useful tool in project evaluation, provided it is used at the right time and for the appropriate project type; but if used too soon or for the wrong projects, it can do much damage. Qualitative and nonfinancial considerations must also enter the decision to move ahead. Therefore, limit your reliance on financial evaluation to "known" projects—line extensions, product modifications, and the like—at the early stages. For more venturesome new products, avoid the use of financial techniques until a later gate in the process.

The Benefits of Benefit Measurement

Benefit measurement methods are generally recommended for many of the gates in the new product process. At the earliest gates, for example, because only a tentative commitment is required (early stages are relatively inexpensive ones) and because available information tends to be limited, benefit methods are the most logical evaluation tool. At Gate 1, the idea screen, some companies use a sorting technique, such as Q-Sort (below) to make gross distinctions between yea and nay project ideas. Checklists are also are a useful Go/Kill decision aid early in the process. And even at later gates—for example, Gate 3—benefit measurement methods, namely, scoring models coupled with checklists, have much to offer.

Our research into project selection methods reveals that of all methods, scoring models have much to commend them and fare remarkably well, in spite of their limited popularity.[14] They yield a strategically aligned portfolio and one that reflects the business's spending priorities; they produce effective and efficient decisions; and they result in a portfolio of high-value projects.

Key Points for Management

Consider the important decision points or *gates* in your new product process:

1. How are new product ideas screened in your business? Is idea screening recognized as a distinct decision point or gate in the process, at which a conscious and deliberate Go/Kill decision is made? Or do ideas sort of meander into the process, almost by osmosis?

2. Look at your other predevelopment decision points (the equivalent of my Gates 2 and 3)—for example, at your decision to open the door to Development. What method is used to make these early but pivotal Go/Kill decisions?

If you're not using any formal or consistent project selection method at all, or if you're relying strictly on a financial analysis, chances are your new product project selection can be improved. Read on to see how you can use benefit measurement methods, better financial approaches, and portfolio models to yield better project selection decisions, especially at the predevelopment gates.

A Closer Look at Benefit Measurement Approaches

Benefit measurement methods are recommended by a number of experts as a way to improve your decision making at Go/Kill gates. Let's take a closer look at various types of approaches useful in screening new product projects. Benefit measurement methods are designed to *integrate subjective inputs of management,* and include comparative approaches, benefit contribution techniques (financial indices), simple checklists, and scoring models.

Comparative Approaches: Q-Sort and Analytic Hierarchy Approaches

Comparative approaches include such methods as Q-sort, project ranking, and paired comparisons. Each method requires the gatekeepers to compare one proposal to another proposal or to some set of alternative proposals. The decision maker must specify which of the proposed new product projects is preferred, and, in some methods, the strength of preferences. In some of these methods, a set of project benefit measurements is then computed by performing mathematical operations on the stated preferences.

The Q-sort method is one of the simplest and most effective methods for rank ordering a set of new product proposals, especially at the idea screening gate.[15] Each member of the gatekeeping group is given a deck of cards, with each card bearing the name or description of one of the projects. Following a discussion on all the projects, each member then sorts and resorts the deck into five categories, from a "high" group to a "low" group (or into simple "Yes" or "No" categories), evaluating each project according to a prespecified criterion. (The criterion could be, for example, expected profitability, or simply Go/Kill.) The gatekeepers' results are anonymously tallied on a chart and displayed to the entire group. The group is then given a period of time to debate the results informally. The procedure is repeated, again on an anonymous and individual basis, followed by another discussion period. By the third round, the gatekeeper group usually moves to consensus on the ranking of the projects on each criterion. The method is simple, easy to understand, and straightforward to implement; it provides for group discussion and debate; and it moves the group toward agreement in a structured way.

Comparative methods such as Q-sort do have their limitations. Perhaps their weakest aspect is that gatekeepers must give an overall or global opinion on a project. Individual facets of each project—for example, size of market, fit with distribution channels, likelihood of technical success—are never directly compared and measured across projects. It is left to each decision maker to consider these individual elements consciously or unconsciously and to arrive somehow at a global assessment. This may be asking too much of some evaluators. Moreover, the group discussion may focus on a few facets of the project and overlook other key elements. A second problem is that no cut-off criterion is provided; projects are merely rank-ordered. It is conceivable that even those projects ranked highest will be mediocre choices in a field of poor ideas. Finally, a complaint voiced at some companies is that the decision process is not very transparent to those people outside the gatekeeping group— the entire process reeks of a political one, without the use of any criteria.

Analytic hierarchy approaches overcome some of the objections to Q-sort above, for example, the lack of decision criteria. These are decision tools based on paired comparisons of both projects and criteria. Software such as *Expert Choice* enables a team of managers to arrive at the preferred set of projects in a portfolio.[16] Voting software and hardware (for example, hand-held wireless voting machines linked to software and a video projector) permit the management team to input their choices quickly and visually.

Benefit Contribution Models: Financial Indices

Benefit contribution models require the gatekeepers to gauge the project attractiveness in terms of its specific contribution to new product or corporate objectives. Since new product objectives are usually financial, the benefit contribution method typically amounts *to simple measures of monetary return.* Various economic indices—quick-and-dirty financial calculations—are employed.

At the early gates in the new product process, simple cost-and-benefit methods can be employed. Such index methods require only the most rudimentary of financial data, and hence are particularly suitable for early gate decisions. The attractiveness of a new product proposal can be measured via the following equation:

$$\text{attractiveness index} = \text{expected benefit to company} \div \text{cost}$$

where:

expected benefit	=	benefit to the firm × probability of success
benefit	=	some simple measure of profits
cost	=	cost to execute the project

As an illustration, one 3M division deliberately avoids the use of complex financial calculations in the early gates. Instead, it uses the following financial index as a "sanity check":

$$\text{attractiveness index} = \text{sales} \times \text{margin} \times \sqrt{\text{life}} \div \text{cost}$$

where:

sales	=	the likely sales for a typical year once the product is on the market
margin	=	the probable margin percent
life	=	the expected market life in years of the product (the square root of life is merely the company's way of discounting the future and particularly long-life products)
cost	=	the cost of getting into the market (Development, Launch costs, and capital expenditures)

This business uses two arbitrary hurdle points, X and Y. If the index exceeds X, the project passes; and if the index is between X and Y, more investigation is required. Below Y, it is killed. Company people view this financial index as "more a check to make sure we're not spending $10 million to enter a $1 million business." In conjunction with this financial index, this business also uses a scoring model approach to assess the qualitative merits of the project.

A financial index approach is clearly a gross simplification of a rigorous financial analysis. But at the early gates, only gross distinctions between good projects and sure losers are required. The method has the advantage of not requiring detailed financial data and thus suits the initial screening and early gate decisions well.

Checklist Methods

One of the simplest approaches to evaluating new product proposals is the checklist method. This approach can be likened to questionnaires that follow a magazine article on some new dreaded disease. At the end of the article is a list of 20 questions. If you answer more than 12 "Yes's" out of 20, then you should see your doctor— there's a good chance you have the disease. These types of diagnostic checklist questionnaires are found in many fields, from medicine to psychology to personal planning. They are the *original expert system*, and have proven to be reasonably accurate in terms of predicting or diagnosing some ailment or condition.

How are checklists developed? A group of experts constructs a list of questions that they believe are useful discriminators in predicting or diagnosing a situation. The system is validated using past cases—does the list of 20 questions really discriminate between the yea and the nay cases? A cut-off score is established—how many "Yes" or "No" answers it takes to indicate the existence of a problem.

Checklists work well in new product evaluation, particularly at the early gates. Many companies use nothing more than a checklist of 10 or less questions as the idea screen at Gate 1 (for example, recall Exxon Chemical's checklist of Gate 1 questions—strategic fit, market attractiveness, technical feasibility, and killer variables in Chapter 4).

In using the checklist, the project is presented to a group of gatekeepers. Following a project briefing, the evaluators answer the set of questions on the checklist, providing "Yes/No" or "Favorable/Unfavorable" answers. The answers are tallied and a profile or score for the project is determined. A suitable pattern of responses (for example, a prespecified number of "Yes" replies) signals a Go decision.

Checklist methods offer an attractive approach to new product evaluation. Implementation is straightforward; a number of criteria are considered, not just a single one; the list ensures that vital considerations are not overlooked; the evaluation is a consistent one, as all projects are subjected to the same set of criteria; and finally, the method does not require detailed financial inputs nor does it rely on a single financial criterion.

There are problems with checklists, however. The choice of questions for the list is arbitrary: they represent the compiler's best guess as to what factors are important to consider in evaluating a project. Some elements are likely to be more important than others (for example, having a sustainable competitive advantage versus having a fit with the business's manufacturing facilities), and the checklist does not build in a weighting scheme. The issue of what constitutes "an acceptable pattern of responses" remains a difficult one. Finally the inputs or answers to the questions are subjective, may be largely conjecture and opinion, and may not even reflect careful thought.

Scoring Models

An extension of the checklist is the scoring model. Here projects are rated on a number of criteria, but this time on rating scales (for example, 0–10 or 1–5 scales). These ratings are then added together in a weighted fashion to yield an overall project score. The scoring model thus overcomes many of the criticisms of the checklist. Specifically:

- the scoring model allows for degrees in each characteristic: it is not just a black-or-white "Yes" or "No";
- it recognizes that some questions are more important than others, and incorporates a weighting scheme; and
- it provides a combining formula that yields a single project score, so that projects can be rank-ordered against each other, or be compared against some cut-off or minimum score.

In using a scoring model, the project is often first subjected to a set of *must-meet* criteria using the checklist approach above. These are the mandatory questions—a single *No* spells a Kill. These questions are relatively easy to answer, and weeding out obviously unsuitable projects is simple. Those projects that pass these *must-meet questions* are then subjected to a set of *should-meet criteria* using a scoring model. Independently of one another, the gatekeepers rate the project on each of a number of characteristics using numeric scales. The scores are tallied across gatekeepers, and an average score for each question is computed. The average score for each question is then multiplied by the weighting factor for that question, and summed across questions to yield a project score. The project score is judged against a minimum cut-off criterion to make the Go/Kill decision, and is also used to rank-order and hence prioritize projects.

Hoechst AG is one of the largest chemical companies in the world, with annual sales in excess of $30 billion U.S. Corporate Research & Technology in the U.S. (HCRT) is a research and technology intensive unit within the corporation whose special mandate is to develop and commercialize new products that lie outside the scope of the traditional business units. It tends to focus on larger, higher-risk, more step-out and longer-term major projects (as opposed to projects designed to maintain and renew a business unit's existing product line). Hoechst-U.S. spends approximately $300 million on R&D, of which a significant portion goes to HCRT. It also uses a *Stage-Gate* new product process—a five stage-and-gate process designed to move projects from the idea stage through to commercialization.[17]

The Hoechst scoring model comprises a list of 19 questions within five major categories. Each question or criterion had been carefully selected and worded, operationally defined, and tested for validity and reliability over some years. We offer their model in Appendix B as an example to other companies.

The five major factors that Hoechst's management considers in prioritizing projects are:

▶ Probability of technical success
▶ Probability of commercial success
▶ Reward (to the company)
▶ Business strategy fit (fit with the business unit's strategy)
▶ Strategic leverage (ability of the project to leverage company resources and skills)

Within each of these five factors are a number of specific characteristics or measures (19 in total), which are scored on 1–10 scales by management at the gate meeting. The 19 scales are anchored (scale points 1, 4, 7, and 10 are defined) to facilitate discussion (see Appendix B for the questions).

Simple addition of the questions within each factor yields the five factor scores. Then the five factor scores are added together in a weighted fashion to yield an overall score for the project, namely, the *program attractiveness* score. This final score is used for two purposes:

1. Go/Kill decisions at gates: Embedded within Hoechst's new product process are predefined decision points or gates. These gates are staffed by a group of senior managers and executives, who review the projects under consideration and make Go/Kill

decisions. The *program attractiveness score* is one input into the Go/Kill decision at each gate: a score of 50 percent of maximum is the cut-off or hurdle. Note that the decision is not quite as simple as a "Yea/Nay" based on this score—there is much animated discussion on each project.

2. *Prioritization:* Immediately following the gate meeting, the portfolio of projects is reviewed. This is where the prioritization of "Go" projects from the gate takes place, and where resources are allocated to the approved projects that were positively rated at the gate meeting. Here, the *program attractiveness* scores for the new projects (versus scores for already resourced projects) determines how the new projects are prioritized in the total list, and whether these new ones receive resources or are placed on hold. Other considerations, besides the computed *attractiveness* score, are:

- appropriate balance or mix of projects;
- resource needs of each project (people, money); and,
- availability of key people and money.

The NewProd™ *Model*

Scoring models have been improved and refined: more user-friendly, more predictive, and more useful output is generated in the form of diagnostics. For example, *NewProd™* is an empirically derived, computer-based new product scoring model, which was developed from the experiences and outcomes of hundreds of past new product launches.*[18] It is premised on the fact that the profile of a new product project, in terms of a number of qualitative characteristics, is a reasonable predictor of success: that *product success is predictable.* These qualitative characteristics include measures of competitive and product advantage, leveraging core competencies and product/company fit, market attractiveness and competitive situation, and so on.

In use, up to 12 evaluators assess the project on each of 30 key questions using 0–10 scales. These questions are proven discriminators between winners and losers. Two answers per question are solicited: an assessment of the project on that characteristic (a rating), and then the

---

*The most recent NewProd-2000 model, including industry-specific versions, is available from the Product Development Institute Inc.: e-mail address: www.prod-dev.com

evaluator's indication of how confident he or she is in his or her answer (a confidence score). The profile of the project, based on these ratings and confidences, is analyzed by computer and, in effect, compared with the profiles of hundreds of projects in the database that have known commercial outcomes. In this way, a likelihood of success and the project's strengths and weaknesses are determined.

NewProd™ attempts to predict whether a new product will be a success or not, and thus is an important input into the Go/Kill and prioritization decisions. The *NewProd*™ model is also a facilitating tool used by the project team to analyze or diagnose a project. *NewProd*™ thus helps the project's evaluators or the project team itself uncover the project's strengths, weaknesses, and uncertainties; it leads to a common understanding of the project; and it helps them develop an action plan for the project.

This commercially available *NewProd*™ model has been adopted as a selection and diagnostic tool in about 100 companies in Europe and North America. It has been successfully validated in Holland, Scandinavia, and North America and yields predictive abilities in the 73 to 84 percent range—not perfect, but considerably better than the typical manager's ability to pick winners![19]

Key Points for Management

Benefit measurement methods, specifically checklists and scoring models, have much going for them. Recent research suggests that, when used at gate meetings, they yield better decisions: high-value projects; solid Go/Kill decisions; and a good balance of projects. Additionally, they fit management's decision-making style and are quite time-efficient. So consider using these methods at your project reviews and gate meetings.

Additionally, checklists and scoring models avoid a total reliance on financial analysis and financial estimates. Recall that businesses that rely strictly on financial methods for project selection achieve the worst results!

A Closer Look at Economic Models

The two most popular financial methods for new products are *payback period* and *discounted cash flow* (DCF, which includes NPV and IRR). Both payback and DCF are cash flow techniques as opposed to traditional accounting accrual methods; hence they avoid disputes such as what can be capitalized and written off versus what must be expensed in year 1; or what depreciation rate to use. Moreover, DCF methods result in the "correct return" or yield from the project.

Payback and Break-Even Times

At gate meetings, senior management often considers *three different measures of time*, all of which are relevant to making Go/Kill decisions (see Figure 5.3):

- *cycle time*—the time from project initiation to market Launch. This metric answers the question: how long before you get to market and begin to see revenue and to recover your investment?
- *payback period*—the time from Launch date to the full recovery of initial expenditures in R&D, capital equipment, and Launch. It answers the question: "how long after Launch before you get all your money back?"
- *break-even time* (BET)—the time from project initiation to when all expenditures were recovered. It answers the question: "from the time you first started spending money, how long before you recover your money?" The BET is simply the addition of the two measures above, namely, cycle time and payback period.

Using payback and BET metrics has four main advantages.

- The methods are simple and easily understood.
- They capture the notion of both risk and return: a faster payback or BET means both a higher return on investment and a lower risk (less need to count on distant, future, and highly uncertain revenues).
- They use a cash flow approach, hence avoid accounting method disputes.
- Projections only as far into the future as the point of cash recovery are required—you don't need 10-year projections as in DCF and NPV methods.

Discounted Cash Flow (DCF or NPV and IRR)

The most rigorous method of financial analysis for new products is *net present value or DCF methods*.[20] DCF analysis requires a year-by-year

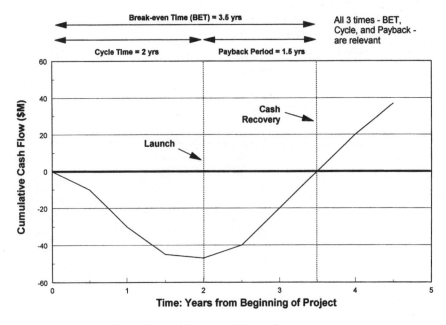

Figure 5.3 Break-Even Time and Payback Period

cash flow projection, but here the net cash flows for each year are discounted to the present using a discount rate (usually the minimal acceptable return or hurdle rate for the company). This stream of future cash earnings, appropriately discounted to the present, are then added; and initial outlays are subtracted to yield the net present value (NPV). If the NPV is positive, the project has cleared the hurdle or discount rate. Most computer spreadsheet programs come with a DCF capability, which also permits the calculation of the internal rate of return (IRR)*— the true yield on the project (as a percentage).

DCF analysis also has certain advantages.

 ‣ It recognizes that time is money—that money has a time value— and it tends to penalize those projects with more distant launch dates and revenue streams.

 ‣ It too is a cash flow method, and avoids the usual problems of accounting and accrual techniques.

---

*In the IRR calculation, the discount rate is determined such that the NPV equals zero.

▶ It yields the "true" return as a percentage.

▶ It tends to place much less emphasis on cash flow projections that are many years in the future (that is, the result is not particularly sensitive to revenue and cost estimates made for many years out, particularly if the discount rate or IRR is high).

To help identity project risks, *sensitivity analysis is* recommended. Sensitivity analysis is quite easy to do, especially if your project data are already in a spreadsheet format. In sensitivity analysis, key assumptions are tested: for example, what if the revenue drops to only 75 percent of projected; what if the manufacturing cost is 25 percent higher than expected; or what if the launch date is a year later than projected? Spreadsheet values are changed, one at a time, and the financial calculations are repeated. Some managements require best-case and worst-case calculations, also done via sensitivity analysis.

If the returns are still positive under these different "what if" scenarios, the conclusion is that the project justification is not sensitive to the assumptions made. However, if certain "what if" or worst-case scenarios yield negative returns, then these assumptions become critical: key project risks have been identified.

In order to accommodate risk and uncertainty, DCF methods have been augmented to include Monte Carlo simulation (where numerous financial scenarios for the project are generated in order to better understand the financial risks); and the use of variable discount rates in the case of higher-risk projects.

Options Pricing Theory

DCF or NPV methods have been recently criticized as being inappropriate for new product decisions: they assume an "all or nothing" decision situation, and hence are appropriate for capital expenditure decisions; but new product projects are *purchased one piece at a time*—in increments (see p. 151, "The Dark Side of NPV"). At each gate, management is in effect *buying options on the project;* and these options cost far less than the full cost of the project, and hence are an effective way to reduce risk. The argument is that options pricing theory rather than NPV is the appropriate way to evaluate the worth of a new product project at each gate.

One way to approximate an incremental or options pricing theory (OPT) approach is to structure the decision problem via a decision tree, according to Kodak.[21] This Expected Commercial Value (ECV) method seeks to determine the value or *commercial worth* of projects (see Figure 5.4) and is one of the more well-thought-out financial models. It features several twists that make it particularly appropriate to evaluating new product projects, in that, unlike traditional NPV or DCF, this method recognizes that new product projects are *investments made in increments.*

ECC International (English China Clay)* is the world's largest producer of clay and clay-related products, with annual sales revenues of about $4 billion (U.S.). U.S. operations are headquartered in Atlanta, Georgia. Even though clay is a rather mature business, ECC's aggressive management has an objective of a 30 percent increase in revenue derived from new products over the next five years.[22]

In this company's ECV method, one determines the value or commercial worth of each project to the corporation, namely, its Expected Commercial Value. This approach is based on a two-stage decision tree shown in Figure 5.4; it considers the future stream of earnings from the project, the probabilities of both commercial success and technical success, along with both commercialization costs and development costs.

A sample calculation is given in Figure 5.5, with a disguised project from the company. Note *how different the ECV is from the NPV;* for example, the project's present-valued income stream is $40 million; and after subtracting Development and Commercialization costs, its NPV becomes $30 million. Thus, at first glance, one might be tempted to place a commercial worth of $30 million on the project. Then introduce probabilities of success, and the probability-adjusted NPV drops to zero—kill the project! But not so, according to the ECV method: the *real value* of the project is $2.5 million—a major difference from either the $30 million or the zero figure! Had we used a five-stage decision process (instead of just the two-stage simplification above), the differences between the probability-adjusted NPV and the EVC approach are even greater, with the ECV value approaching over $5 million. The point is that merely rating or ranking projects according to NPV, and even the probability-adjusted NPV, is very misleading.

*Kodak too uses this ECV or OPT approach.

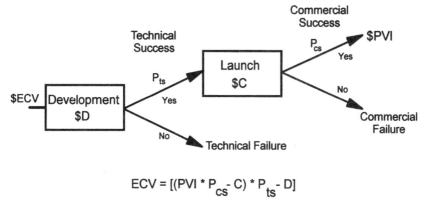

$$ECV = [(PVI * P_{cs} - C) * P_{ts} - D]$$

ECV = Expected Commercial Value of the project

P_{ts} = Probability of Technical Success

P_{cs} = Probability of Commercial Success (given technical success)

D = Development Costs remaining in the project

C = Commercialization (Launch) Costs

PVI = Present Value of project's future income or earnings (discounted to today)

Figure 5.4 Determining the Expected Commercial Value (ECV)

Reprinted with permission from Perseus Books (at the time of publication, Addison-Wesley), Reading, Mass. R. G. Cooper, Edgett, S. J. & Kleinschmidt, E. J., *Portfolio Management for New Products* (Reading, Mass: Addison-Wesley, 1998).

Key Points for Management

Financial methods are a must, especially at Gates 3, 4, and 5 in the process, where expenditures are large and revenue and cost estimates start to become more reliable. But some words of caution:

- Don't rely exclusively on financial methods for project selection—the businesses that do achieve inferior results!
- Financial estimates may be more reliable by Gate 3, but they're still a long way from being very predictive. So continue to use these projections with caution.
- Don't rely heavily on financial methods too early in the process or for step-out, high-risk projects.
- Consider switching from traditional NPV or DCF methods to the more suitable ECV or OPT approach, especially when evaluating higher-risk projects.

The Situation:

Income stream, PVI (present valued)	$40 million
Commercialization costs (launch & capital)	5M
Development costs	5M
Probability of commercial success	50%
Probability of technical success	50%
Here the overall probability of success is	25%

Traditional NPV, no probabilities:
　The NPV is simply $40 - 5 - 5 =$　　　　　　　　　　$30 M

NPV with probabilities:
　probability of success × payoff, minus
　probability of failure × costs of failure
　which is: $.25 \times 30 - .75 \times 10$　　　　　　　　zero

The right way—the ECV or OPT way:
　according to the formula and chart in Figure 5.3
　$\{[(40 \times .5) - .5] \times 5\} - 5$　　　　　　　　　　$2.5 M

Bottom line: The NPV method, without considering probabilities, wildly overestimates the value of the project. With probabilities, the NPV method understates its value. The project should be killed according to NPV; but not so, according to the ECV (OPT—options pricing theory) method

---

Figure 5.5　Illustration Using NPV and ECV Methods

Designing the Gates: How Gates Work

How should your business go about designing and implementing effective gate meetings in your new product process? In this section, I look at some prerequisites—at the purpose of gates and requirements for a good gating system—and then move to the design of gate—structure, criteria, roles and rules of the game. If you are to be an effective gatekeeper, it is important that you understand how gates work, or, more important, how they *should* work!

Purpose of a Gate

Gates provide an assessment of the quality of the project, ensuring that your business does the right projects . . . and does them right! Gates deal with three *quality* issues: quality of execution; business rationale; and the quality of the action plan:

Quality of Execution: Have the steps in the previous stage been executed in a quality fashion? Have the project leader and team done their job well?

Business Rationale: Does the project (continue to) look like an attractive one from an economic and business standpoint?

Action Plan: Are the proposed action plan and the resources requested reasonable and sound?

Note that these three questions are separate issues, and should be debated separately. For example, often a project team does a superb job, but has their project put on hold, simply because there are better projects to do. Unless the debate on "quality of execution" is separated from "business rationale," the team may have the impression that they are being chastised by senior management for the job they did.

Requirements of Effective Gate Methods

Many approaches to project evaluation and idea selection have been developed, as you have seen earlier in this chapter. When designing an approach to project evaluation and selection, and when electing the method that best suits your business, be sure to consider these points:

Each decision point is only a tentative commitment in a sequential and conditional process. Each Go/Kill decision is only one in a sequence of such decisions.[23] A Go decision is not an irreversible one, nor is it a decision to commit all the resources for the entire project. Rather, gate decisions can be viewed as a series of *options decisions,* beginning with a flickering green light at the idea screen, with progressively stronger commitments made to the project at each successive decision point. In effect, you buy discrete pieces of the project at each gate: the entire new product project is incrementalized in order to reduce risk.

The gating procedure must maintain a reasonable balance between the errors of acceptance and errors of rejection. Too weak an evaluation procedure fails to weed out the obvious losers and misfits, and results in misallocation of scarce resources and the start of a creeping commitment to the

wrong projects. On the other hand, a too rigid evaluation procedure results in many worthwhile projects—perhaps your next "blockbuster
product"—being stopped or rejected. This is especially true at the very
early gates, where the project is little more than an idea: here it is
extremely fragile and vulnerable, and often too easy to kill.

*Project evaluation is characterized by uncertainty of information and the ab-
sence of solid financial data.* The initial decisions to move ahead with a
project amount to decisions to invest that must be made in the absence
of reliable financial data.[24] The most accurate data in the project are not
available until the end of the development stage or even after testing
and validation and as the product nears commercialization—information on manufacturing costs, capital requirements, and expected revenue.[25] But at the early gates, data on projected sales, costs, and capital
requirements are little more than educated guesses (if they exist at all).
This lack of reliable financial data throughout much of the new product
process emphasizes the *substantial differences* in the methods needed for
new product screening and predevelopment gate evaluations versus
those required for conventional commercial investment decisions.[26]

*Project evaluation involves multiple objectives and therefore multiple deci-
sion criteria.* The criteria used in project Go/Kill decisions should reflect
the business's overall objectives, and in particular its goals for its new
product efforts. Obviously new product objectives are to contribute to
business profitability and growth. But there could be other specific ones,
including opening up new windows of opportunity, operating within
acceptable risk boundaries, focusing on certain arenas of strategic
thrust, or simply complementing existing products. Moreover, as was
seen in Chapter 3, many qualitative characteristics of a new product
project—such as product advantage, market attractiveness, and synergy—are correlated with success and financial performance, and hence
should be built in as goals or "desired characteristics" as part of the
evaluation criteria.

The evaluation method must be realistic and easy to use. Project evaluation
tools must be user-friendly. In short, they must be sufficiently simple
and time-efficient that they can be used by a group of managers in
a meeting setting. Data requirements, operational and computational
procedures, and interpretation of results must all be straightforward.

The Royal Bank of Canada has used a scoring model in project selection and portfolio management, not unlike Hoechst's in Appendix B.
But collecting the data at the gate meeting presented problems: multiple projects, a number of criteria per project, and multiple gatekeep-

ers in the room created a data handling nightmare at gate meetings. The solution: the company has adopted a computer-assisted voting system, whereby gatekeepers use a wireless voting machine, which feeds their scores directly to a PC.* The scores—means and ranges—are displayed for each question on a large screen via a computer projector. This electronic scoring has greatly facilitated gate meetings and reduced wasted time, ensuring closure on questions and also an immediate display of results.

At the same time, the evaluation method must be realistic: for example, it cannot entail so many simplifying assumptions that the result is no longer valid. Many operations research evaluation tools fail on this point, largely because their simplifying assumptions render the method unrealistic, while some of the bubble diagram approaches are viewed as a little simplistic.

The Structure of a Gate

A little structure at gate meetings goes a long way toward improving the effectiveness and efficiency of your leadership team's decision making. Well-designed gates and gate meetings have a common format with three main components:

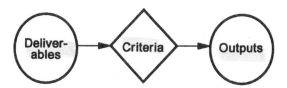

1. *Deliverables:* Too often, project leaders do not understand the expectations of senior management. Hence they arrive at gate meetings lacking much of the information that senior management needs in order to make a timely Go/Kill decision. So gates must define *visible deliverables in advance*. These are what the project leader and team must deliver to the gate—they are the results of actions in the preceding stage. The list of deliverables for a gate

*Available from: Saunders Consulting Group, Toronto, Canada.

becomes the *objectives* of the project leader and team. A *standard menu of deliverables* is specified for each gate. As well, at the preceding gate, both the path forward and the deliverables for the next gate are decided. A fairly typical menu of deliverables for the vital "money gate," Gate 3, is shown in Table 5.1. (See also Table 4.3).

At Exxon Chemical, although each gate has a menu of standard required deliverables, the gatekeepers devote considerable attention toward the end of each gate meeting reaching consensus with the project team regarding just what will be delivered for the next gate. In this way, the expectations are made very clear for the project team.

2. *Criteria:* In order to make good decisions, your leadership team needs decision criteria—criteria that are operational (that is, are really used at gate meetings), visible, and clearly understood by all gatekeepers. These criteria are what the project is judged against in order to make the Go/Kill and prioritization decisions. These criteria are usually a standard list for each gate, but change somewhat from gate to gate. They include both financial and qualitative criteria, and are broken down into required (must-meet) characteristics versus desired characteristics (should-meet).

Table 5.1 Typical Deliverables for Gate 3 (The Go-to-Development Decision Point)

- Results of detailed market analysis.
- User needs, wants, and benefits desired (based on customer interviews) defined.
- Concept test results and purchase intent data.
- Competitive analysis (who, shares, pricing).
- Preliminary marketing plan (one page).
- Results of technical analysis (technical feasibility demonstrated).
- Probable technical route; risks identified.
- Product definition: target market, positioning, price point, product requirements.
- Estimates of likely R&D costs, timing, resources.
- Probable manufacturing route.
- Estimates of manufacturing costs, equipment, and capital requirements.
- Legal, regulatory, environmental assessments.
- Financial analysis (IRR, NPV, sensitivity analysis).
- Plan of action for next stage (in detail).
- Tentative plan through to Launch (with extraordinary items flagged).

3. *Outputs:* Too often, project review meetings end with a rather vague decision. Ask any three people who attended the meeting about what decisions were made, and you're likely to hear three different answers. Thus gates must have clearly articulated outputs. Outputs are the results of the gate meeting, and include a decision (Go/Kill/Hold/Recycle) and a path forward (an approved project plan, and a date and the list of required deliverables for the next gate). There are only four* possible decisions from a gate meeting; the decision cannot be to "defer the decision":

- *Go* means just that—the project is approved, and the resources are committed by the gatekeepers, both people and money.
- *Kill* means "terminate the project"—stop all work on it, and spend no more time or money here. And don't resurrect the project under a new name in a few months' time!
- *Hold* means that the project passes the gate criteria—it's a good project—but that better projects are available and resources are not available for the current project. A Hold decision is a prioritization issue.
- *Recycle* is analogous to "rework" on a production line: go back and do the stage over again, this time doing it right. Recycle signals that the project team has not delivered what was required of them.

Types of Gate Criteria

Each gate has it own list of criteria for use by the gatekeepers. These criteria are what the gate decision is based on, and can be Go/Kill and/or project prioritization criteria. Gate criteria are of two types:

- *Must-Meet:* these are Yes/No questions; a single No can signal a Kill decision. Checklists are the usual format for must-meet items.
- *Should-Meet:* these are highly desirable project characteristics, but a No on one question won't kill the project; rather these questions are scored and a point count or project score is determined. Scoring models handle the should-meet questions well .

*Although in next generation *Stage-Gate*™ processes, with fuzzy gates, a fifth decision is possible, namely, "Conditional Go" (Chapter 4: Third-Generation *Stage-Gate*™ Processes).

Note that criteria can be *quantitative* (for example, IRR > 22 percent) as well as *qualitative*, capturing issues such as the strategic alignment of the project.

In the design of a gating scheme, the must-meet criteria or *checklist questions* typically capture strategic issues, feasibility questions, and resource availabilities. Examples:

- Does the new product project fit the strategic direction of the business?
- Is its development technically feasible?
- Do you have the resources required to undertake the venture?

A No to these questions—for example, a lack of strategic fit—is enough to kill the project.

By contrast the should-meet criteria or *scoring model questions* describe the relative attractiveness of the project. Examples:

- How large is the market?
- How fast is it growing?
- To what degree can the product utilize existing plant and production equipment/technology?
- To what extent does the product have sustainable competitive advantage?

A *No* or *negative* answer to any one of these should-meet questions certainly won't kill the project. But *enough low scores* may indicate that the project is simply not attractive enough to pursue.

Gate criteria are designed to be used by you, the leadership team, at the gate meeting. After the project is presented and debated, the criteria should be discussed one-by-one, scored, and a decision based on the criteria reached. Progressive companies use score-cards or computer-assisted scoring at gate meetings, so that scores can be displayed and differences debated.

Key Points for Management

Gates have three main components:

- a menu of deliverables (defined for each gate)—clear expectations!

- criteria on which the Go/Kill and prioritization decisions will be made.
- outputs—Go/Kill/Hold/Recycle and resources approved.

Consider using a set of must-meet questions in a checklist format as culling quetions, followed by a list of should-meet questions in a scoring model format to help determine relative project attractiveness. Be sure to use these criteria at your gate meeting, discussing each question and reaching closure on it. If you do this, chances are your gatekeeping group will make more objective, more reasoned, and better decisions.

A Two-Part Decision at Gates: Resource Allocation

The real issue in project evaluation is allocating scarce resources across various projects, each at different stages of completion. In practice, the gate decision breaks down into a two-part decision (see Figure 5.6).

The first decision is: is the project a good one? If this were the only project available, would you proceed with it? Here the project is evaluated on its own merits against a set of standards. Think of this decision as a Pass-versus-Kill decision.

The second decision at gates is a prioritization one: given that the project is a good one, and considering the other projects already under way or on hold and the resources available, what is the priority of this project? Is it high priority: a strong green light and an emphatic Go—one you commit resources to? Or is it a Hold—one you put on the shelf until resources become available at a later date?

The first decision—Pass-versus-Kill—is conceptually a much simpler one. The second decision, the prioritization one, is more problematic conceptually, as it involves this one project versus all the other projects in the pipeline, both active and currently on-hold. Project prioritization is the issue here, along with resource allocation among many projects competing for the same resources. Thus issues of *portfolio management* (next chapter) also start to surface at the gate meeting.

Culling Questions: Must-Meet Criteria

As you think about the gating process, remember that project selection is a culling process. The approach is to subject projects initially to simple, easy-to-ask questions; in this way, you pare down the list of

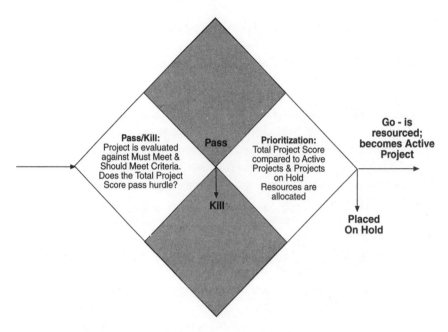

Figure 5.6 The Two-Step Decision Process at Gates

projects to a more manageable subset, which you then subject to more thorough evaluation.

The first part of each gate—the initial culling questions—is a simple *quality check* that the deliverables are in place, and that the activities that underlie these deliverables have been executed in a quality fashion. Next, a set of must-meet questions determine whether the project meets minimum standards in terms of strategic alignment, magnitude of the opportunity, technical feasibility, and so on. These questions are designed more to weed out obvious loser and misfit projects rather than to give a strong green light. Table 5.2 shows my recommended set of must-meet questions for Gates 1, 2, and 3; this is a composite list based on the experiences and gate designs at a number of leading companies. These gate questions are applied in a relatively gentle fashion at Gate 1, but with increasing rigor at successive gates.

Prioritization Questions

The next set of questions asks whether the project is a good business proposition: they confirm that the project yields positive value for the company. No project scores top marks on every business criterion, so

Table 5.2 Sample Gates 1, 2, 3 Culling Criteria—Must-Meet Questions

- Strategic Alignment (fits the business's strategy).
- Existence of Market Need (minimum size).
- Reasonable Likelihood of Technical Feasibility.
- Product Advantage (unique customer benefits, good value for money for the customer).
- Meets SHEL Policies (safety, health, environmental, legal).
- Positive Return versus Risk.
- No Show-Stoppers (killer variables).

here is where the should-meet or scored criteria apply . . . a point count system based on a scoring model. In your scoring model, you should try to capture criteria that you and the leadership team believe are characteristics of a "good" or "high-priority" project. Strategic fit and strategic importance along with financial attractiveness are obvious criteria. But you might also want to include some of the factors that drive performance (from Chapter 3), for example, product and competitive advantage, synergies and ability to leverage core competencies, and market attractiveness. The list shown in Table 5.3 is a well-crafted list of Gate 3 criteria, based on criteria used at leading companies and on my critical success factors. You can abbreviate the list for earlier gates.

Another tried-and-proven list of scoring or should-meet questions, used by Hoechst-U.S., is provided in Appendix B.

The Gatekeepers

Who Are the Gatekeepers?

Who are the people that staff these critical gates—the gatekeepers who make the Go/Kill and resource allocation decisions and who are essential to making the new product process work? Obviously the choice of the gatekeepers is specific to each business and its organizational structure. But here are some rules of thumb:

- The first rule is simple: the gatekeepers at any gate must have the *authority to approve the resources* required for the next stage. That is, they are the owners of the resources.
- To the extent that resources will be required from different functions, the gatekeepers must *represent different functional areas*— R&D, marketing, engineering, manufacturing, and perhaps sales,

Table 5.3　Gate 3 Should-Meet Prioritization Criteria (Scored 0–10 or 1–5)

1. **Strategic:**
   - degree to which project aligns with the business's strategy.
   - strategic importance of project to the business.
2. **Product Advantage:**
   extent to which the new product . . .
   - offers unique benefits to users/customers (not available from competitive products).
   - meets customer needs better than competitive products.
   - provides excellent value for money to the customer.
3. **Market Attractiveness:**
   - market size.
   - market growth rate.
   - competitive situation (tough, intense, price-based competition is a low score).
4. **Synergies (Leverages Core Competencies):**
   - leverages our business's marketing, distribution, and selling strengths/resources.
   - leverages our technological know-how, expertise, and experience.
   - leverages our manufacturing/processing capabilities, expertise, and facilities.
5. **Technical Feasibility:**
   - size of the technical gap (small gap is a high score).
   - complexity of the project, technically (less complex is a high score).
   - technical uncertainty of outcome (high certainty is a high score).
6. **Risk versus Return:**
   - expected profitability (magnitude: NPV in $000).
   - percent return (IRR percent or ROI percent).
   - payback period (or BET)—how fast you recover your initial expenditure/investment (years).
   - certainty of return/profit/sales estimates (from "pure guess" to "highly predicable").
   - degree to which project is low-cost and fast to do.

These should-meet items are scored (for example, 1–5 or 0–10 point scales) and added (in a weighted or unweighted fashion) to yield six factor scores. Each factor score must clear a hurdle for a pass. They are also added (again, weighted or unweighted) to yield the project score. This project score must pass a minimum hurdle for a pass, and is also used to rank projects against each other.

purchasing, and quality assurance. There's not much sense having a gatekeeper group just from one functional area, such as marketing or R&D!

▶ The gatekeepers usually *change somewhat from gate to gate.* Typically Gate 1, the initial screen, is staffed by a small group, perhaps three or four people who need not be the most senior in the organization. Here, the spending level is quite low. By Gate 3, however, where financial and resource commitments are substantial, the gatekeepers typically include more senior managers, for example, the leadership team of the business.

▶ There should also be some *continuity of gatekeepers* from gate to gate. In short, the composition of the evaluation group should not change totally, requiring a total start-from-the-beginning justification of the project at each gate. For example, some members of the leadership team—the heads of marketing and R&D, for example— might be at Gate 2, with the full leadership team at Gate 3.

Critical projects, or projects with major strategic implications, often involve the senior gatekeepers at earlier gates, even at Gate 1 in some businesses. The argument voiced by senior people is: "we don't want any projects starting that may ultimately involve hundreds of millions in expenditures without our early approval!" In other businesses, the leadership team is happy to review projects at Gate 3 and on, leaving the earlier gate decisions to a more junior group; but they do want to be informed of these early gate decisions!

Different magnitude projects also require different levels of gatekeeper groups in some businesses. For example, Business Banking in Royal Bank of Canada has two levels of gatekeepers from Gate 3 on:

- a senior gatekeeping group—for larger, riskier projects (total cost > $500,000).
- a middle-level gatekeeping group—for lower-risk and/or smaller projects.

A final issue is the need for the same gatekeeping groups across all projects. Two companies I have worked with both implemented their *Stage-Gate™* processes with *different gatekeeping groups* for different projects. At Kodak, each project had its own gatekeeping team, but no one gatekeeper group had an overview picture of all the projects; the result was that resource allocation across projects became impossible. At Telenor, the Norwegian telephone system, the situation was similar, with each project having its own gatekeeper group; these evaluation teams quickly turned into steering committees and "cheerleaders" so that no projects were ever killed! Both companies have revised their gatekeeping methods, and have moved toward "standing gatekeeper groups" that review all Gate 3, 4, and 5 projects.

Gatekeeper Roles and Responsibilities

The critical role of gatekeepers is to *facilitate* the *rapid commercialization* of the *best projects*. It is your job to ensure that projects receive a timely and fair hearing, that objective and consistent decisions are made, that resources are allocated and commitments kept, and that roadblocks are cleared out of the way. Good gatekeepers achieve these goals by . . .

- *making timely, firm, and consistent Go/Kill decisions.* Too often I witness gatekeeping teams that cancel gate meetings or fail to make the decision in a timely fashion. Yet they are the first to complain about long cycle times and projects taking too long to reach the marketplace.

- *prioritizing projects objectively.* Projects must be prioritized at gate meetings—is this a strong green light project, or a weak green, or a yellow? And these prioritizations must be made on the basis of objective, visible criteria, and supported by facts, not just opinion of the gatekeepers. There is no room for politicking and opinioneering at gate meetings!

- *establishing visible deliverables for successive gate meetings.* Deliverables are based on a standard menu for each gate. But each project is unique, and may deviate from the standard deliverables list. The gatekeepers must agree to a list of needed deliverables for the project in question, and ensure that the project leader understands what is required of her.

- *committing and ensuring availability of necessary resources.* Resource commitments must be made at gates. There's no sense in having a gate meeting, deciding on "Go," but failing to assign the needed resources. Recall that the gatekeepers are the people who "own" the resources required for the next stage, and hence are in a position to make the resource allocation decision right at the gate meeting.

- *mentoring and enabling project teams.* The traditional notion of a gatekeeper as "judge and critic" is obsolete in progressive businesses. Rather, the gatekeeper is very much an enabler, helper, and mentor, providing resources and assistance, and facilitating the rapid execution of the project.

▶ *setting high standards for quality of execution of project tasks.* Gatekeepers are also the quality assurers in the process, ensuring that projects unfold as they should. Recall the comment from the VP at Hoechst in Chapter 2: "As a member of the executive and also a key gatekeeper, I view my role, not so much as judge and critic, but more as a *quality assurer.*"

The five key roles of the gatekeepers are outlined in Table 5.4.

Making the Gates Work

Most businesses' leadership teams develop and agree to their "rules of the game" and also to the procedures for gate meetings. These might sound a bit of a nuisance, and not the most exciting task you face. But at best, gate meetings are tricky affairs to make work well, so perhaps your leadership team should take the time to review and develop these rules.

Gate procedures typically deal with how the project information will be presented, how the project will be evaluated or scored, and how the decision will be made. Note the importance of these gate decisions, so a little structure that promises to promote effectiveness is a desirable element. I provide a typical gate format or procedure in Appendix C.

Table 5.4   The Five Roles of Gatekeepers

The Bankers: to make Go/Kill and prioritization decisions and to provide the needed resources for the project.

The Enforcers: to ensure that the new product process works—to instill discipline.

The Quality Assurers: to ensure that projects are unfolding as they should—in a quality fashion—DIRTFooT (do it right the first time).

The Mentors: to help project teams chart their path forward, to provide advice, and to share their wisdom.

The Godfathers: to help project teams get things done—removing red tape and other obstacles to the timely completion of the project.

One of the thorny issues that often arises at gate meetings is this: just how firm are the resource commitments made at each gate meeting? If a better project comes along next month, shouldn't you allocate resources to it, and cancel your commitments to projects already approved? The issue is a controversial one, and has arguments on both sides—see below "How Firm Are Resource Commitments."[27]

How Firm Are Resource Commitments?

Different firms employ different rules of thumb. There are four possible rules.

1. Resources committed at gates are infinitely flexible. In short, if a better project comes along, resources can be readily stripped from projects already under way. There is no such thing as a "firm resource commitment"!

2. Resources are only firm between one gate and the next. At every gate, the project is "up for grabs" and can be reprioritized, or even put on hold, if it does not score as high as other projects in the pipeline or those in the hold tank. Exxon Chemical employs this rule.

3. Resources are firm, starting at a certain gate. That is, as long as the project continues as a good one—meets timelines, budgets, and all successive gate criteria—then the project leader team can expect continued funding. Even if a newer and better project comes along, top management will resist the temptation to strip resources from the already approved project. The Network Systems Division of GTE employs this rule.

4. Resources are firm, starting at a certain gate. The project is expected to pass all successive gates. Thus, gate reviews are largely perfunctory. That is, once the project is commissioned, the expectation is that it will reach the marketplace.

I recommend either Rule 2 or Rule 3. Rule 1—infinitely flexible resources—may be great in economic theory (efficient allocation of resources), but plays havoc with project teams and morale. Moreover, newcomer projects always look better than ones that are three-quarters complete; hence, resources tend to be stripped from the latter. Taken to an extreme, no project ever gets completed! Rule 4 is seen far too often. It is the express-train approach, where gates become "project reviews" but there's never any intention or will to stop a mediocre project.

Rules of the Game

Your leadership team must work toward becoming an effective gatekeeping group if you want to see new products prosper in your business. Recent research has revealed what members of effective gatekeeper teams in leading companies say is the *secret to their success*. (This research was undertaken in business units of major firms. Effective gatekeepers and gatekeeping teams were questioned about what made them perform so well; here's a summary of what they said):[28]

Consensus: Gatekeepers must work together as a team to reach consensus decisions. Once the decision is made, all gatekeepers agree to support the decision. Alignment among the members of the leadership team is vital. It makes no sense to have the head of marketing strongly supporting the project, while the head of R&D is against it and refuses to commit the needed resources.

Strategy and criteria: Gatekeepers must reach agreement on several key items in advance. They must agree on a business strategy and the arenas of strategic focus (Chapter 7). They must also agree on the criteria against which the project will be assessed, and commit to making decisions based on these criteria.

Rules of the game: Effective gatekeeping teams have developed "rules of the game," and then agree to live by these. These rules cover expected behaviors of the members of the gatekeeping group, and are clearly visible to each gatekeeper as well as to project teams and leaders. (Table 5.5 provides a sample set of rules of the game that I have gathered from various companies over the years. Review these and see how many your leadership team can endorse).

Prioritization method: Gatekeepers must also develop or agree to live with a prioritization process for projects—just how projects will be prioritized and resources allocated, especially when there are more good projects than resources available (more on the topic of prioritization and portfolio management in the next chapter). And since resources must be committed at gate meetings, the gatekeepers need a solid understanding of commitments already made—the priorities of the active projects and the resource commitments made to them, as well as projects on-hold, awaiting resources.

Understanding the process: Gatekeepers must possess a solid understanding of their business's new product process: what activities are expected within stages, and in particular what the required deliverables are for each gate.

Ten Ways to Ruin Gate Meetings

I end this chapter with a somewhat tongue-in-cheek look at all the ways the leadership team manages to ruin an otherwise effective new product process—how they literally snatch defeat from the jaws of victory! If you and your leadership team are guilty . . . well, read on . . .

1. Miss most meetings. When you do come, start reading the materials (deliverables) as the meeting starts.
2. Don't give the project team a chance to make their presentation. Attack with tough questions as soon as they put their first overhead up.
3. Always ask for information that has not been specifically requested—this way you keep the project team off balance.
4. Attack the project team with vicious, rude questioning. Make sure these junior people really live in fear of the gatekeepers.
5. Ignore the stated criteria at the gates. Make the decision from the gut. And ignore the facts—use your own opinion instead.
6. Dwell only on the financial projections. Spend at least three-quarters of the meeting arguing over numbers. The rest of the information doesn't matter.
7. Your role is that of a judge. Never offer any help or advice.
8. If in doubt, don't make a decision. Keep the team waiting around for several weeks. It shows who's boss.
9. Don't prioritize projects. Just keep adding projects to the active list. There's lots of slack in the organization that needs cutting out.
10. Demand that the project team reduce their timelines and resources requested. And committed resources can be rescinded at any time.

Table 5.5   Typical Gatekeeper "Rules of the Game"—Learn to Live by These

---

1. Gatekeepers must hold the gate meeting and be there. Postponed or cancelled meetings are not an option. If you cannot attend, your vote is "Yes" (or you can send a designate with your "proxy vote").
2. Gatekeepers must have read the materials (deliverables) and prepared for the meeting. Contact the gate facilitator or project team if there are show-stoppers or killer variables—no "surprise attacks" at the gate meeting.
3. Gatekeepers cannot request information or answers beyond that specified in the deliverables: no playing "I gotcha." Gates are not a forum to demonstrate your machoism, political clout, or intellectual prowess.
4. Gatekeepers cannot "beat up" the presenter. Give the project team an uninterrupted period to present. The question-and-answer session must be fair, not vicious.
5. Gatekeepers must make their decision based on the criteria for that gate. Gatekeepers must review each criterion and reach a conclusion. Each gatekeeper should use a scoring sheet.

Table 5.5 *(continued)*

6. Gatekeepers must be disciplined: no hidden agendas; no invisible criteria; decisions based on facts and criteria, not emotion and gut feelings!
7. All projects must be treated fairly and consistently: they must pass through the gate—no special treatment for executive-sponsored or "pet" projects; all are subjected to the same criteria and the same rigor.
8. A decision must be made, within that working day! If the deliverables are there, you cannot defer the decision—this is a system built for speed.
9. The project team must be informed of the decision—immediately and face-to-face.
10. If the decision is Go, the gatekeepers support the agreed-to action plan: commit the resources (people and money); and agree to release times for people on the project team. (*Note:* no one gatekeeper can override the Go decision or renege on agreed-to resources.)
11. If the decision is Hold, the gatekeepers must try to find resources. The project cannot remain on hold for more than three months—up or out! (This rule puts pressure on gatekeepers to make tougher decisions— some real Kills—or to commit more resources.)

Key Points for Management

Remember: in striving for better new product performance, the *greatest change in behavior* usually occurs not at the project team level, but *with the gatekeepers.* So, as a member of your leadership team, bring some needed discipline to your group, and start moving toward professional gatekeeping in your business. Define your roles as a group; and spell out some rules of the gate—either the list in Table 5.5, or some other set you agree to live with. And try to refrain from any of the practices outlined in my "ten ways to ruin gate meetings."

In Chapter 1, I challenged the leadership team to be the enablers and facilitators of product development—to set the stage for product innovation. The roles, rules, and practices outlined in this chapter are some of the simpler things you can do to work toward effective gatekeeping. They're not costly, but they make a world of difference.

6

Managing Your New Product Portfolio

In many lines of work, it isn't how much you do that counts, but how much you do well and how often you decide right.
—William Feather

Take calculated risks. That is quite different from being rash.
—George S. Patton, U.S. General

More Than Just Project Selection

A vital question in the new product battleground is: how should the corporation most effectively invest its R&D and new product resources?[1] That's what *portfolio management* is about—resource allocation to achieve your business's new product objectives. Portfolio management is more than simply project selection, the topic of the previous chapter. Rather, it's about the entire mix of projects and new product or R&D investments.

Project selection deals with the fingers: Go/Kill decisions on individual projects.

Portfolio management deals with the fist: looking at the entire set of project investments together.

Much like a stock market portfolio manager, those senior managers who succeed at optimizing their new product investments—selecting the winning new product projects, achieving the ideal balance of projects, and building a portfolio that supports the business's strategy—will win in the long run.

So, What Is Portfolio Management?

Portfolio management and project prioritization is about resource allocation. That is, which new product projects shall the corporation fund from the many opportunities it faces? And which ones will receive top priority and be accelerated to market? It is also about business strategy, for today's new product projects decide tomorrow's product/market profile of the business. Note that an estimated 33 percent of companies' sales today come from new products introduced within the past five years.[2] Finally, it is about balance, namely, the optimal investment mix between risk versus return; maintenance versus growth; and short-term versus long-term new product projects.

Portfolio management is defined as follows:[3]

Portfolio management is a dynamic decision process, whereby a business's list of active new product (and R&D) projects is constantly up-dated and revised. In this process, new projects are evaluated, selected and prioritized; existing projects may be accelerated, killed or de-prioritized; and resources are allocated and re-allocated to active projects. The portfolio decision process is characterized by uncertain and changing information, dynamic opportunities, multiple goals and strategic considerations, interdependence among projects, and multiple decision-makers and locations. The portfolio decision process encompasses or overlaps a number of decision-making processes within the business, including periodic reviews of the total portfolio of all projects (looking at all projects holistically, and against each other), making Go/Kill decisions on individual projects on an ongoing basis, and developing a new product strategy for the business, complete with strategic resource allocation decisions.

New product portfolio management sounds like a fairly mechanistic exercise of decision making and resource allocation. But there are many unique facets of the problem that make it perhaps the most challenging decision making faced by the modern business:

- First, new product portfolio management deals with *future events* and opportunities; thus much of the information required to make project selection decisions is at best uncertain, and at worst very unreliable.
- Second, the decision environment is a very *dynamic* one: the status and prospects for projects in the portfolio are ever-changing, as new information becomes available..

▶ Next, projects in the portfolio are at *different stages* of completion, yet all projects compete against each other for resources, so that comparisons must be made between projects with different amounts and "goodness" of information.

▶ Finally, *resources* to be allocated across projects are limited: a decision to fund one project may mean that resources must be taken away from another; and resource transfers between projects are not totally seamless.

Portfolio Management and Project Selection Methods: Best Practices Study

This investigation into project selection and portfolio management methods, mentioned in the last chapter, is the first large-scale investigation into this topic. It was conducted in two phases:

Phase I: looked at a small number of leading firms, and identified what portfolio management methods they are using. Many of these best practices are reported in this chapter.

Phase II: looked at a much broader cross-section of businesses (203 business units). It investigated their portfolio management practices, managements' views, and results achieved. I also report some results from this phase of the study here.[1, 4]

Why So Important?

Portfolio management is a critical and vital senior management challenge, according to our recent study of project selection and portfolio management best practices—see Figure 6.1 and list on page 189.[4] Note how important the topic is rated by the senior executives in the business as well as the chief technology person. Additionally, higher-performing businesses also tend to rate the importance of portfolio management much higher than poorer performers.

Portfolio management is important to you, the leadership team of your business, for three main reasons:

▶ First, a successful new product effort is *fundamental to business success* as you move into the next century. More than ever, senior management recognizes the need for new products, especially the *right* new products. This logically translates into portfolio management:

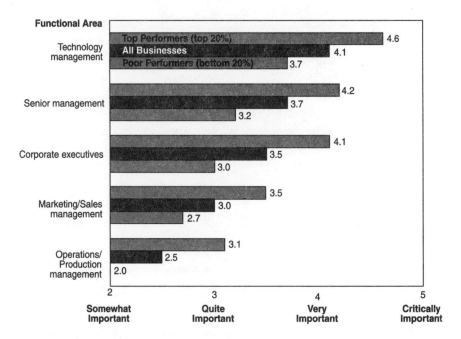

Figure 6.1   Importance of Portfolio Management

Reprinted with permission from: R. G. Cooper, Edgett, S. J. and Kleinschmidt, E. J., "R & D portfolio management best practices study: methods used & performance results achieved," *Research-Technology Management*, July–August 1998, © Industrial Research Institute, Inc.

the ability to select today's projects that will become tomorrow's new product winners.

▶ Second, new product development is the *manifestation of your business's strategy*. One of the most important ways you operationalize strategy is through the new products you develop. If your new product initiatives are wrong—the wrong projects, or the wrong balance—then you fail at implementing your business strategy.

▶ Third, portfolio management is about *resource allocation*. In a business world preoccupied with value to the shareholder and doing more with less, technology and marketing resources are simply too scarce to allocate to the wrong projects. The consequences of poor portfolio management are evident: you squander scarce resources on the wrong projects, and as a result, starve the truly meritorious ones.

Specific reasons for the importance of portfolio management, derived from our study, are noted below: "Portfolio Management is Important Because . . ."[5]

Portfolio Management Is Important Because . . .

There are *eight key reasons* why portfolio management is a *vital management task,* according to managers in the study:

1. financial—to maximize return; to maximize R&D productivity; to achieve financial goals.
2. to maintain the competitive position of the business—to increase sales and market share.
3. to properly and efficiently allocate scarce resources.
4. to forge the link between project selection and business strategy: the portfolio is the expression of strategy; it must support the strategy.
5. to achieve focus—not doing too many projects for the limited resources available; and to resource the "great" projects.
6. to achieve balance—the right balance between long- and short-term projects, and high-risk and low-risk ones, consistent with the business's goals.
7. to better communicate priorities within the organization, both vertically and horizontally.
8. to provide better objectivity in project selection—to weed out bad projects.

Top performers emphasize the link between project selection and business strategy, and downplay the need to be careful (and avoid failures) as the reasons why they view portfolio management as important.

Three Goals in Portfolio Management

Regardless of the portfolio management method employed, there are three common denominators across businesses when it comes to portfolio management: three macro or *high-level goals.* The goal you wish to emphasize most will in turn influence your choice of portfolio methods. These three broad or macro goals are:

‣ *Value Maximization:* Here the goal is to allocate resources so as to maximize the value of your portfolio in terms of some business objective (such as long-term profitability; or return on investment; likelihood of success; or some other strategic objective).

▶ *Balance:* Here the principal concern is to develop a balanced portfolio—to achieve a desired balance of projects in terms of a number of parameters; for example, the right balance in terms of long-term projects versus short-term ones; or high-risk versus lower-risk, sure bets; across various markets, technologies, product categories, and project types* (for example, new products, improvements, cost reductions, maintenance and fixes, and fundamental research); and finally in terms of numbers of projects versus the company's capacity to handle them.

▶ *Strategic Direction:* The main goal here is to ensure that, regardless of all other considerations, the final portfolio of projects truly reflects the business's strategy—that the breakdown of spending across projects, areas, markets, and so on, is directly tied to the business strategy (for example, to areas of strategic focus that management has previously delineated); and that all projects are "on-strategy."

What becomes clear is the potential for conflict between these three high-level goals. For example, the portfolio that yields the greatest NPV or IRR may not be a very balanced one (it may contain a majority of short-term, low-risk projects; or is overly focused on one market); similarly, a portfolio that is primarily strategic in nature may sacrifice other goals (such as expected short-term profitability). While you and your leadership team may not explicitly state that one goal takes precedence over the other two, the nature of the portfolio management tool that you elect will indicate a hierarchy of goals. This is because certain of the portfolio approaches are much more applicable to some goals than others: for example, the visual models (such as portfolio bubble diagrams) are most suitable for achieving a balance of projects (visual charts being an excellent way of demonstrating balance); whereas scoring models may be poor for achieving or even showing balance, but most effective if the goal is maximization against an objective. Thus the choice of the

---

*Although the focus here is on portfolio management for new products, to the extent that technology resources used in new products are also required for other types of projects, portfolio management must consider the fact that new product projects compete against process developments, product maintenance projects, and even fundamental research projects.

"right" portfolio approach depends on which goal your leadership team has explicitly or implicitly highlighted.

What methods do companies find most effective to achieve the three portfolio goals? The next sections outline the methods, complete with strengths and weaknesses, beginning with the goal of maximizing the value of the portfolio.

Key Points for Management

Portfolio management is holistic: it deals with the entire set of new product projects (rather than just making project selection decisions, one at a time).

Portfolio management is deemed important by senior management for a number of vital reasons, most notably: to maximize financial return on R&D spending; to maintain the competitive position of the business; to properly allocate scarce resources; and to forge the link between project selection and the business's strategy.

There are three main goals in portfolio management:

- to maximize the value of the portfolio;
- to achieve the right balance of projects; and
- to ensure that projects are on-strategy and spending breakdowns mirror the business's strategy.

Note the potential for conflict among these three goals.

Goal #1: Maximizing the Value of the Portfolio

A variety of methods can be used to achieve this goal, ranging from financial models to scoring models. Each has its strengths and weaknesses. The end result of each method is a rank-ordered list of "Go" and "Hold" projects, with the projects at the top of the list scoring highest in terms of achieving the desired objectives: the value in terms of that objective is thus maximized.

Expected Commercial Value

This method seeks to maximize the "value" or *commercial worth* of your portfolio, subject to certain budget constraints. The ECV method determines the value or commercial worth of each project to the corporation, namely, its *Expected Commercial Value*. Recall from Chapter 5 the calculation of the ECV (Figure 5.3). This calculation is based on a decision tree analysis, and considers the future stream of earnings from the project, the probabilities of both commercial success and technical success, along with both commercialization costs and development costs. Let's continue with the example I used in Chapter 5, English China Clay.

In order to arrive at a prioritized list of projects, English China Clay considers scarce resources. In their case, capital resources are thought to be the constraining or scarce resource (note that many of ECC's projects are very capital-intensive). Other companies may choose to use R&D people or work-months, or R&D funds, as the constraining resource. ECC takes the ratio of what it is trying to maximize—namely, the ECV— *divided by the constraining resource*, namely, the capital cost per project (Table 6.1). Projects are rank-ordered according to this ECV/capital ratio until the total capital limits are reached: those projects at the top of the list are Go, while those at the bottom (beyond the total capital limits) are placed on hold. The method thus ensures the greatest "bang for buck": that is, the ECV is maximized, for a given capital budget.*

This ECV model has a number of attractive features: it recognizes that the Go/Kill decision process is an incremental one (the notion of purchasing options); all monetary amounts are discounted to today (not just to Launch date), thereby appropriately penalizing projects that are years away from Launch; and it deals with the issue of constrained resources and attempts to maximize the value of the portfolio in light of this constraint.

The major weakness of the method is the *dependency on financial* and other quantitative data. Accurate estimates must be available for *all* projects' future stream of earnings; for their commercialization (and capital) expenditures; for their development costs; and for probabilities of success—estimates that are often unreliable, or at best, simply not available early in the life of a project. One seasoned executive took great exception to multiplying two very uncertain probability figures together: "This will always unfairly punish the more venturesome projects!" A second weakness is that the method *does not look at the balance* of the portfolio—

---

*This decision rule of rank order according to the ratio of what one is trying to maximize divided by the constraining resource seems to be an effective one. Simulations with a number of random sets of projects show that this decision rule works very well, truly giving "maximum bang for buck"!

Table 6.1 ECC's Rank-Ordered List According to ECV/Development Cost

Project Name	ECV	Development Cost (Dev)	ECV/Dev	Sum of Dev	
Beta	19.5	5	3.90	5.0	
Echo	15.7	5	3.14	10.0	
Alpha	5.0	3	1.67	13.0	limit
Foxtrot	15.5	10	1.55	(23.0)	
Delta	1.5	1	1.50	14	
Gamma	2.1	2	1.05	15	

Criterion: Ratio of what you are trying to maximize divided by constraining resource (yields maximum "bang for buck").

at whether the portfolio has the right balance between high- and low-risk projects, or across markets and technologies. A third weakness is that the method considers only *a single criterion*, the ECV, for maximization.

Productivity Index

The *Productivity Index* (PI) is similar to the ECV method described above, and shares many of ECV's strengths and weaknesses. The PI tries to maximize the financial value of the portfolio for a given resource constraint, and is used in leading firms from consumer products (Procter & Gamble) to very high-technology businesses (British Nuclear Fuels).[6]

The Productivity Index is the following ratio:

$$PI = ECV \times P_{ts}/R\&D$$

Here, the definition of *Expected Commercial Value* is different than that used by English China Clay. In the Productivity Index, the *Expected Commercial Value* (ECV) is a probability-adjusted NPV. More specifically, it is the probability-weighted stream of cash flows from the project, discounted to the present, and assuming technical success, less remaining R&D costs.* P_{ts} is the probability of technical success, while *R&D* is the

*There are various ways to adjust for risks or probabilities: via a risk-adjusted discount rate used to determine the NPV; or via applying probabilities to uncertain estimates in calculating the NPV; or via Monte Carlo simulation to determine NPV.

R&D expenditure *remaining* to be spent on the project (note that R&D funds already spent on the project are sunk costs and hence are not relevant to the prioritization decision). Projects are rank-ordered according to this productivity index in order to arrive at the preferred portfolio, with projects at the bottom of the list placed on hold.

Dynamic Rank-Ordered List

This method overcomes the limitation of relying on only a single criterion to rank projects, such as ECV or PI: it can rank-order according to several criteria concurrently, without becoming as complex and as time-consuming as the use of a full-fledged, multiple-criteria scoring model. These criteria can include, for example, profitability and return measures; strategic importance; ease and speed to do; and other desirable characteristics of a high-priority project. The four criteria used by Company G, a major hardware/software supplier, are (see Table 6.2):

▶ *Strategic importance* of the project, namely, how important and how aligned the project is with the business's strategy, is gauged on a 1–5 scale, where 5 = critically important.

▶ *NPV* (net present value) of the future earnings of the project, less all expenditures remaining to be spent on the project. Here the NPV has built into it probabilities of commercial success (in the calculation of the NPV, sales revenues, margins, and so on, have all been multiplied by probabilities to account for uncertainties).

▶ *IRR* (internal rate of return), calculated using the same data as the NPV, but gives the percent return.

▶ *Probability of technical success* as a percent—some projects in Company G are very speculative technically, so technical success probabilities are often less than 100 percent.

How are projects prioritized or ranked on four criteria simultaneously? Simple: first, the probability of technical success is multiplied by each of the IRR and NPV to yield an adjusted IRR and NPV (Table 6.2). Next projects are ranked independently on each criterion: adjusted IRR; adjusted NPV; and strategic importance (see numbers in parentheses in Table 6.2). The final overall ranking—the far right column in Table 6.2—is determined by calculating the *average of the three rankings*. For example, in Exhibit 2, for Project Alpha, which scored first on strategic importance, and second on each of IRR and NPV, the average of these three

Table 6.2 Company G's Dynamic Rank-Ordered List

Project Name	IRR*PTS	NPV*PTS	Strategic Importance	Ranking Score[a]
Alpha	16.0 (2)	8.0 (2)	5 (1)	1.67 (1)
Episilon	10.8 (4)	18.0 (1)	4 (2)	2.33 (2)
Delta	11.1 (3)	7.8 (3)	2 (4)	3.33 (3)
Omega	18.7 (1)	5.1 (4)	1 (6)	3.67 (4)
Gamma	9.0 (6)	4.5 (5)	3 (3)	4.67 (5)
Beta	10.5 (5)	1.4 (6)	2 (4)	5.00 (6)

[a]The final column is the mean across the three rankings. This is the score that the six projects are finally ranked on. Project Alpha is number 1 while Project Beta is last.
Note:

- Both IRR and NPV are multiplied by Probability of Technical Success (PTS).
- Projects are then ranked according to the three criteria. Numbers in parentheses show the ranking in each column. Projects are ranked-ordered until there are no more resources.

rankings is 1.67 . . . which places Alpha at the top of the list. Simple perhaps, but consider the list of projects in Table 6.2, and try to arrive at a better ranking yourself—one that maximizes against all three criteria!

The major strength of this dynamic list is its simplicity: rank-order your projects on each of several criteria, and take the average of the rankings! Another strength is that the model can handle several criteria concurrently, without becoming overly complex. Its major weakness is that the model does not consider constrained resources (as did the ECV or PI methods above, although conceivably Company G could build this into its rank-ordering model); and, like the ECV and PI models, it is largely based on uncertain, often unreliable financial data. Finally, it fails to consider the balance of projects.

Scoring Models as Portfolio Tools

Scoring models have long been used for making Go/Kill decisions at gates, as shown in the previous chapter. But they also have applicability for project prioritization and portfolio management. Projects are scored at gate meetings, and the total project scores become the basis for developing a rank-ordered list of projects, much as Hoechst does (Chapter 5).

Scoring models generally are praised in spite of their limited popularity. Recall from the previous chapter that research into project selection methods reveals that scoring models produce a strategically aligned portfolio that reflects the business's spending priorities; and they yield effective and efficient decisions, and result in a portfolio of high-value projects. But there are some pitfalls when using scoring models as a portfolio tool to prioritize projects:

▶ *Imaginary precision:* Using a scoring model may impute a degree of precision that simply does not exist; as one executive at Hoechst exclaimed: "they're trying to measure a [soft] banana with a micrometer!"

▶ *Halo effect:* This was a concern at the Royal Bank of Canada, which over the years has whittled their list of multiple criteria in their scoring model down to five key criteria. Why? Management argues that if a project scores high on one criterion, it tends to score high on many of the rest—a halo effect.

▶ *Efficiency of allocation of scarce resources:* A missing ingredient in scoring models is to ensure that the resulting list of Go projects indeed achieves the highest possible scores for a given total expenditure. For example, an artefact of one firm's scoring model was that much larger projects tended to rise to the top of the list; however, if the ranking criterion had been "Project Score/R&D Spend" instead of just "Project Score," then some smaller but efficient projects—ones that required much fewer R&D resources—would have risen to the top.

Key Points for Management

The value maximization methods outlined above have much to commend them. Specific weaknesses—obtaining data, reliability of data, overreliance on financial criteria, dealing with multiple objectives, imaginary precision, and halo effects—have been outlined. As a group, their greatest weakness is that they fail to ensure that the portfolio is strategically aligned and optimally balanced. For example, the resulting portfolio of projects generated via any of the methods above might maximize profits or some project score, but yield a very unbalanced list of projects (for example, too many short-term ones) or fail to mirror the strategic direction of the business. These goals—balance and strategic alignment—are highlighted below.

In site of these weaknesses, maximization of the portfolio's value is still a very worthwhile objective. You can argue about balance and philosophize about the strategic direction of your portfolio. But if the projects in the portfolio are poor ones—poor profitability, low likelihoods of success, or poor attractiveness scores—then the portfolio exercise is rather academic. First and foremost, the portfolio must contain "good" projects, and that is where the maximization methods outlined above excel. One cannot ignore these methods . . . they must be part of your repertoire of portfolio methods.

Goal #2: A Balanced Portfolio

The second major goal sought by some businesses is a balanced portfolio—a balanced set of development projects in terms of a number of key parameters. The analogy is that of an investment fund, where the fund manager seeks balance in terms of high-risk versus blue chip stocks; and balance across industries, in order to arrive at an optimum investment portfolio.

Visual charts are favored in order to display balance in new product project portfolios. These visual representations include portfolio maps or bubble diagrams (Figure 6.2)—an adaptation of the four-quadrant BCG (Star; Cash Cow; Dog; Wildcat) diagrams that have seen service since the 1970s as strategy models—as well as more traditional pie charts and histograms.

A casual review of portfolio bubble diagrams will lead some to observe that "these new models are nothing more than the old strategy bubble diagrams of the 1970s!" *Not so.* Recall that the BCG strategy model, and others like it (such as the McKinsey/GE model), plotted *business units* on a "market attractiveness" versus "business position" grid.[7] Note that the unit of analysis is the SBU—an existing business, *what is*—and whose performance, strengths, and weaknesses are all known. By contrast, today's new product portfolio bubble diagrams, while they may appear similar, plot individual new product projects—future businesses or *what might be.* As for the dimensions of the grid, here too the "market attractiveness" versus "business position" dimensions used for existing SBUs may not be as appropriate for new product possibilities; so other dimensions or axes are extensively used.

Which Dimensions to Consider

What are some of the parameters that your business should plot on these bubble diagrams in order to seek balance? Different pundits

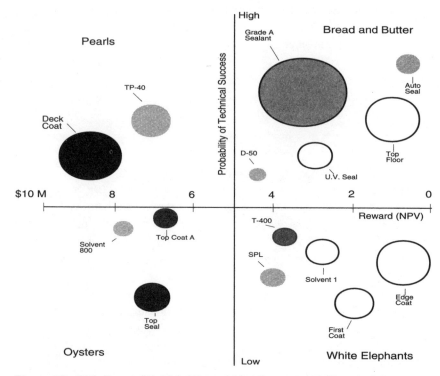

Figure 6.2   Risk-Reward Bubble Diagram for Company T: Chemical Company
Reprinted with permission from Perseus Books, Reading, Mass. R. G. Cooper, Edgett,
S. J., & Kleinschmidt, E. J., *Portfolio Management for New Products* (Reading, Mass:
Perseus Books, 1998).

recommend various parameters and lists, and even suggest the "best
plots" to use. Table 6.3 provides a list of the most popular bubble diagram plots (from our study of portfolio practices).[8]

No two companies, however, seem to agree on what is the best plot to
use in senior management meetings. So, in this section, I'll simply share
with you some examples from leading companies, and you consider
which might be best for you. Later in the chapter, I have some recommendations.

Risk–Reward Bubble Diagrams

The most popular bubble diagram is a variant of the *risk–return chart*
(see Figure 6.2). Here one axis is some measure of the *reward* to the company, the other is a *success probability:*

Table 6.3   Popular Bubble Diagram Plots (rank-ordered by popularity)

Rank	Type of Chart	First dimension plotted		Second dimension plotted	Percent of businesses using bubble diagrams
1	Risk vs. Reward	Reward: NPV, IRR, benefits after years of launch, market value	BY	Probability of success (technical, commercial, overall)	44.4%
2	Newness	Technical newness	BY	Market newness	11.1%
3	Ease vs. Attractiveness	Technical feasibility	BY	Market attractiveness (growth, potential, consumer appeal, life cycle)	11.1%
4	Strength vs. Attractiveness	Competitive position (strengths)	BY	Attractiveness (market growth, technical maturity, years to implementation)	11.1%
5	Cost vs. Timing	Cost to implement	BY	Time to implement	9.7%
6	Strategic vs. Benefit	Strategic focus or fit	BY	Business intent, NPV, financial fit, attractiveness	8.9%
7	Cost vs. Benefit	Cumulative reward	BY	Cumulative development costs	5.5%

‣ One approach is to use a *qualitative estimate* of reward, ranging from "modest" to "excellent."[9] The argument here is that too heavy an emphasis on financial analysis can do serious damage, notably in the early stages of a project. The other axis is the probability of overall success (probability of *commercial* success times probability of *technical* success).

‣ In contrast, other firms rely on very quantitative and financial gauges of reward, namely, the probability-adjusted NPV* of the project.[10] Here the probability of *technical* success is the vertical axis, as probability of commercial success has already been built into the NPV calculation.

*See footnote, page 193.

A sample bubble diagram is shown in Figure 6.2 for a division of a major chemical company, Company T. The size of each bubble shows the annual resources spent on each project (in Company T's case, this is dollars per year; it could also be people or work-months allocated to the project).

The four quadrants of the portfolio model in Figure 6.2 are:

- *Pearls* (upper left): These are the potential star products—projects with a high likelihood of success, and which are also expected to yield a very high reward. Most businesses desire more of these. Company T has two such Pearl projects, and one of them has been allocated considerable resources (denoted by the sizes of the circles).

- *Oysters* (lower left): These are the *long-shot* projects—projects with a high expected payoff, but with low likelihoods of technical success. They are the projects where technical breakthroughs will pave the way for solid payoffs. Company T has three of these; none is receiving many resources.

- *Bread and Butter* (upper right): These are small, simple projects—high likelihood of success, but low reward. They include the many fixes, extensions, modifications, and updating of products; most companies have too many. Company T has a typical overabundance of such projects (note that the large circle here is actually a cluster of related renewal projects). More than 50 percent of spending goes to these Bread and Butter projects in Company T's case.

- *White Elephants* (lower right). These are the low-probability and low-reward projects. Every business has a few White Elephants—they inevitably are difficult to kill; but Company T has far too many. One-third of the projects and about 25 percent of Company T's spending falls in the lower-right White Elephant quadrant.

Given that Company T is a star business seeking rapid growth, a quick review of the portfolio map in Figure 6.2 reveals many problems. There are too many White Elephant projects (it's time to do some serious pruning!); too much money spent on Bread and Butter, low-value projects; not enough Pearls; and greatly underresourced Oysters.

One feature of this bubble diagram model is that it forces senior management to deal with the resource issue. Given finite resources (for example, a limited number of people or money), *the sum of the areas of the circles must be a constant.* That is, if you add one project to the diagram, you must subtract another; alternatively, you can shrink the size of several circles. The elegance here is that the model forces management to consider the resource implications of adding one more project to the list—that some other projects must pay the price!

Also shown in this bubble diagram is the product line that each project is associated with (via the shading or cross-hatching). A final breakdown that Company T reveals via color is timing (not shown in my black-and-white map). Hot red means "imminent launch" while blue is cold and means "an early-stage project." Thus, this apparently simple risk–reward diagram shows a lot more than simply risk and profitability data: it also conveys resource allocation, timing, and spending breakdowns across product lines.

Variants of Risk–Reward Bubble Diagrams: Dealing with Uncertainties

3M's ellipses: One problem with the bubble diagram employed by Company T is that it requires a point estimate of both the reward, namely, the likely or probable NPV, as well as the probability of success. Some businesses at 3M use a variant of the bubble diagram to effectively portray uncertain estimates.[11] In calculating the NPV, optimistic and pessimistic estimates are made for uncertain variables, leading to a range of NPV values for each project. Similarly, low, high, and likely estimates are made for the probability of technical success. The result is Figure 6.3, where the sizes and shapes of the bubbles reveal the uncertainty of projects: here, very small bubbles mean highly certain estimates on each dimension, whereas large ellipses mean considerable uncertainty (a high spread between worst case and best case) for that project.

Monte Carlo simulation: Procter & Gamble and Company M, a U.S. medical products firm, use Monte Carlo simulation to handle probabilities. P&G's portfolio model is a three-dimensional portfolio model, created by three-dimensional CAD software (Figure 6.4);* the three axes are:

- NPV—a measure of the project's expected reward (probability adjusted);
- time to launch (the longer the time, the higher the risk and the more distant the reward); and

*This unique three-dimensional portfolio diagram is still experimental at P&G, and is being developed by Corporate New Ventures.

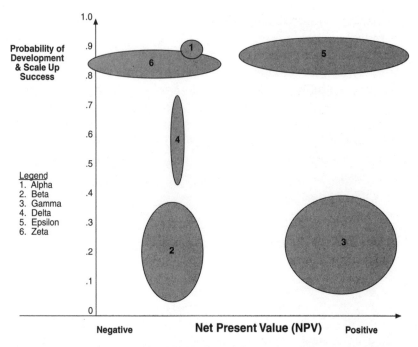

Figure 6.3 3M's Risk-Reward Bubble Diagram Showing Uncertainties
Reprinted with permission from Perseus Books, Reading, Mass. R. G. Cooper, Edgett, S. J. & Kleinschmidt, E. J., *Portfolio Management for New Products* (Reading, Mass: Perseus Books, 1998).

- the probability of commercial success (as calculated from P&G's customized version of the NewProd™ model—see Chapter 5).

Similarly, Company M uses an NPV-versus-probability-of-success portfolio model similar to Company T's in Figure 6.2.

In both firms, in order to account for commercial uncertainty, every variable—revenues, costs, Launch timing, and so on—requires three estimates: high, low, and likely. From these three estimates, a *probability distribution curve* is calculated for each variable. Next, random scenarios are generated for the project using these probability curves as variable inputs. Thousands of scenarios are computer-generated (hence the name Monte Carlo: thousands of spins of the wheel), and the result is a distribution of financial outcomes. From this, the expected NPV and its range is determined—an NPV figure that has had all commercial out-

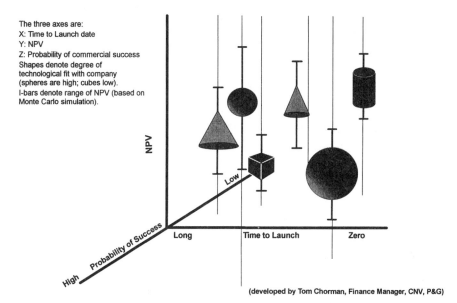

The three axes are:
X: Time to Launch date
Y: NPV
Z: Probability of commercial success
Shapes denote degree of
technological fit with company
(spheres are high; cubes low).
I-bars denote range of NPV (based on
Monte Carlo simulation).

NPV

Low

Probability of Success

High

Long

Time to Launch

Zero

(developed by Tom Chorman, Finance Manager, CNV, P&G)

Figure 6.4 Procter & Gamble's 3-Dimensional Risk-Reward Bubble Diagram
Reprinted with permission from Perseus Books, Reading, Mass. R. G. Cooper, Edgett,
S. J. & Kleinschmidt, E. J., *Portfolio Management for New Products* (Reading, Mass:
Perseus Books, 1998).

comes, and their probabilities, figured in. P&G shows this range of
NPVs simply as an I-bar drawn vertically through the spheres.

Portfolio Maps with Axes Derived from Scoring Models

A somewhat simpler risk–reward diagram is used by Reckitt & Colman (R&C), one of the many visual charts that comprise their portfolio
method. The most useful portfolio map, in management's view, is their
"ease versus attractiveness" chart. Here the axes are "concept attractiveness" and "ease of implementation" (Figure 6.5). Both axes are constructed from multi-item scored scales generated by scoring models
used at R&C's gate meetings.

Concept attractiveness is made up of scores on six items, including, for
example, purchase intent, product advantage, sustainability of advantage, and international scope. Similarly, *ease of implementation*, the second axis, is comprised of scored items, as the business's technological
strengths and the expected absence of problems in terms of development, registration, packaging, manufacturing, and distribution. R&C
uses a scoring model at its gate meetings, and the scores on two factors

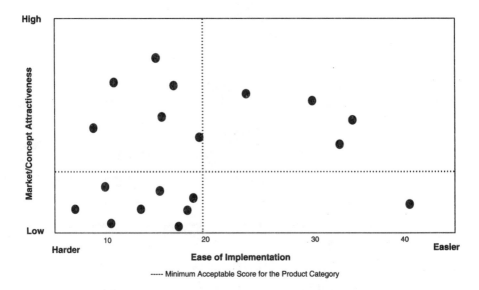

Figure 6.5 Reckitt & Colman—Market/Concept Attractiveness vs. Ease of Implementation

Reprinted with permission from Perseus Books, Reading, Mass. R. G. Cooper, Edgett, S. J. & Kleinschmidt, E. J., *Portfolio Management for New Products* (Reading, Mass: Perseus Books, 1998).

in the model—attractiveness and ease—are used to construct the axes of its two-dimensional portfolio bubble diagram.

A variant on this scoring approach is employed by Speciality Minerals, a spin-off company from Pfizer. A scoring model is used to make Go/Kill decisions at gates and also to rank-order projects on a prioritization list. Here, seven factors are considered in the firm's scoring model: business unit interest, customer interest, sustainability of competitive advantage, technical feasibility, credibility of the business case, fit with technical/manufacturing capabilities, and financial attractiveness. These *same factors* then provide the input data to construct the bubble diagram (Figure 6.6). For example:

- The vertical axis, labeled "value to the corporation," is comprised of the financial attractiveness and competitive advantage factors, added together in a weighed fashion.
- The horizontal axis is "probability of success" and is made up of three factors: customer interest, technical feasibility, and fit with technical/manufacturing capabilities (again, a weighted addition).

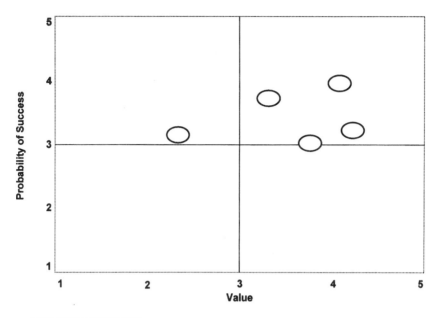

Based on Gate 3 Scoring Results
Value = .66 (Profitability) + .34 (Comp Adv)
Prob of Success = .25 (Cust Int.) + .5 (Tech Feasibility) + .25 (Fit)

Figure 6.6   Specialty Minerals' Risk-Reward Bubble Diagram Using Scored Axes

Reprinted with permission from Perseus Books, Reading, Mass. R. G. Cooper, Edgett, S. J. & Kleinschmidt, E. J., *Portfolio Management for New Products* (Reading, Mass: Perseus Books, 1998).

The unique feature here is that this company's seven-factor scoring model does double duty: it is the basis for Go/Kill decisions at gate reviews. It also provides five factors (and data) to construct the two axes of the portfolio bubble diagram. The gate decisions are thus closely linked to portfolio reviews.

Traditional Charts for Portfolio Management

There are numerous parameters, dimensions, or variables across which one might wish to seek a balance of projects. As a result, there is an endless variety of histograms and pie charts that help portray portfolio balance. Some examples:

Timing is a key issue in the quest for balance. One does not wish to invest strictly in short-term projects, nor totally in long-term ones. Another timing goal is for a steady stream of new product launches spread out over the years—constant "new news," and no sudden logjam of product launches all in one year. Figure 6.7 captures the issue of timing and portrays the distribution of resources to specific projects according to years of Launch. For example, for Company T, 35 percent of funds are allocated to four projects—all due to be launched within the year (year 1). Another 30 percent of resources are being spent on four projects whose projected Launch date is the following year (year 2); and so on.

Another timing issue is *cash flow*. Here the desire is to balance one's projects in such a way that cash inflows are reasonably balanced with cash outflows in the business. R&C thus produces a timing histogram that portrays the total cash flow per year from all projects in the portfolio over the next few years (not shown).

Project types is yet another vital concern. What is your spending on genuine new products versus product renewals (improvements and replacements), or product extensions, or product maintenance, or cost reductions and process improvements? And what should it be? Pie charts effectively capture the spending split across project types.

% of Resources (this year)

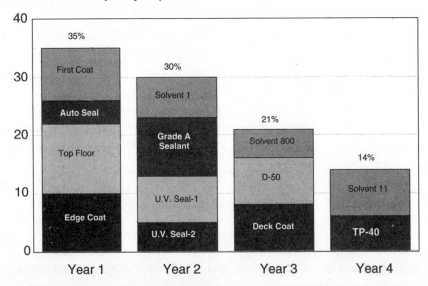

Figure 6.7 Timing of Product Launches

Reprinted with permission from Perseus Books, Reading, Mass. R. G. Cooper, Edgett, S. J. & Kleinschmidt, E. J., *Portfolio Management for New Products* (Reading, Mass: Perseus Books, 1998).

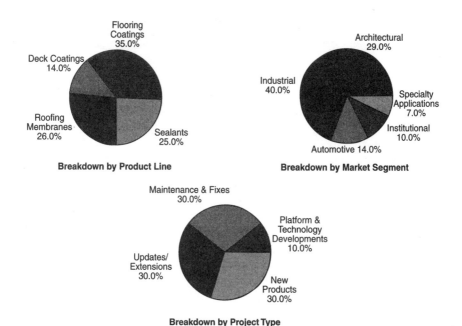

Breakdown by Product Line

Breakdown by Market Segment

Breakdown by Project Type

Figure 6.8 Breakdown of Resources Spent by Product Line, Market Segment, & Project Type

Reprinted with permission from Perseus Books, Reading, Mass. R. G. Cooper, Edgett, S. J. & Kleinschmidt, E. J., *Portfolio Management for New Products* (Reading, Mass: Perseus Books, 1998).

Markets, products, and technologies provide another set of dimensions across which managers seek balance. The question faced is: do you have the appropriate split in R&D spending across your various product lines? Or across the markets or market segments in which you operate? Or across the technologies you possess? Pie charts are again appropriate for capturing and displaying this type of data (Figure 6.8).

Number of projects versus the *capacity of the business* to handle them is a vital issue, and is shown in some of the charts above. Recall that bubble diagrams display allocation of available resources across projects (size of the bubbles), and deal in part with the resource demand-versus-availability balance. Traditional diagrams that capture resource commitment include bar chart displays of departments (or people) and their project workloads as a percentage of their availability. Such charts signal bottlenecks or logjams in the process. To construct such charts, it is first necessary to determine availability of resources for new product projects (people, by department), and also to determine current and future resource needs by project.

Key Points for Management

There is much to be said for achieving the right balance of projects in the portfolio. That is, there is more to life than simply achieving a high-value portfolio. Balance is also an issue. The trouble is that achieving balance—or selecting an appropriate tool to help achieve balance—is easier conceptually than in practice.

In spite of the many intricate and ingenious methods and diagrams, there remain problems with the quest for balance:

▶ First, some of the more popular bubble diagrams suffer the same fate as the maximization models previously outlined, namely, they rely on substantial financial data, when often financial data are either unavailable, or at best, highly uncertain.

▶ Second, there is the issue of information overload. "Maps, endless maps!" was the complaint of one exasperated executive, as he leafed through more than a dozen maps plotting everything versus everything in his business's portfolio method.

▶ Third, these methods are information display, not decision models per se. Unlike the value maximization methods, the result is not a convenient rank-ordered list of preferred projects.

▶ Finally, often it's not clear what the "right balance" of projects is. Your leadership team can stare all they want at various charts, but unless a portfolio is obviously and extremely out-of-balance (as in Company T's in Figure 6.2), how does one know whether one has the right balance?

The fact that portfolio balance methods are far from perfect does not mean they be dismissed outright. *Certainly not.* But such approaches should be used with some forethought: the choice of maps (which axes to use in the plots, for example) and charts (which parameters to show) must be well-thought-out. Avoid the temptation of portraying too many maps and charts. And be sure to test their use in portfolio reviews or gate meetings before adopting them.

Goal # 3: Building Strategy into the Portfolio

Strategy and new product resource allocation must be intimately connected. *Strategy begins when you start spending money!* Until one begins allocating resources to specific activities—for example, to specific development projects—strategy is just words in a strategy document.

The mission, vision, and strategy of the business is made operational through the decisions it makes on where to spend money. For example, if a business's strategic mission is to "grow via leading-edge product development," then this must be reflected in the number of new product projects under way—projects that will lead to growth (rather than simply to defend) and projects that really are innovative. Similarly, if the strategy is to focus on certain markets, products, or technology types, then the majority of R&D spending must be focused on such markets, products, or technologies.

One business unit's senior executive claimed that "my SBU's strategy is to achieve rapid growth through product leadership"; yet when we examined his breakdown of R&D spending, the great majority of resources was going to maintenance projects, product modifications, and extensions. Clearly this was a case of a disconnect between *stated strategy* and *where the money* is spent.

Linking Strategy to the Portfolio: Approaches

Two broad issues arise in the desire to achieve *strategic alignment* in the portfolio of projects:

- ▶ *Strategic fit:* The first is: are all your projects consistent with your business's strategy? For example, if you have defined certain technologies or markets as key areas to focus on, do your projects fit into these areas—are they in bounds or out of bounds?
- ▶ *Spending breakdown:* The second is: does the breakdown of your spending reflect your strategic priorities? That is, if you say you are a growth business, then the majority of your R&D spending ought to be on projects that are designed to grow the business. In short, when you add up the areas where you are spending money, are these totally consistent with your stated strategy?

There are two ways to incorporate the goal of strategic alignment:

1. *Bottom-up—building strategic criteria into project selection tools:* here strategic fit is achieved simply by including numerous strategic criteria in the Go/Kill and prioritization tools; and
2. *Top-down—Strategic Buckets method:* this begins with the business's

strategy and then moves to setting aside funds—envelopes or *buckets of money*—designated for different types of projects.

Bottom-Up—Strategic Criteria Built into Project Selection Tools

Not only are scoring models effective ways to maximize the value of the portfolio, they can also be used to ensure strategic fit. One of the multiple objectives considered in a scoring model, along with profitability or likelihood of success, can be to *maximize strategic fit*, simply by building into the scoring model a number of strategic questions.

In the scoring model used by Hoechst (Appendix B), two major factors out of five are strategic; and of the 19 criteria used to prioritize projects, six, or almost one-third, deal with strategic issues. Thus, projects that fit the business's strategy and boast strategic leverage are likely to rise to the top of the list. Indeed, it is inconceivable how any "off-strategy" projects could make the active project list at all: Hoechst's scoring model naturally weeds them out.

Similarly, Reckitt & Colman subjects all projects at gate meetings to a list of must-meet criteria before any prioritization consideration is given. At the top of this must-meet list is *strategic fit:* projects that fail this criterion are knocked out immediately. Next, a set of should-meet criteria is used via a scoring model. Unless the project scores a certain minimum point count, again it is knocked out. Embedded within this scoring model are several strategic direction criteria. Finally, in R&C's bubble diagram (where *concept attractiveness* is plotted versus *ease of implementation*—see Figure 6.5), of the six parameters that make up *concept attractiveness*, two capture important strategic directions—ability to build the brand and franchise; and geographic scope. Thus R&C builds strategic fit and direction in throughout its scoring and bubble diagram portfolio approaches.

My list of must-meet and should-meet gate criteria in the previous chapter does much the same thing—introduces a number of strategic criteria so that off-strategy projects won't pass the gate, while high-strategic-fit projects receive high scores (Tables 5.2 and 5.3).

Top-Down Strategic Approach—Strategic Buckets Model

While strategic fit can be achieved via a scoring model, a top-down approach is the only method designed to ensure that the eventual portfolio of projects *truly reflects* the stated strategy for the business: that where the money is spent mirrors the business's strategy.

The Strategic Buckets Model operates from the simple principle that *implementing strategy equates to spending money on specific projects.* Thus, setting portfolio requirements really means "setting spending targets."

The method begins with the business's strategy, and requires the senior management of the business to make forced choices along each of several dimensions—choices about how they wish to allocate their scarce money resources. This enables the creation of "envelopes of money" or "buckets." Existing projects are categorized into buckets; then one determines whether actual spending is consistent with desired spending for each bucket. Finally, projects are prioritized within buckets to arrive at the ultimate portfolio of projects—one that mirrors management's strategy for the business.

Sounds simple, but the details are a little more complex. Senior management first develops the vision and strategy for the business. This includes defining strategic goals and the general plan of attack to achieve these goals—a fairly standard business strategy exercise. Next, they make forced choices across key strategic dimensions. That is, based on this strategy, the management of the business allocates R&D and new product marketing resources across categories on each dimension. Some common dimensions are:

- *Strategic goals:* Management is required to split resources across the specified strategic goals. For example, what percent should be spent on Defending the Base? On Diversifying? On Extending the Base? and so on.
- *Product lines:* Resources are split across product lines: for example, how much to spend on Product Line A? On B? On C? A plot of product line locations on the product life cycle curve was used in one firm to help determine this split. Rhode & Schwarz, a sizable German computer and electronics firm, uses a scoring model to allocate resources across product lines.
- *Project type:* What percent of resources should go to new product developments? To maintenance-type projects? To process improvements? To fundamental research? One SBU within Exxon Chemical uses the standard *product/market newness* matrix to visualize this split (see Figure 1.6). Here, the six different types of projects defined on this matrix each receive a certain percentage of the total budget.

A somewhat simpler breakdown is used at Allied Signal, Engineered Materials Division. The chief technology officer explains: "We have our 'Mercedes Benz star' method of allocating resources. We [the leadership team of the business] begin with the business's strategy and use the Mercedes star emblem [the three-point star] to help divide up the resources. There are three categories: fundamental research and platform development projects which promise to yield major breakthroughs and new technology platforms; new product developments; and maintenance—technical support, product improvements and enhancements, and so on [Figure 6.9]. We divide up the R&D funds into these three categories, and then rate and rank projects against each other within a category. This way, we ensure that we end up spending money according to our strategy."

- *Familiarity Matrix:* What should be the split of resources to different types of markets and to different technology types in terms of their *familiarity to the business?* Both Dow Corning and Eastman Chemi-

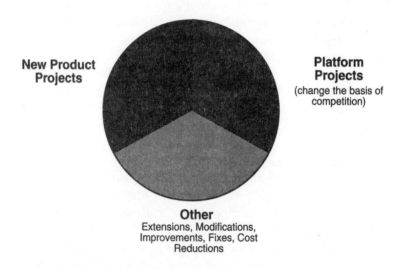

New Product Projects

Platform Projects
(change the basis of competition)

Other
Extensions, Modifications, Improvements, Fixes, Cost Reductions

The business's strategy dictates the split of resources into buckets; projects are rank ordered within buckets, but using different criteria in each bucket (method used by Allied Signal).

Figure 6.9 Mercedes Benz Star Method of Portfolio Management

Reprinted with permission from Perseus Books, Reading, Mass. R. G. Cooper, Edgett, S. J. & Kleinschmidt, E. J., *Portfolio Management for New Products* (Reading, Mass: Perseus Books, 1998).

cal use variants of the "familiarity matrix" proposed by Roberts—technology newness versus market newness—to help allocate resources (Table 6.4).[12]

- *Geography:* What proportion of resources should be spent on projects aimed largely at North America? At Latin America? At Europe? At the Pacific? Or aimed globally?

Now, management develops *strategic buckets.* Here the various strategic dimensions (above) are collapsed into a convenient handful of buckets. For example, buckets might be . . .

- Product Development Projects for Product Lines A and B;
- Cost Reduction Projects for all product lines;
- Product Renewal Projects for Product Lines C and D;

and so on (see Table 6.5). Next, the desired spending by bucket is determined: the *"what should be."* This involves a consolidation of desired spending splits from the strategic allocation exercise above.

Next comes a gap analysis. Existing projects are categorized by bucket and the total current spending by bucket is added up (the *"what is"*). Spending gaps are then identified between the *"what should be"* and *"what is"* for each bucket.

Finally, projects within each bucket are rank-ordered. You can use either a scoring model or financial criteria to do this ranking within buckets (Table 6.5). Portfolio adjustments are then made, either via immediate pruning of projects, or by adjusting the approval process for future projects.

Table 6.4 Familiarity Matrix—Technology and Market Newness

Technology Newness	Market Newness	
	Existing/Base	New
New Step-Out	Step-Out Product Development	New Business & New Ventures
New But Familiar	New items (existing lines)	Market Development
Base	Defend and/or Penetrate	Market Expansion (customer application projects)

Note: Resources are split across project types via the familiarity matrix.

Table 6.5   Table Showing Four Strategic Buckets, Desired Resource Alloctions Across Buckets, and Ranking of Projects within Buckets

New Products: Product Line A Target Spend: $8.7M		New Products: Product Line B Target Spend: $18.5M		Maintenance of Business Product Lines A & B Target Spend: $10.8M		Cost Reductions: All Product Lines Target Spend: $7.8M	
Project A	4.1	Project B	2.2	Project E	1.2	Project I	1.9
Project C	2.1	Project D	4.5	Project G	0.8	Project M	2.4
Project F	1.7	Project K	2.3	Project H	0.7	Project N	0.7
Project L	0.5 limit	Project T	3.7	Project J	1.5	Project P	1.4
Project X	1.7	**Gap = 5.8**		Project Q	4.8	Project S	1.6 limit
Project Y	2.9			Project R	1.5 limit	Project U	1.0
Project Z	4.5			Project V	2.5	Project AA	1.2
Project BB	2.6			Project W	2.1		

Projects ran ordered within column according to a financial criterion: NPV × Probability of Success; or ECV; or a scoring model (Chapter 5); see endnote 1.

The major strength of the Strategic Buckets Model is that it firmly links spending to the business's strategy. Over time, the portfolio of projects, and the spending across strategic buckets, will equal management's desired spending levels across buckets. At this point, the portfolio of projects will truly mirror the strategy for the business.

Another positive facet of the strategic buckets model is the recognition that *all development projects that compete for the same resources should be considered in the portfolio approach.* For example, product development projects must compete against cost reduction projects, because both utilize R&D resources.

Finally, different criteria can be used for different types of projects. That is, one is not faced with comparing and ranking very different types of projects against each other—for example, major new product projects versus minor modifications. Because this is a two-step approach—first allocate money to buckets, then prioritize like projects within a bucket—it is not necessary to arrive at a universal list of scoring or ranking criteria that fits all projects.

The major weakness of the approach is the burden it places on senior management of the business: this is a very time-consuming, arduous exercise. Further, making forced choices on resource splits, in the absence of consideration of specific projects, may be a somewhat hypothetical exercise. Finally, there are often too many dimensions across which resource splits must be made. One way to avoid this problem is *to focus on only a few of the most relevant dimensions,* as defined by your strategy (and these will vary by business, even within the same corporation).

The view expressed by the head of strategic planning for R&D at Rohm and Haas is *not* to split spending along every possible dimension, as illustrated in Table 5.3. Rather, the secret is *selective breakdowns:* "The key is to define the areas of *strategic thrust* of the business. That is, a business must have its strategy clearly defined . . . whether it be in terms of markets or product lines, or technology areas. For example, if a particular strategic initiative is to 'grow via development of products aimed at China,' then 'products aimed at China' is the definition of an area of strategic thrust. Then the leadership team must define how much effort [or money] it wishes to spend against each area of strategic thrust . . . that's the essence of portfolio management!"

A Variant on Strategic Buckets: Target Spending Levels Instead of Buckets

Some companies use an approach similar to Strategic Buckets, but arrive at a resource allocation guide or Target Spending Levels instead of Buckets. After developing the business's strategy, spending splits are agreed across relevant dimensions. For example: "Our target spending split is 40 percent for Market A and 60 percent for Market B." Thus far, the method is identical to the Strategic Buckets approach.

The major difference is that there is only a *single portfolio list of projects,* a list that covers all markets, product lines, project types, and so on (unlike Strategic Buckets, which has multiple portfolios, one portfolio list per bucket). A running count or tally of the breakdown of spending is kept during the year, so that actual spending along dimensions (for example, by product line or by project type) can be compared to the Target Spending Level, and adjustments made as the year progresses. The pie charts, which portray balance along various dimensions, are useful display methods here (see Figure 6.8), but with spending targets added: the *what should be* versus the *what is.*

Top-Down and Bottom-Up: A Combined Approach

In an attempt to overcome the deficiencies outlined in both top-down (Strategic Buckets) and bottom-up methods, some firms adopt a hybrid approach, namely, a top-down, bottom-up method. The method is similar to the Strategic Buckets Model, as follows:

▶ The top-down, bottom-up method begins with the business's strategy: mission, strategic arenas, and priorities.

▶ Next, flowing from this strategy, tentative target breakdowns of spending splits across different categories are developed (for example, tentative spending splits across product lines, or markets, or technologies, or project types, or across some or all of these).

So far the method closely resembles a top-down approach.

Now the method moves to a bottom-up approach:

▶ All existing or active projects and all on-hold projects (potential projects) are rated and ranked. This ranking is achieved via a maximization method, for example, a scoring model or some other criterion or method outlined earlier in this chapter. Some businesses use the scores, ratings, or data from most recent gate meetings to do this. Others rescore all projects. In this respect, the method is similar to that employed by Hoechst.

▶ This exercise yields a single prioritized list: a ranking of all projects and potential projects that are in the pipeline. Those projects near the top of the list are obvious "Go" projects; those near the bottom (or below the cut-off line) are obvious Kills . . . at least, on this first iteration.

The final step is to merge top-down and bottom-up outcomes. Note that frequently the list of projects generated by the bottom-up ranking yields splits in resources that are quite inconsistent with the top-down tentative or desired spending splits—the two methods do not coincide on the first iteration.

The strategic planning exercise used within Business Banking at Royal Bank of Canada (RBC) is fairly typical. Like Hoechst, RBC uses a scoring model to rate and rank projects. One check that the firm has built into its scoring technique to ensure that project spending is linked to strategy is their "StratPlan" exercise.

StratPlan is a macro-level, *strategic planning exercise.* Each of the 12 Product Groups (product lines) within the business are assessed via a strategic exercise, resulting in strategies for each. StratPlan scores these 12 Product Groups and classes them according to a McKinsey-style grid: Stars product lines, Cash Cows, Dogs, and Question-Marks.*

Independently, all active and on-hold new product projects are scored and rank-ordered via a scoring model, much like Hoechst's method in Appendix B. The cut-off point on the rank-ordered list is the point where total spending equals the total budget: all projects above this cut-off line are a "first-cut Go." This list of Go projects is then broken down by Product Group, and the total proposed expenditures by Product Group are determined. These totals, as a percentage of revenue, are next compared across Groups, seeking inconsistencies with each Product Group's strategy. Gaps are identified between new product spending levels per Product Group versus the desired spending. For example, if a Product Group were classified as a "maintain and defend" product line, yet received a rather large percentage of development spending via the scoring model, a gap exists. A second round of project prioritization ensues, with some projects that originally had been "Go" now removed from the list. This moves the portfolio closer to the one dictated by the StratPlan exercise. Several rounds are required before the final list of Go projects is agreed to. At this point, the prioritized list contains very good projects, according to the scoring model; and the spending allocations correctly reflect the various strategies of each Product Group.

This top-down, bottom-up method thus checks that the resulting list of projects (and their spending breakdowns) is indeed consistent with the business's strategy and with the tentative desired spending breakdowns. At the same time, the method fully considers what projects—active and on-hold—are available, and their relative attractiveness.

This StratPlan exercise resembles the Strategic Buckets Model in that desired spending levels per area (in this example, by Product Line Group) are decided, gaps identified, and the portfolio of projects arranged accordingly. However, the method reverses the order of steps (projects are prioritized first, and then spending splits are checked for consistency with strategy after), is somewhat easier to implement, and is less demanding on senior management.

---

*RBC uses somewhat different nomenclature than the standard model; but the meaning of the four quadrants is the same.

Moving Toward an Integrated Portfolio Management Process

Which portfolio management process is right for you? This is not an easy question, as there is no single right answer. But here are some recommendations based on our best practices study, what appears to work, and managements' views about the various methods.

Three Decision Processes

Our recommended integrated Portfolio Management Process consists of three decision processes (see Figure 6.10).* Each is linked to the other, and all three decision processes must work in harmony if the objective is effective portfolio management.

1. *Strategy development at the business unit (BU) level (top of Figure 6.10):* Ideally the BU's business strategy also includes a new product strategy, which specifies new products goals (for example, percentage of sales to be derived from new products), arenas of focus (for example, those markets, technologies, and product areas where new products will be developed), and even attack plans and relative priorities (for example, the desired breakdown of spending across markets, technologies, product categories, and project types[†]). This is the topic of Chapter 7.

2. *The BU's Stage-Gate™ New Product Process (right side of Figure 6.10):* The formal process or roadmap that drives new product projects from idea to new product Launch is part of an integrated portfolio management system. Real-time portfolio decisions are being made here: the gates are where Go/Kill decisions are made on individual projects, and hence where resources are allocated.

   Recall from Chapter 5 that prioritization takes place at gates, as resources must be allocated (one can no longer wait for semi-annual reviews to make these resource allocation decisions, given the desire for cycle time reduction!). Resource allocation is made

---

*"Our" refers to my two close colleagues, Professors Elko Kleinschmidt and Scott Edgett, and myself. Our proposed approach is outlined in greater detail in our recent portfolio management book—see note 1.

[†]Project types: for example, genuine new products; product improvements, enhancements, and extensions; new applications and market developments; customer support projects; cost reductions and process developments; fundamental research; and trouble-shooting or plant support.

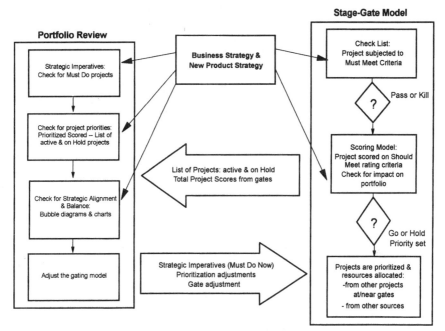

The Portfolio Review feeds the Stage-Gate Model; and the Stage-Gate Model feeds the Portfolio Review. Both models are in sync and driven by Strategy.

Figure 6.10   The Total Portfolio Management Process Linking Strategy, the Portfolio Review, and the NP Process or *Stage-Gate™* Model

Reprinted with permission from Perseus Books, Reading, Mass. R. G. Cooper, Edgett, S. J. & Kleinschmidt, E. J., *Portfolio Management for New Products* (Reading, Mass: Perseus Books, 1998).

by comparing the proposed project to the active projects already in the pipeline, as well as to those "on-hold" awaiting resources.

3. *The Portfolio Review (left side of Figure 6.10):* This is the periodic review of the portfolio of all projects. It is here where all projects—active and even on-hold—are reviewed and compared against each other. Here, the vital question for the leadership team of the business is: Do you have the right set of active projects here? Is this really where you want to spend your money?

The Portfolio Review should be a periodic check on the decisions made via the gating process, and held semiannually or quarterly. If the gates are working well, the Portfolio Review should be merely a course correction. But if too many Go and Kill decisions are made at this Portfolio Review, then look hard at your stage-gate process . . . something is wrong there!

The Portfolio Review considers all projects together: it is holistic. Think of the gate decisions, that deal with individual projects, as the fingers; and the Portfolio Review as the fist. At Portfolio Reviews, be sure to check that your portfolio of projects meets the three goals of portfolio management: maximum value to the business; balance; and strategic link. We recommend the following portfolio models for use at the Portfolio Review:

▶ *To achieve maximum portfolio value:* The gate scoring model, suggested in Chapter 5, is an excellent way to rate and rank projects at the Portfolio Review, yielding a prioritized list of the best projects, much like Hoechst and RBC do. Consider using criteria similar to those in Table 5.3 or in Appendix B—they're proven and they work! Alternatively, if your business is very financially driven, and if financial projections for new products are quite predicable, use a financial index or metric to rank projects, such as the ECV/Project Cost ratio (Figures 5.4 and 5.5 and Table 6.1).

▶ *To achieve balance:* Balance is best portrayed by the various visual charts:

  • Use bubble diagrams (for example, reward versus risk). If there are goals in addition to financial ones, and if financial estimates are uncertain, place less reliance on these financial numbers, and utilize a bubble diagram whose axes are derived from the scoring model factors (as does Reckitt & Colman, Figure 6.5, and Specialty Minerals, Figure 6.6). Otherwise, use the standard NPV versus Probability of Success bubble diagram (as in Figure 6.2, 6.3, or 6.4).
  • Use pie charts and histograms, which capture split of spending across markets, product categories, technologies, project types, and Launch timing (as in Figure 6.8).

▶ *To achieve strategic alignment:* Consider using the Strategic Buckets approach in order to preallocate funds to various buckets: for example, across project types or across markets, technologies, or product lines. The "Mercedes-star" method proposed by Allied Signal seems to suit many senior managements (Figure 6.9). Alternately, use the top-down, bottom-up approach to ensure that the spending breakdown mirrors strategic priorities. Additionally, be sure to build in strategic criteria—fit and importance—into your gate scoring model in order to drive on-strategy projects toward the top of the list (see Table 5.3).

An Illustration: The Agro Division

Let's illustrate the integrated portfolio management process via a real but disguised example of a business unit in a large corporation: the Agro division, a moderate-sized higher technology business unit in the agricultural chemical industry, within a much larger corporation.

New Product Strategy at Agro

The Portfolio Management Process is driven by strategy (see the box at the top of Figure 6.10). Why? Because strategy begins when you start spending money. Up to that point, strategy is just words on paper. Since portfolio choice is about allocating resources and making Go/Kill decisions on projects—in short, where you spend your money—then *portfolio choices must begin with strategy.*

After all, strategy guides and directs a business. It defines what is in or out of bounds; and it defines arenas of focus as well as their relative emphasis. The *manifestation of strategy* is decisions about where you will spend your money: the portfolio decisions.

Senior management at Agro reviewed the strategic mission and vision for the BU, undertook a strengths, weaknesses, opportunities, threats (SWOT) analysis, and performed a market-by-market analysis and core competency assessment that yielded a set of product line and market segment priorities. Then management moved to the issue of *new product strategy* for the BU, which logically evolved from the business's strategy. Management went through a difficult exercise of splitting the development budget across these prioritized markets and product lines for the BU—making forced choices, much like the top-down buckets approach outlined above. The result of this new product strategy session is summarized in Figure 6.11, where Target Spending Levels across product lines and markets are shown (top two pie charts) and Strategic Buckets across project types are also displayed (bottom pie chart).

Agro's **Stage-Gate**™ *New Product Process*

Agro relies on a five-stage, five-gate new product process, much like the one in Figure 4.2. The business uses a combination checklist and scoring model at the various gates. Gate 3 is a vital decision point, where the project becomes a full-fledged Development project. It is also where their "portfolio model" kicks in. The Gate 3 gatekeepers are the

- BU mission: rapid growth; aggressively gain market share in this growing business.
- Strategy overview: growth via leading-edge product development utilizing the BU's existing technology base; broaden distribution domestically and abroad.
- NP goals: 75% increase in sales via new products over the next three years.
- Market priorities and spending splits (see pie chart, left)
- Product line priorities and spending splits (see pie chart, right)
- Project type splits (see pie chart, bottom)

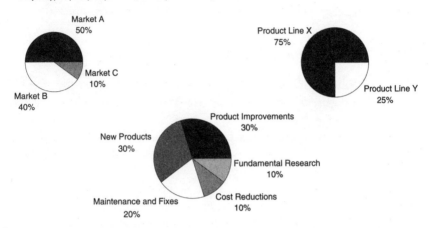

Figure 6.11   Summary of Agro's Business & New Product Strategy
Reprinted with permission from Perseus Books, Reading, Mass. R. G. Cooper, Edgett, S. J. & Kleinschmidt, E. J., *Portfolio Management for New Products* (Reading, Mass: Perseus Books, 1998).

leadership team in Agro, and the meeting is chaired by the general manager of the business. The checklist and scoring models used at Gate 3 are quite similar to the samples shown in Tables 5.2 and 5.3.

Consider a real project of Agro's at the Gate 3 decision point, namely, *Bio-55*. The project has had a small two-person team working on it for the past four months. Market studies have been completed. Some preliminary technical (laboratory) work has been undertaken, enough to establish a reasonable likelihood of technical feasibility. And the Business Case has been prepared. The product has been defined (target market, product benefits, price point, technical requirements, and high-level specs); the project justified, namely, the financial analysis and business rationale; and the project plan or action plan mapped out for the next stages of the project.

At Gate 3, senior management reviews the *Bio-55* project against a set of must-meet criteria (as in Table 5.2). *Bio-55* passes all of them: there are no negative votes here. Next, the project is scored on the should-meet items (as in Table 5.3). Out of a possible 60 points, the project scores 45.5, for a Total Project Score of 76 percent. The *Bio-55* project scores very well and clears all the Gate 3 hurdles, including the 60 percent hurdle on the Total Project Score. It looks like a Go—or is it?

The Prioritization Decision at Gates

Bio-55 is in a market area, namely, Market B, deemed vital to Agro—a high-priority market. Also, because it is a genuine new product (and not just another modification or extension), it is also higher-priority. Recall that management had developed a desired split in R&D spending across markets via its strategic exercise (see Figure 6.11), where it was decided that Market B should receive about 40 percent of spending (currently Market B only accounts for about 28 percent of spending, so that a *considerable gap* exists). Similarly, management wants to spend about 30 percent on new products; currently only 19 percent is being spent there. So *Bio-55* is an even more desirable project than the scoring model suggests, simply *because it helps move the portfolio toward the desired balance* and toward achieving strategic alignment.*

But where and how does one decide in the first place that there are too many of Market C and not enough Market B projects? Or too many line extensions and not enough genuine new product projects? Surely not at each and every gate meeting—that would be too cumbersome. Defining gaps is one role of the Portfolio Review, below.

The outcome of the checklist and scoring model exercise at the gate is a decision: the project is either a Kill—it fails the criteria and hurdles— or a Pass. Merely being a Pass does not guarantee that the project will be immediately resourced, however. There is still the question of finding the resources for the project. Recall that the gate meeting is conceptually

---

*Agro employs a "correction factor," called the Portfolio Balance Factor (PBF), to their scoring model results, to favor projects that drive the portfolio more into balance. Thus the PBF for projects aimed at Market B (such as *Bio-55*) was set at 1.1. Multiplying *Bio-55*'s total project score of 76 percent by 1.1 now makes *Bio-55* an even more attractive project, with a Total Project Score of 84 percent, simply because *Bio-55* brings the portfolio closer to achieving strategic alignment.

a two-part decision process (Figure 5.5). The first part rates and scores the project, leading to a Kill or Pass decision. The second facet of the gate meeting deals with prioritization and the decision to allocate resources to the Go projects.

The gatekeepers face two choices here: either they resource the project—it becomes (or continues as) an active or Go project; or they place it on hold. Projects in the hold tank are good projects; it's just that resources are scarce and other projects are better. At this point, the project under review must be compared to other projects—both active projects already under way as well as projects in the hold tank. If the project under consideration rates better than projects in the hold tank, and equal to active projects, then it should be resourced. The Total Project Score from the scoring model is used to make this comparison. Recall that this Total Project Score captures the value of the project to the business (strategic importance and fit, reward, and probability of success) as well as how well the project helps balance the portfolio. A useful chart to assist this discussion is the Prioritized Scored List (see example in Figure 6.12), which portrays the rank-ordered list of active and on-hold projects, together with their Total Project Scores.

Agro's *Bio-55* achieved a very positive score of 76 percent, which is adjusted upward to 84 percent at Gate 3, simply because *Bio-55* helps balance the portfolio.* This score of 84 percent places *Bio-55* above other projects in the hold tank, and indeed among the better projects on the active list (see Figure 6.12).

So the decision is Go. Indeed, the decision is a strong Go, and maximum resources are allocated to *Bio-55*. Resources are acquired from several sources. First, the two-person team already on the project is assigned to continue as key team players. Other technology players are added from another project, soon to be entering the Launch phase, where their services are no longer required full-time. Finally, a project with several people assigned is approaching a Gate 4 meeting, and may be cancelled, potentially freeing up a few more people for *Bio-55*. They are also tentatively earmarked for *Bio-55*.

*The adjustment or correction factor applied was 1.1 (the Portfolio Balance Factor). See footnote on page 223.

Project Name	Rank (Priority Level)	Total Project Score	Portfolio Balance Factor	Adjusted Total Project Score
Soya-44	1	80	1.10	88
Encapsulated	2	82	1.00	82
Legume N-2	3	70	1.10	77
Spread-Ease	4	75	1.00	75
Charcoal-Base	5	80	0.90	72
Projects on Hold				
N2-Fix	1	80	1.00	80
Slow-Release	2	70	1.10	77
Multi-Purpose	3	75	.90	68
etc.	etc.			

The Adjusted Total Project Score is the Total Project Score multiplied by the correction factor, the Portfolio Balance Factor (PBF). The PBF scores those projects that are "good" for the portfolio more points.

Figure 6.12   Agro's Prioritized Scored List of Active & On Hold Projects (New Products Bucket Only)

Reprinted with permission from Perseus Books, Reading, Mass. R. G. Cooper, Edgett, S. J. & Kleinschmidt, E. J., *Portfolio Management for New Products* (Reading, Mass: Perseus Books, 1998).

Key Points for Management

1. Ensure that your business has an effective gating process in place—the right side of Figure 6.10. Do not expect Portfolio Reviews to correct the problems created by a broken gating process!
2. Gates should have clearly defined, consistent, prespecified, and visible criteria for making Go/Kill and prioritization decisions, as outlined in Chapter 5.
3. Gates achieve portfolio balance and strategic alignment in four ways:

   - via Strategic Buckets or Target Spending Levels;
   - by building strategic criteria into the scoring model used at the gate;
   - by utilizing the Prioritized Scored List and various bubble diagrams and charts at gate meetings (maps and lists that show other projects in the portfolio, and the impact of adding the current project); and
   - by using an adjustment or correction factor to the project score.

The Portfolio Review

The Portfolio Review is a holistic review of all projects in the portfolio, is held periodically, and is staffed by the leadership team of the business. This review monitors the decisions made at gates and makes needed adjustments both to the portfolio of projects and to the gating decision process (this Portfolio Review is the box on the left side of Figure 6.10).

Ideally, Portfolio Reviews are merely *course corrections*. If the gating process and gate criteria are well designed and effectively applied, Portfolio Reviews should not witness multiple cancellations of projects and numerous approvals of others: this is *not* a project selection meeting! Portfolio Reviews look at projects *in aggregate*, not typically at *individual projects*. The hope is that the gates are working well and doing a good job of selecting and prioritizing individual projects throughout the year.

Strategic Imperatives

First, there is a review of the BU's strategy and identification of any *strategic imperatives;* that is, projects that are absolutely essential to achieving the strategy. Agro management has a Portfolio Review meeting twice a year. Here, each of the key strategic thrusts and arenas is discussed. One question focuses on the need to move ahead right now with any projects essential to the BU's strategy.

Maximizing the Value of the Portfolio

Next, there is a check that projects are ranked and prioritized appropriately—that those projects that score highest on the key criteria (those with the greatest value to the business) are indeed being given top priority and maximum resources. If too many projects in the hold tank score higher than active projects, something is amiss! The Total Project Score for each project becomes the ranking criterion for use in a Prioritized Scored List. This Prioritized Scored List is simply a rank ordered list of active and on-hold projects (see Figure 6.12).

Agro's list of active and funded new product projects past Gate 3—the Prioritized Scored List—is shown in Figure 6.12. This table also shows projects in the hold tank (below the line). All projects are rank-ordered on this Prioritized Scored List according to the Total Project Score. Note that these scores have been adjusted in order to push projects that bring the portfolio closer to strategic alignment and proper balance toward the top. For example, the project *Legume N-2*, with an initial score of 70, might not have made the active list, except for the adjustment, which drives its score up to a respectable 77.

Management now checks to ensure that projects at the top of the list are indeed receiving the right priorities in terms of resource allocation, and that the active projects have higher scores than on-hold projects. Several projects on hold have excellent scores, namely, N2-Fix and *Slow-Release*. Indeed, they both have better adjusted scores than some active and funded projects, specifically *Spread-Ease* and *Charcoal-Base*. But both *Spread-Ease* and *Charcoal-Base* are well on their way through Testing and moving toward Launch. Both still have good scores and continue to clear the gate hurdles. So the decision is to continue with *Spread-Ease* and *Charcoal-Base*, and to seek resources for the two top-rated Hold projects, *N-2 Fix* and *Slow-Release*, resourcing these as soon as people become available.

Checking for Balance and Strategic Alignment

Here the key question is: when all the active or Go projects are considered together, is the resulting portfolio strategically aligned and properly balanced? Recall that:

- strategically aligned means all projects are on-strategy, and the spending breakdown across projects is consistent with the business's priorities and strategies; and
- properly balanced means that there exists the appropriate breakdown in spending (or numbers of projects) across markets, product types, technologies, and project types.

Various visual displays are recommended to portray the existing portfolio of active projects and to check for balance.

Bubble diagrams to display balance:

The bubble diagrams for Agro in Figures 6.13 and 6.14 portray the risk–reward snapshot of the portfolio. Agro has three clear Pearls—high-reward, high-probability projects. Not surprisingly, they were also at the top of the Prioritized Scored List of new product projects in Figure 6.12. One new product project is a long-shot, or Oyster, namely, *Legume N-2*. Bread and Butter projects are numerous, and include one low-risk major new product with a modest reward (*Charcoal-Base*) and one with a major reward (*Slow-Release-4*), a product improvement on an existing Agro product. Smaller projects in this

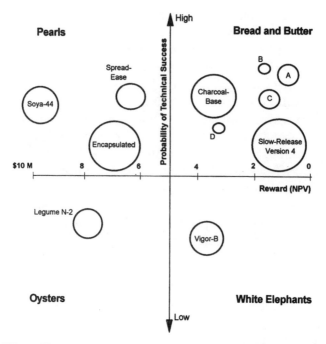

Adapted from SDG method[6].

Circle Sizes = resources (annual) per project

Figure 6.13   Agro's Risk-Return Bubble Diagram (2 buckets)

Reprinted with permission from Perseus Books, Reading, Mass. R. G. Cooper, Edgett, S. J. & Kleinschmidt, E. J., *Portfolio Management for New Products* (Reading, Mass: Perseus Books, 1998).

Bread-and-Butter quadrant are A, B, C, and D. All are product improvements. There is one White Elephant, *Vigor-B*, a product improvement that has run into trouble. This project began life with a higher likelihood of success, but technical problems arose and the project had drifted into the White Elephant quadrant.

Overall, management's assessment of the distribution of projects in the bubble diagram in Figure 6.13 was positive, unlike Company T's in Figure 6.2. The risk–reward pattern showed no obvious patterns for concern. For example, one long-shot Oyster project was deemed about right. The one White Elephant was discussed, and the decision was to call for an immediate gate meeting for an imminent Go/Kill decision. Within weeks, *Vigor-B* was killed.

The bubble diagram in Figure 6.14 shows essentially the same informa-

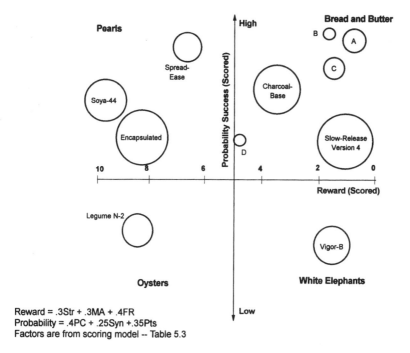

Figure 6.14 Alternate Version of Agro's Risk-Return Diagram (2 buckets)
Reprinted with permission from Perseus Books, Reading, Mass. R. G. Cooper, Edgett,
S. J. & Kleinschmidt, E. J., *Portfolio Management for New Products* (Reading, Mass:
Perseus Books, 1998).

tion as Figure 6.13. In Figure 6.14, reward is portrayed in nonfinancial
terms, with both axes derived from the scoring model results.

Pie charts to display breakdowns and balance:

These charts show splits in resources being spent, or numbers of projects, across key dimensions, compared against the ideal or desired
spending pattern. These charts provide a check for *strategic alignment.*
Spending displays can be broken down by:

- *product type, product category, or product line.* Figure 6.15 (see left pie
  chart) reveals that projects for Product Line X account for about 67
  percent of spending, versus a desired 75 percent. This 8 percent gap
  is relatively small as a percent, so no corrective actions were taken.
- *market or segment* (right pie chart, Figure 6.15). Projects targeted at

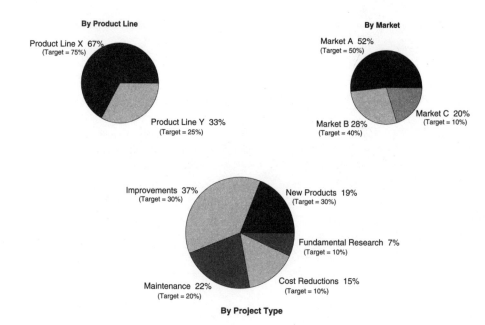

Figure 6.15 Agro's Spending Breakdowns
Reprinted with permission from Perseus Books, Reading, Mass. R. G. Cooper, Edgett, S. J. & Kleinschmidt, E. J., *Portfolio Management for New Products* (Reading, Mass: Perseus Books, 1998).

Market B account for 28 percent of the spend; this is far short of the goal of 40 percent. Further, projects for Market C account for far more than the goal (20 percent versus a target of 10 percent). Corrections were agreed to here: for example, all projects aimed at Market B would be given a boost by scoring them somewhat higher.

▶ *types of projects:* genuine new products, modifications and improvement, customer request projects, and product maintenance projects or fixes (bottom pie chart, Figure 6.15). Strategic Buckets were established a priori for the six project types. As shown in Figure 6.15, the desired spending levels are not achieved. Too much is going to product improvements and not enough to genuine new products. Management decided to remain with these desired splits, and took action to stimulate the conception of more high-quality new product projects for the next year.

♦ *project newness via the "newness" matrix* (not used for Agro; see Table 6.4 or Figure 1.6 for examples).

Key Points for Management

1. In addition to a sound new product process with effective gates, you must also have periodic Portfolio Reviews (left side of Figure 6.10). Recall that gates look at individual projects—the fingers; Portfolio Reviews look at all projects together and in aggregate— the fist.
2. Here are the important steps in the Portfolio Review:

    *   Check for strategic imperatives—"must do now" projects.
    *   Check project priorities: use the Prioritized Scored List and spot inconsistencies.
    *   Check for balance and alignment: use the recommended bubble diagrams, charts, and maps.
    *   Define adjustments needed to the gating process (for example, a correction factor to be applied to the gate scoring model).

3. Recommended charts and maps to use at Portfolio Reviews include:

    *   the risk–reward bubble diagram (NPV versus probability; or nonfinancial reward versus success probabilities; or scored axes); and
    *   pie charts showing splits in resources (versus Strategic Buckets or Target Spending Levels).

In Conclusion: Your Integrated Portfolio Management Process

Three vital decision processes take place within the business unit that comprise the Portfolio Management Process. They are: business unit strategy development, the new product process with its stages and gates, and the Portfolio Review (shown in Figure 6.10).

These three decision processes ideally are integrated, are in harmony, and feed each other (refer to Figure 6.10). For example, the business's strategy (top) drives the gating method by providing key criteria for the scoring model. It also provides key criteria for the Portfolio Review, helps establish the targets for various spending breakdown or buckets (for balance), and even identifies strategic imperatives ("must do now" projects).

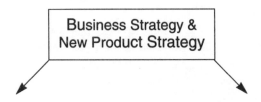

Similarly, and referring to Figure 6.10, the gating process (right) feeds the gate decisions and project scores to the Portfolio Review (horizontal arrow, heading left—see sketch below). Finally, the Portfolio Review (left box in Figure 6.10—see sketch next page) feeds strategic project decisions (imperatives) and gate adjustments to the gating process (horizontal arrow, heading right in Figure 6.10). These gate adjustments simply adjust the gate criteria or scoring model to favor project types that are deemed "desirable but underrepresented" in the portfolio, and moves the project portfolio toward the ideal balance.

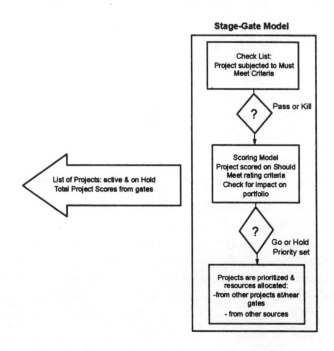

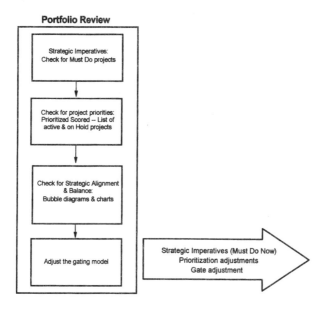

Portfolio Review

If all three elements of the Portfolio Management Process—the business's strategy and the defined spending splits, the new product process with its gates in place and working well, and the Portfolio Review, with its various charts and lists—are in place, then a harmonized system should yield excellent portfolio choices: projects that deliver economic payoffs to the business, that mirror the business's strategy and direction, and that achieve the business's new product goals. But if any piece of the process in Figure 6.10 is not working—for example, if there is no clearly defined new product strategy for the business, or if the new product process and gating method is broken—the results are less than satisfactory.[13]

Key Points for Management

New products are the leading edge of your business strategy. The product choices you make today determine what your business's product offerings and market position will be in five years. Making the right choices today is paramount: portfolio management and new product project selection is fundamental to business success. Make sure that you have the tools you need to make these right choices—an effective Portfolio Management Process—in your business!

7

A New Product Strategy for Your Business: What Markets, Products, and Technologies?

I find the great thing in this world is not so much where we stand, as in which direction we are moving: To reach the port of heaven, we must sail sometimes with the wind and sometimes against it but we must sail, and not drift, and not lie at anchor.
—Oliver Wendell Holmes, The Autocrat of the Breakfast Table, 1858.

Win the Battle, Lose the War?

What if . . .

What if your leadership team had overseen the implementation of a *Stage-Gate*™ new product process to guide projects to market?

And what if all your business's new product projects followed the process and were executed well—good up-front homework, solid marketing input, tough Go/Kill gates, and so on?

And what if your business committed the necessary resources to product development—both quality and quantity of resources?

Would the result be a high-performing business unit? Not necessarily. One of the three cornerstones of success in new product warfare is still missing, and that cornerstone makes the difference between winning individual battles and winning the entire new product war.

The missing cornerstone is the *business's new product strategy*. And it's lacking in too many businesses I have studied. The new product strategy charts the strategy for the business's entire new product initiative. It is the master plan: it provides the direction for your enterprise's new product efforts, and it is the essential link between your product development effort and your total business strategy.[1]

This chapter begins with a look at the need for a new product strategy and the hard evidence in support of strategy—facts that make it imperative that you and your leadership team develop a new product strategy for your business. The components of an innovation strategy are then defined, followed by a glimpse into some of the broad strategic options or scenarios that your business might elect in product innovation. I then reveal the benchmarking evidence to see what types of product development strategies appear to deliver the best results, and to understand what strategic success factors the winners had in common. Next, approaches to developing a new product strategy are outlined—approaches where you define and elect arenas of strategic thrust for your new product efforts and possible attack plans. So let's move forward, elevating ourselves above the battle—above the level of the individual new product project, tactics, and the *Stage-Gate*™ process—and play the role of the general, looking at strategy and direction for the business's entire new product effort. Let's go win the war!

The Importance of a New Product Strategy for Your Business

Businesses that are most likely to succeed in the development and launch of new products are those that implement a company-specific approach, driven by business objectives and strategies, with a *well-defined new product strategy* at its core. This was one of the findings of an extensive study of new product practices by Booz-Allen & Hamilton: the new product strategy was viewed as instrumental to the effective identification of market and product opportunities.[2]

Our benchmarking studies also reveal that having an articulated new product strategy for the business is one of the three important drivers of new product performance. Recall the three cornerstones of performance from Chapters 1 and 2. Businesses with a defined new product strategy—one that specifies goals and the role of new products, defines arenas of strategic thrust, and has a longer-term orientation—achieve better new product results: these businesses meet their new product sales and profit objectives more; they boast new product efforts with a much greater positive impact on the business; and they achieve higher success rates at launch.

A number of companies do develop such innovative strategies. For example, *product innovation charters* were described by Crawford in his study of 125 firms.[3] He notes that managements are now beginning to pull *all the multifunctional elements together* in one document, which specifies the types of markets, products, technologies, and orientation the company will pursue with its new product strategy.

What Is a New Product Strategy?

A new product strategy is a strategic master plan that guides your business's new product war efforts. But how does one define or describe a new product strategy? The term "strategy" is widely used in business circles today. The word is derived from the ancient Greek word meaning "the art of the general." Until comparatively recently, its use was confined to the military. In a business context, strategy has been defined as "the schemes whereby a firm's resources and advantages are managed (deployed) in order to surprise and surpass competitors or to exploit opportunities."[4] More specifically, strategic change is defined as "a realignment of firm's product/market environment."[5] Strategy is closely tied to product and market specification: Corey argues that strategy is about choosing your *markets to target,* and choosing the *products to target them* with.[6]

Business strategy here refers to the *business unit's* strategy; and *new product strategy* is a component of that business strategy.[7] By *business and new product strategy,* I do not mean a vaguely worded statement of intent, one that approaches a vision or mission statement. Rather, I mean operational, action-specific strategies. Recall from Chapter 6 that strategy is about where you spend money. Thus, a business's new product strategy includes:

1. the goals for your business's total product development efforts;
2. the role of product development: how new products tie into your business's overall goals;
3. arenas of strategic focus, including priorities;
4. spending splits across these arenas (R&D funds, possibly marketing and capital funds for developments); and
5. how to attack each arena.

Let's elaborate on these five strategy elements:

1 & 2—Goals and role: The business's new product strategy specifies the goals of the new product effort, and it indicates the role that product innovation will play in helping the business achieve its business objectives. It answers the question: how do new products and product innovation fit into your business's overall plan? A statement such as "By the year 2005, 30 percent of our business's sales will come from new products" is a typical goal. Performance goals can also be stated, such as the desired number of new product introductions, expected success rates, and acceptable financial returns from new products.

3— *Arenas and strategic thrust:* The concept of *strategic arenas* is at the heart of a new product strategy. A business and new product strategy, at minimum, specifies clearly defined *strategic arenas* for the business to focus on, including how it will focus its product development efforts. That is, it defines the types of markets, applications, technologies, and products on which the business's new product efforts will focus. The specification of these arenas—what's "in bounds" and what's "out of bounds"—is fundamental to spelling out the direction or *strategic thrust* of the business's product development effort, and is the result of identifying and assessing new product opportunities at the strategic level.

These strategic arenas can be defined in terms of dimensions such as:

- markets or market segments; and/or
- product types, product lines, or product categories; and/or
- technologies and technology platforms.

4—*Spending priorities:* Strategy definition goes further, however: it indicates the relative emphasis, or strategic priorities, accorded each arena of strategic focus. For example, if Markets A, B, and C are identified as "strategic arenas," the *relative priorities* of these markets should be part of the strategy. This means that the strategy must be translated into *deployment decisions:* the relative spending priorities or splits (allocation of resources across arenas: for example, how much to spend in each of Markets A, B, and C).

5—*Plan of attack or entry strategy:* The issue of *how to attack* each strategic arena should also be part of the business's new product strategy. For example, for one arena, the strategy may be to be the industry innovator—the first to the market with new products; and in another arena, the attack plan may be to be a "fast follower," rapidly copying and improving on competitive entries. Other strategies might focus on being low-cost versus the differentiator versus a niche player; or on emphasizing certain strengths, core competencies, or product attributes or advantages. The attack plans logically lead to spending decisions regarding how much to spend on different types of projects (spending split by project types, such as platform developments versus new products versus maintenance and renewal projects). Additionally, entry strategies might be outlined and can include internal product development, licensing, joint venturing, and even acquisitions of other firms.

Why Have a New Product Strategy at All?

Developing a new product strategy is hard work. It involves many people, especially top management. Why, then, go to all the effort? Most of us can probably name countless companies that do not appear to have a master plan for their new product efforts. How do they get by?

Doing Business Without a Strategy

Running an innovation program without a strategy is like conducting a war without a military strategy. There's no rudder, there's no direction, and the results are often highly unsatisfactory. You simply drift. On occasion, such unplanned efforts do succeed, largely owing to good luck or perhaps brilliant tactics.

A new product initiative without a strategy will inevitably lead to a number of ad hoc decisions made independently of one another. New product and R&D projects are initiated solely on their own merits and with little regard to their fit into the grander scheme (portfolio management is all but impossible, for example). The result is that the business finds itself in unrelated or unwanted markets, products, and technologies: there is no focus.

Goals and Role: The Necessary Link to Business Strategy

What types of direction does a new product strategy give a business's new product efforts? First, the goals of your new product strategy tie your product development effort tightly to the overall business strategy. New product development, so often viewed in a "hands-off" fashion by senior management, becomes a central part of the business strategy, a key plank in the business's overall strategic platform.

The question of spending commitments on new products is dealt with by defining the role and goals of the new product effort. Too often the R&D or new product budget is easy prey in hard economic times. Development and new product marketing spending tend to be viewed as discretionary expenditures—something that can be slashed if need be. Establish product innovation as a central facet of your business's overall strategy, and firmly define the role and goals of product innovation, however, and cutting this R&D budget becomes much less arbitrary: there is a continuity of resource commitment to new products.

The Strategic Arenas: Guiding the War Effort

The second facet of the new product strategy, the definition of arenas, is critical to guiding and focusing your new product efforts. The first step in the *Stage-Gate™* new product process is idea generation. But where does one search for new product ideas? Unless the arenas are defined, the idea search is undirected, unfocused, and ineffective.

Your businesses's new product strategy is also fundamental to project selection and portfolio management. That's why I show strategy as the top box in the portfolio management process of Figure 6.10—strategy overarches the entire decision and selection process. For example, the first gate in the new product process is idea screening. The key criterion for this early Go/Kill decision is whether the proposed project has strategic alignment. This usually translates into "Is this the kind of market, product, and technology that we as a business have decided is *fair game* for us?" Without a definition of your playing fields—arenas of strategic thrust—good luck in trying to make effective screening decisions! The strategic alignment question remains a vital criterion for project selection at almost every gate throughout the *Stage-Gate™* process, and also helps dictate spending splits and the desired balance of the portfolio of projects; hence it is critical to portfolio management.

The definition of arenas also guides long-term resource and personnel planning. If certain markets are designated top-priority arenas, then the business can acquire resources, people, skills, and knowledge to enable it to attack those markets. Similarly, if certain technologies are singled out as arenas, the business can hire and acquire resources and technologies to bolster its abilities in those fields. Resource building doesn't happen overnight. One can't buy a sales force on a moment's notice, and one can't acquire a critical mass of key researchers or engineers in a certain technology at the local supermarket. Putting the right people, resources, and skills in place takes both lead time and direction.

The Evidence in Support of Strategy

The argument in favor of a deliberate assessment of opportunities and the development of a new product strategy, although logical, may be somewhat theoretical. One can't help but think of all those companies that have made it without a grand strategy. Further, the notion of deciding what's in bounds versus what's out of bounds is foreign to many businesses: after completing his large sample study on innovation charters, Crawford notes that "the idea of putting definitive restrictions on new product activity is not novel, but the use of it, especially sophisticated use, is still not widespread."[8] Quinn's work on how managers *really* develop corporate strategy concludes that "the approaches they [managers] use frequently bear little resemblance to the rational-analytical systems so often described in the planning literature."[9] He goes on: "Overall corporate strategy tended to evolve as internal decisions and external events flowed together to create a new consensus for action." He argues that strategies evolve and crystallize over time, often in a piecemeal fashion and based on interim decisions. His argument is not that businesses have no strategies, but the way the strategy is developed often does not hinge on formal planning methods.

Regardless of how strategy is developed, the question remains: does a new product strategy really matter? Perhaps current practice observed by Quinn is not ideal, and senior people *ought to* approach strategy development a little more formally! So where's the evidence in support of having a new product strategy? The studies that have looked at businesses' new product strategies have a clear and consistent message: new product strategies at the business unit or company level are critical to success, and some strategies clearly work better than others. Consider these facts:

▶ Booz-Allen & Hamilton's study of new product practices found that "successful companies are more committed to growth through new products developed internally" and that "they are more likely to have a strategic plan that includes a certain portion of growth from new products."[10] The authors of this study go on to explain why having a new product strategy is tied to success:

"A new product strategy links the new product process to company objectives, and provides focus for idea/concept generation and for establishing appropriate screening criteria. The outcome of this strategy analysis is a set of strategic roles, used not to generate specific new product ideas, but to help identify markets for which new products will be developed. These market opportunities provide the set of product and market requirements from which new product ideas are generated. In addition, strategic roles provide guidelines for new product performance measurement criteria. Performance thresholds tied to strategic roles provide a more precise means of screening new product ideas" (p. 22).

▶ How various new product strategies are tied to performance was studied by Nystrom and Edvardsson in a number of industrial product firms.[11] Strategies emphasizing the synergistic use of technology, a responsive R&D organization, and an externally oriented R&D effort are generally more successful. While the study was limited to a handful of strategy dimensions, the message is clear that strategy and performance are closely linked.

▶ The *performance impact of product innovation strategies* in 120 businesses was investigated in one of my own studies.[12] This study is one of the first investigations undertaken on a large number of businesses that considers many strategy dimensions, and how the strategy of the business's entire new product effort is tied to performance results. The overriding conclusion is that product innovation strategy and performance are strongly linked. The types of markets, products, and technologies that firms elect and the orientation and direction of their product innovation efforts have a pronounced impact on success and profitability. Strategy really does count.

▶ Ten best practices were identified by management in a recent study of 79 leading R&D organizations.[13] Near the top of the list is "use a formal development process," an endorsement of the use of stage-and-gate processes. Even higher on the list is "coordinate long-range business planning and R&D plans"— a call for a new product or R&D plan for the business that meshes with the business plan. Although adoption of these best practices varies widely by company, the study revealed that high performers tend to embrace these best practices more than do low performers.

The #2 Cornerstone of Performance: A Clear and Well-Communicated New Product Strategy for the Business

Do you have a clearly articulated new product strategy for your business?[14] If so, you're in the minority. But businesses that boast such a strategy do better, according to our most recent benchmarking study.[15] Recall from Chapter 2 that having a new product strategy—a clear and visible one—is the #2 driver of businesses' new product performance. Businesses that have articulated new product strategies fare much better than those found lacking here: 32 percent higher new product success rates; meet sales objectives more (42 percent better); and meet profit objectives more (39 percent better)—see Figure 7.1 for detailed results. And the ingredients of a solid new product strategy are also correlated with both the impact and profitability of the business's total new product efforts (Figure 7.2).

Here are the *four main ingredients* of a positive new product strategy uncovered in this benchmarking study:

Met Objectives Score (0-100)

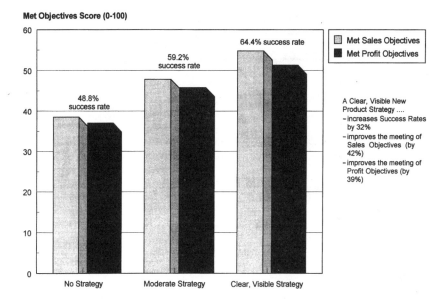

Figure 7.1   Impact of New Product Strategy on Business's Performance
Reprinted with permission from: R. G. Cooper & Kleinschmidt, E. J. "Benchmarking firms' new product perfromance and practices," *Engineering Management Review* 23, 3, Fall 1995, 112–120. © 1995 IEEE.

> *There are goals or objectives for the business's total new product efforts; for example, what sales, profits, and the like new products will contribute to the business goal.*

This ingredient of strategy—having clear goals—would seem to be fairly basic. What surprised us is how many businesses lack clear, written goals for their overall new product efforts. Note the mediocre average proficiency scores in Figure 7.2: only 58.8 points out of 100. By contrast, leading firms, such as 3M, make new product goals such as "30 percent of our division's sales will come from new products introduced over the next three years" an explicit part of every division's business goals. What's more, 3M ties the achievement of these goals to senior management's compensation, which may partially explain 3M's stunning track record in product innovation!

Ironically having new product goals drives the *impact* of the business's new product effort, but not so much its *profitability*. This is perhaps a reflection of the fact that these goals are most often stated as "percentage of the business's sales to be generated by new products"; hence the result is felt in terms of sales impact, not profit. One might

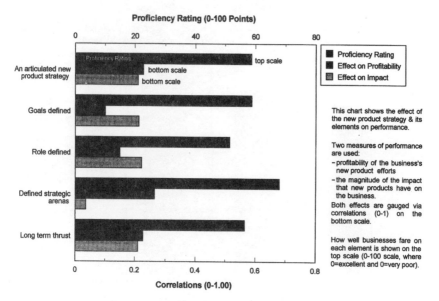

Figure 7.2 Ratings of Strategy Ingredients & Effect on Performance

argue that goals expressed in terms of profit and return on R&D spending might also appropriate here.

> *The role of new products in achieving the business's goals is clearly communicated to all.*

The whole point of having goals is so that everyone involved in the activity—in this case, new products—has a common purpose . . . something to work toward. Yet, far too often, personnel who work on new product projects are not aware of their business's new product objectives or the role that new products play in the total business objectives. This is the *weakest ingredient* of new product strategy (note the low score in Figure 7.2: only 51.5 points out of 100).

> *There are clearly defined arenas—specified areas of strategic focus or strategic thrust, such as specific product areas, markets, or technologies—to give direction to the business's total new product effort.*

The new product strategy specifies where you'll attack, or perhaps more important, where you won't attack. Without arenas defined, the search for specific new product ideas or opportunities is unfocused. Over time, the portfolio of new product projects is likely to contain a lot of unrelated projects, in many different markets, technologies, or product-types—a scatter-gun effort. And the results are predicable: a not-so-profitable new product effort. Note the positive correlation that defined arenas has on new product profitability (Figure 7.2).

> One Du Pont polymers business faced exactly this problem: much money spent on R&D, but no focus because there was no strategy or defined arenas. Management recognized the deficiency: they then identified a number of possible arenas (product/market/technology areas that might be "in bounds"); assessed each in terms of their market attractiveness and the opportunity for leveraging the division's core competencies; selected several arenas; and then began to focus their new product initiatives within these chosen arenas.

In spite of its importance, this definition of strategic arenas for the new product effort is only a modestly rated area on average, with a score of only 68.0 points out of 100 (Figure 7.2).

The new product effort has a long-term thrust and focus, including some longer-term projects (as opposed to just short-term, incremental projects).

This is a fairly weak ingredient of the four strategy ingredients with a score of only 56.5 out of 100 across all businesses (Figure 7.2). The short time horizon of businesses' new product efforts has been a criticism widely voiced. Ironically, this one ingredient is *the most important* of the four strategy ingredients and is significantly linked to four important performance metrics: meeting sales and profit objectives, and the impact of the program on both company sales and profits, as well as to the two performance dimensions, new product profitability and impact.

Key Points for Management

Doing business without strategy is like trying to sail a ship without a rudder. Our benchmarking study's results support this adage. So do other studies. Clearly those businesses that lack goals for their total new product effort, where arenas or areas of strategic thrust have not been defined, where the strategy and projects are short-term in nature, and where the strategy is not well communicated to all, are at a decided performance disadvantage.

Do what 3M does. *Set goals* for your business's new product effort (for example, percentage of sales, profit, or growth that new products will contribute over the next X years). Make these goals clear to everyone involved. And consider tying them to senior management's compensation!

Emulate the Du Pont example, and *specify strategic arenas*—areas of strategic focus, defined in terms of markets, technologies, and product types or categories. Base these choices on a strategic exercise. And consider going one step further: move toward portfolio management, and decide priorities and *ideal expenditure splits* across these arenas.

Strategy Types: Prospectors, Analyzers, Defenders, Reactors

One way of looking at strategy is via a typology based on the speed that an organization responds to changing market and external conditions via altering its products and markets. There are four strategy types, according to Miles and Snow,[16] and you may wish to elect one as the scenario or vision for your own business. Which one are you? And which one should you be?[17]

Prospectors: These businesses are the industry innovators. They value being first in with new products and are first to adopt new technologies, even though there are risks and not all such efforts are profitable. Prospectors respond rapidly to early signals that point to emerging or new opportunities. In the automobile business, Honda and Chrysler are considered to be prospectors.

Analyzers: These businesses are fast followers. By carefully monitoring the actions of major competitors, and by moving quickly, they often are able to bring a superior product to market—more cost-efficient or with better features and benefits—than the prospector's product. But analyzers are rarely first to market. Toyota and Ford are analyzer companies.

Defenders: Defenders attempt to locate and maintain a secure position or niche in a relatively stable product or market area. They protect their domain by offering higher-quality, superior service or lower prices. These businesses ignore industry changes that have no direct influence on their current operations. General Motors, Nissan, and Mazda are defenders.

Reactors: These firms are not as aggressive in maintaining established products and markets as competitors. They respond only when forced to by strong external or market pressures. Subaru was considered a reactor (although its strategy may have changed).

These four types of businesses are useful descriptors when you and your leadership team are trying to envision which type of product developer you aspire to be. Additionally, the way resources are split across project types varies by business, with prospectors undertaking proportionately more new-to-the world projects as a percentage of their total portfolio. Average breakdowns by project type are shown in Table 7.1 for each of the four strategies, and may provide a useful guide or point of comparison for your business.[18]

Key Points for Management

New product strategy pays off. If your organization does not have an explicit, written new product strategy, complete with measurable goals and specification of arenas as a guide to your business's new product efforts, now is the time to begin developing one.

What strategy type is your business—prospector, analyzer, defender, or reactor? And which type should you be? Or is your strategic approach to new products a hit and miss affair—no strategy at all? Then read on to see what strategic types, thrusts, and arenas appear to yield superlative results.

Table 7.1 Project Types by Business Strategy Type

Project Type	Prospector	Analyzer	Defender	Reactor
New-to-the-world	30%[a]	6%	7%	0%
New-to-the-firm	15%	16%	17%	8%
Additions to existing product line	22%	42%	40%	48%
Improvements to existing products	11%	16%	11%	13%
Repositionings	8%	8%	9%	11%
Cost reductions	15%	17%	21%	12%
Number of firms	30	22	22	4

[a]Reads: 30 percent of the products that Prospectors develop are classed as "new-to-the-world." Adds to 100 percent down a column.
Source: Griffin and Page; see endnote 17.

Winning New Product Strategies and Their Performance Impacts

What are the secrets of a successful new product strategy? To answer this question, I observed the product innovation strategies of 120 business units, measured on 66 strategy variables.[19] These strategy variables describe the types of markets, products, and technologies that the businesses elected for their new product efforts, and their direction, orientation, and commitment to this initiative. The performance of each business's new product efforts was measured on 10 different performance metrics. The conclusions, set out below, are based on concrete data and the results of a scientific investigation, not on wishful thinking, conjecture, or speculation. And they'll prove useful to you in the formulation of your new product strategy.

Conclusion 1. There is a strong connection between the new product strategy a business elects and the performance results it achieves. New product strategy and performance are closely connected. Four strategic thrusts and five different strategy types or scenarios were uncovered, and each is strongly tied to performance. One strategy—Type A, the Differentiated strategy—achieves remarkable results, and serves as a model to other businesses.

The implications of this strategy–performance link are critical to the management of a business's new product efforts. The existence of this link points to the need to define clearly your business's new product strategy as a central and integral part of your overall business plan. The development of a new product strategy becomes a pivotal task for the leadership team of your business.

Conclusion 2. There are four strategic thrusts or orientations that impact on performance, and should be considered as you develop your business's new product strategy.

▶ *Technologically sophisticated strategies* do better. Businesses that are strong on this dimension employ sophisticated development technologies, and develop high-technology, technically complex new products. These businesses are strongly R&D-oriented, proactive in acquiring new development technologies, and proactive in generating new product ideas. They develop innovative, higher-risk, venturesome products that offer unique features and benefits to customers. They employ state-of-the-art development and production technologies, and the business's product innovation effort is viewed by management as offensive (as opposed to defensive) and as a leading edge of the business's total strategy.

♦ *Market-oriented and marketing-driven strategies* do better. Businesses that are strong on this marketing dimension feature a new product process that is strongly market-oriented and one dominated by marketing people. These enterprises are proactive in market-need identification and new product ideas are primarily market-derived. The picture emerges here of a business whose new product effort is highly responsive and sensitive to market needs and wants, and where products are developed that are closely in tune with market wants.

♦ A *focused new product effort* is more successful. Strongly focused businesses develop new products that are closely related to each other—the opposite of a highly diverse or scatter-gun approach. The products that these businesses develop employ related development technologies and related production methods. They are aimed at closely related markets, and the new products themselves are closely tied to each other.

♦ An *offensive orientation* outperforms a defensive stance. Businesses with an offensive orientation view their new product initiatives as aggressive ones—aimed at growth and gaining market share (rather than merely protecting a position). Their new product efforts feature an active search effort for new product ideas, and are proactive in terms of market-need identification.

Conclusion 3. There are five separate strategy types or scenarios that businesses elect for their new product strategies. In order of performance, they are:

Type A— The Differentiated strategy (15.6 percent of businesses studied): These businesses boast a technologically sophisticated and aggressive effort, a high degree of product fit and focus, and a strong market orientation (three of the four thrusts above). They target attractive high-growth, high-potential markets where competition is weaker. Resulting new products are premium-priced and feature strong differentiation and competitive advantage: high-quality products that meet customer needs better than competitors'; and products with a strong customer impact that offer unique features and benefits to the customer.

Not surprisingly, this strategy leads to the best results: the highest percentage of sales by new products (47 percent versus 35 percent for the other businesses); the highest success rates at Launch; a higher profitability level; and greater new product impact on the business's sales and profits.

Type B—The Low-Budget Conservative strategy (23.8 percent of businesses): These organizations feature low R&D spending and develop copycat, me-too, undifferentiated new products. Their new product efforts are focused and highly synergistic with the base business, tending toward a "stay-close-to-home" approach. New products match the business's production and technological skills and resources; fit into the business's existing product lines; and are aimed at familiar and existing markets.

In spite of their lack of spending, organizations adopting this strategy achieve moderately positive results: a high proportion of successes, and low failure and kill rates. The new product effort is profitable, but yields a low proportion of sales by new products and has a low impact on the business's sales and profits. This conservative strategy results in an efficient, safe, and profitable new product initiative, but one lacking a dramatic impact on the business.

Type C—The Technology Push strategy: This is the most popular strategy, elected by 26.2 percent of the businesses studied. Businesses here feature a technologically driven approach to product innovation, and are technologically sophisticated, technology-oriented, and innovative. But their new product effort lacks a strong market orientation, and there is little fit, synergy, or focus in the types of products and markets exploited. Moreover, the markets targeted tend to be unattractive ones.

This *Technology Push strategy* generally leads to mediocre performance results: it fails to meet the business's new product objectives; it yields a high proportion of project cancellations and product failures; and it is less profitable than Type A or B above. This strategy results in a major new product impact on the business's sales, however. In sum, the *Technology Push strategy* produces a technologically aggressive, moderately high-impact initiative, but is costly, inefficient, and plagued by failures because of a lack of focus and a lack of marketing orientation and input.

Type D—The Not-in-the-Game strategy (15.6 percent of businesses): Business that adopt this strategy simply lack technological sophistication; they develop new products that are low-technology, me-too, and low-risk, and rely on simple, mature technologies. These developments prove to be a poor fit with the existing technology and production base of the business. These enterprises lack an offensive stance, and attempt to serve market needs that they haven't served before.

Predictably, Type D results are dismal. New products represent a low proportion of their annual sales, and a high proportion of their new products fail commercially. Finally, their new product initiatives are rated the lowest in terms of meeting the business's objectives and in their impact on the organization's sales and profits.

Type E—The High-Budget Diverse strategy (18.9 percent of businesses). This is the "bull-in-a-china-shop strategy." It features heavy spending on R&D, but in a scatter-gun fashion; there is no direction, no synergy, no focus, no fit. These businesses attack new markets and new technologies, and use unfamiliar production technologies—a clear case of not sticking to their knitting. These businesses are tied with Type D as the worst performers.

Conclusion 4. One strategy—Type A, the Differentiated strategy— yields exceptional performance results. The strategy that outperforms the others calls for a balance between *technological sophistication* and aggressiveness and *a strong market orientation.* The performance results of the businesses that elect this balanced strategy are dramatically better than the four other strategy groups in terms of:

- new product success versus competitors' efforts;
- generating business unit sales (47 percent of sales from new products versus 35 percent for all other businesses);
- meeting the business's new product objectives and impact on the business's sales and profits; and
- the overall success of the effort.

Several characteristics distinguish these Type A high performers from the rest. First, they develop new products that have competitive advantage or differentiation in two ways: high-quality, superior products (superior to competing products in meeting customer needs); and products that offer unique features and benefits with a high customer impact. These products also tend to be premium-priced. New products fit into the businesses' current product lines and are closely related to each other. To achieve this level of differentiation, these businesses feature a strongly market-oriented and marketing-dominated new product effort; they are technologically sophisticated, technologically oriented, and aggressive; and they are highly focused. Finally, they select familiar markets with needs that the organization has served before; their targeted markets are high-potential and high-growth ones, but are not intensely competitive.

The orientation of these businesses' strategies serves as a guide to others. Differentiated-strategy businesses are the only ones to achieve a combination of a *strong market orientation* and a high level of *technological sophistication and aggressiveness.* These businesses possess technological prowess comparable to that of many other enterprises, yet they base their new product efforts on the needs and wants of the marketplace. Their new product ideas are derived from the marketplace; a proactive search effort is made for market need identification; a dominant marketing group is involved in the new product process; and the entire process has a strong market orientation.

Finally, the *Differentiated strategy* yields positive results regardless of the characteristics of the business's industry or the business itself. Industry growth rate, technology level, and technological maturity of the industry all affect performance, but the most important factor is the choice of the right strategy. Moreover, this Differentiated strategy gives consistently positive results regardless of enterprise type or industry. This winning strategy is also a *universally applicable* strategy.

Conclusion 5. Adopting some, but not all, of the elements of the winning strategy is not sufficient. Certain elements of the balance strategy can be found in other strategy types. None of those types perform nearly as well as Type A, however. For example:

▶ Strategy B, the *Low-Budget Conservative* approach, shares certain elements with A, namely, a good product fit and focus. Type B businesses also possess a high degree of technological and marketing synergy between their new product projects and the business's resource base. The result is second best, but far short of the winning strategy. In particular, while the success, failure, and kill rates of new products are positive, the low-budget, technologically unaggressive strategy simply lacks the R&D commitment and technological prowess of Strategy A. The result is a low-impact new product initiative: a case of winning the battle, but losing the war.

▶ Strategy C, *Technology Push*, businesses adopt a technologically aggressive stance, like the winning Type A businesses. But they lack a market orientation, develop products that are a poor fit with their marketing resources, and tend to target low-growth, low-need markets. The result is a moderately high-impact new product effort, but one with poor success, failure, and kill rates.

The conclusion is that a technologically driven and dominated strategy, on its own, is wrong. Equally wrong for most organizations is a conservative, stay-close-to-home approach to new products. The most successful strategy is one that marries technological prowess, a strong market orientation, and a high degree of fit and focus: Strategy A, the Differentiated strategy.

Conclusion 6. The Low-Budget Conservative strategy yields fairly positive results, especially for some types of businesses and industries. Strategy B—the *Low-Budget Conservative* approach—is one of the most popular strategies. It works well only for *some types of businesses*, however. Organizations adopting this conservative strategy . . .

- leverage their competencies in terms of development technology and production expertise;
- have very focused development efforts (focused on few markets, product types, or technologies);
- develop products that fit into the existing product line (a stay-close-to-home approach); and
- tend to target markets where the business can leverage its marketing strengths.

But these businesses . . .

- have a low level of R&D spending;
- are relatively unsophisticated technologically and lack a strong technological orientation;
- develop products with the fewest advantages and the least differentiation: me-too products in their customer impact and features; and parity (undifferentiated) products in terms of quality and meeting customer needs;
- compete on price (new products are priced lower than competitors'); and
- target highly competitive markets.

On average, businesses adopting this *Low-Budget Conservative strategy* achieve positive results in profitability (returns versus expenditures on new products) and new product success rates. The end result is a low-impact new product effort, however, with a lower-than-average percentage of sales from new products (31 percent versus 38 percent for all the other businesses). For certain types of enterprises, the Low-Budget Conservative strategy works particularly well. Businesses with strengths in marketing (strong sales force, channel system, advertising, and market research skills) and businesses in technologically mature, slower-growth industries perform extremely well by adopting this strategy. Sound performance is restricted to their profitability and success rates, however; the total new product effort is still low-impact.

One conclusion is that organizations that possess certain distinctive or core competencies—marketing prowess, for example—might rely on those strengths as the key to moving relatively ho-hum new products to the market. But the results for these Type B businesses are still inferior to the *Differentiated strategy* enterprises that face similar markets and have similar strengths. Moreover, for businesses lacking key strengths or facing developing, higher-growth industries, the *Low-Budget Conservative strategy* typically yields results far inferior to the *Differentiated strategy*. Further, while a conservative strategy may work well for some businesses and over the medium term, if markets or technologies change dramatically, these businesses are caught in a vulnerable position—victims of the "product life-cycle trap."[20]

Conclusion 7. Certain types of arenas yield better performance. Certain arenas or battlefields, when attacked or targeted, tend to result in victory. The characteristics of these "winning battlefields" or arenas—the kinds of markets, technologies, and products that successful businesses focus their innovation efforts on—provide a list of vital criteria that are useful in the evaluation and selection of arenas. There are two broad factors or main themes that distinguish high-performance arenas, according to the study:

- the magnitude of opportunities in the arena—for example, whether markets in the arena are growing or not, and the existence of major market and technological opportunities in the arena; and
- the strength or ability of the business to exploit the arena—for example, whether the business brings the right resources and skills to the table.

I use these criteria later in the chapter to assess strategic arenas as part of the strategy development process.

Key Points for Management

Four major strategic thrusts are the common denominators in businesses that are successful at new products. These thrusts are:

- technological sophistication;
- a strong market orientation and a market-driven process;
- focus; and
- an offensive (versus a defensive) stance.

Have you built these orientations or thrusts into your new product strategy?

Now, take a step back for a moment, and consider your business's new product efforts and strategy. Which of the five strategy scenarios—Type A through Type E—comes closest to describing your business's approach? And how do your performance results compare?

Next, compare your business's explicit or implicit new product strategy to Type A, the Differentiated strategy. Do you share the same orientations? Do you select the same types of markets? Do you develop similar types of products? Go through the list of distinguishing characteristics of these Type A businesses, and see how you rate on each item. This exercise should shed light on your strategic strengths and weaknesses.

Is your business a Type B, facing mature markets, but with key marketing strengths? Have you elected the *Low-Budget Conservative* approach to new products? If so, and if you're typical, the results of your new product efforts are probably adequate. But they could be even better if you adopt the *Differentiated strategy* approach. And watch out for the long run, that you aren't blindsided by changing markets and technologies.

Developing a New Product Strategy for Your Business: Setting Goals

A few years ago, I boarded an early morning flight on a major airline. The captain began his announcement: "Welcome aboard flight 123 en route to . . . ah . . . ah . . . " There was a long pause. The pause was punctuated by laughter and wisecracks from the passengers; the captain didn't know where the flight was going! Fortunately, within 30 seconds, he remembered our destination. If he hadn't, the plane probably would have emptied. Who would stay on a plane where the captain didn't know his destination? Many of us, however, seem content to stay on board new product efforts that have no destination.

Defining goals for your product development strategy is essential. Most of us accept that premise. My strategy study and our benchmarking investigations both reveal that many organizations lack written and measurable goals for their innovation effort.

What types of goals should be included in an innovation strategy? First, the goals should be measurable so that they can be used as benchmarks against which to measure performance. For example, Booz-Allen

& Hamilton notes that firms are now measuring the results of their innovation efforts.[21] Second, the goals should tie the business's new product initiatives tightly to its business strategy. Finally, they must give
you, your leadership team, as well as project teams a sense of direction
and purpose, and be criteria for gate decision making.

Goals That Describe the Role of New Products

One type of new product goals focuses on the role that the new product effort will play in achieving the business goals. Some examples:

- The percentage of your business's sales in Year 5 that will be derived from new products introduced in that five-year period. (Five
  years is a generally accepted time span in which to define a product
  as "new," although given today's pace, three years is more appropriate for many businesses.) Alternately, one can speak of absolute
  sales—dollars in Year 3 from new products—rather than relative
  sales or percentages.

- The percentage of your business's profits in Year 3 or 5 that will be
  derived from new products introduced in that time span. Again,
  absolute dollars can be used instead of relative profits.

- Sales and profits objectives expressed as a percentage of business
  growth. For example: 70 percent of growth in your business's sales
  over the next three years will come from new products introduced
  in this period.

- The strategic role, such as defending market share, exploiting a
  new technology, establishing a foothold in a new market, opening
  up a new technological or market window of opportunity, capital-
  izing on a strength or resource, or diversifying into higher-growth
  areas.[22]

- The number of new products to be introduced. (There are problems
  with this type of objective, however: products could be large-
  volume or small-volume ones, and the *number* of products does not
  directly translate into sales and profits.)

The specification of these goals gives a strong indication of just how important new products are to the total business strategy. The question of
resource allocation and spending on new product efforts can then be
more objectively decided.

Performance Goals

A second type of goals deals with the expected performance of the new product effort. Such goals are useful guides to managers within the new product group. Examples include

- success, failure, and kill rates of new products developed;
- number of new product ideas to be considered annually;
- number of projects entering Development (or in Development) annually; and
- minimum acceptable financial returns for new product projects.

Many of these performance goals flow logically from the role goals. For example, if the business wants 70 percent of sales growth to come from new products, how does that figure translate into number of successful products, number of development projects, success, failure, and kill rates, and number of ideas to be considered annually?

How to Set the Goals

Setting these goals is no easy task. The first time through, the exercise is often a frustrating experience. Yet these goals are fundamental to developing an innovation strategy, not to mention a logically determined R&D budget figure. New product goal setting usually begins with a strategic planning exercise for the entire business, much as was outlined for the Agro division in the previous chapter. The business's growth and profit goals are decided, along with areas of strategic thrust. These business goals and thrusts are then translated into new product goals, often via *gap analysis*.

Senior management at Guinness (Ireland) developed a strategic plan for their brewing business. Ambitious growth and profit goals were decided on. A review of current products and markets worldwide revealed that gaps would exist between projected sales and the goals. That is, current products and markets were projected into the future, and expected revenues and profits were compared to the desired level of sales and profits (the business goals). The gaps would have to be filled by new markets, new products, or new businesses. From this, a set of new product goals were determined.

Here are the types of metrics most often used by various types of businesses for their new product efforts, and which might prove useful in setting your new product goals:[23]

Prospector businesses—the innovators—most often use:

- percentage of profits from new products.
- percentage of sales from new products.
- ability to open up new windows of opportunity.

Analyzer enterprises—the fast followers with competitive advantage— look to:

- ROI from Development efforts.
- whether the innovation effort fits or supports the business's overall strategy.
- percentage of profits from new products.
- success/failure rates.

Defender organizations measure:

- ROI from Development efforts.
- fit with or support of the business's strategy.

Reactor businesses rely on:

- ROI from Development efforts.
- success/failure rates.
- fit with or support of the business's strategy.

Additionally, Table 7.1, showing the breakdown of projects by type, is a useful guide to your discussion on goals: what types of new products—from new-to-the-world through to cost reductions—do you want for your business?

Defining Target Arenas for Your Business

The specification of strategic arenas or battlefields provides an important guide to your product innovation efforts. As Day notes, "what is needed is a strategy statement that specifies those areas where development is to proceed and identifies (perhaps by exclusion) those areas that are off limits."[24] The arenas guide the search for new product ideas; they help in project selection (for example, as noted in Chapter 5, a typical and important must-meet criterion in project selection is: does the project fit within our business's strategy? The strategy is defined in part by the arenas). Finally, delineation of where the business wishes to focus its new product efforts is critical to long-term planning, particularly for resource and skills acquisition.

Defining the target arenas answers the question: on what business, product, market, or technology areas should the business focus its new product efforts? Conceptually, the task is one of *opportunity identification* followed by *opportunity assessment.*

Two issues immediately arise. First, one may question the need for focus at all. Note, however, that new product focus has been found to be an important ingredient of successful innovation strategies.[25] Focus provides direction for idea generation, criteria for project selection, and targets for resource acquisition.[26] A second criticism is that focus will inhibit creativity: some of the best ideas, which may lie outside the target arenas, might be rejected. The counterargument is that focus improves creativity by targeting energies on those areas where the payoff is likely to be the greatest.[27] Further, significant new product breakthroughs outside the bounds of the new product strategy statement can usually be readily accommodated in an ongoing project screening process, or via free-time or scouting projects. Finally, inevitably there will be products that "got away" in any new product effort, just as there will be the proverbial "fish that got away." But there will continue to exist ample opportunities within the defined arenas for the business to exploit, provided management has done a credible job at arena definition.

There are two steps to defining the target arenas. The first is developing a comprehensive list of possible arenas: opportunity identification. The second is paring the list down—assessing the opportunities to yield the target arenas.

What Is a New Product Arena?

How does one define a new product opportunity or arena? Corey proposes that we build two-dimensional matrices, with the dimensions labeled "products" and "markets" in order to identify new business arenas.[28] He notes that markets, together with the products that can be developed in response to needs in these markets, define the opportunities for exploitation: the arenas.

Telenor, the Norwegian telephone system, uses a product/market matrix to help visualize strategic choices, and to define arenas on which to focus its new product efforts. One dimension of the matrix is *market segments:* Home Office; Small Business; Residential; and so on. The other dimension is the *product offering* or product categories: Telephone; Internet; ISDN; and so on. The roughly 10 by 10 matrix identifies 100 cells or possible arenas; some are ruled out immediately as unfeasible. The remaining set is evaluated, and priorities are established. The top-priority or "star" arenas are singled out for more intensive product development efforts.

In *Defining the Business*, Abell takes this matrix approach one step further by proposing that a business be defined in terms of *three* dimensions:[29]

1. *Customer groups served.* For a computer manufacturer, customer groups might include banks, manufacturers, universities, hospitals, retailers, and the like.
2. *Customer functions served.* These might include applications support, services, software, central processing, core memory storage, disk storage, and the like.
3. *Technologies utilized.* For core memory storage, several existing and new technologies might have application.

The result is a three-dimensional diagram, with new product arenas defined in this three-dimensional space.

Finally, Crawford's study of firms' innovation charters points to several ways in which managers define new product arenas in practice.[30] Arenas are specified by:

- product type (for example, liquid pumps);
- by end-user activity (process industries);
- by type of technology employed (rotary hydraulics); or
- by end-user group (oil refineries).

On its own, each of these arena definition schemes has its problems. For example, a product-type definition is limiting: product classes or types die. Similarly, an end-user group definition could lead the business into a number of unrelated technologies, products, and production systems.

Agro's management (in the previous chapter) simply uses market segments and product lines or product types as the dimensions of strategic arenas. In their agricultural chemical business, a market segment is defined by both geography (country and region) as well as crop type. The end result of the strategic exercise is a matrix of crop types and geographies across the top, and product lines and types down the side. Although in a very different business, Agro's management have elected a product/market matrix similar to that employed by Telenor (in the telephone business).

A review of these and other schemes for defining a business arena reveals that a single-dimension approach is likely too narrow. A two- or three-dimensional approach, variants of Corey's or Abell's, probably will suit most business contexts.[31] For example, a new product arena can be defined in terms of:

- Who: the customer group to be served (markets or market segments).
- What: the application (or customer need to be served).
- How: the technology required to design, develop, and produce products for the arena.

These three dimensions—who, what, and how—provide a useful starting point for describing new product arenas. Sometimes, the latter two dimensions—what and how—can be simply combined into a single dimension, product line, or product type.

Defining Arenas: A Blow-by-Blow Illustration

Let's look more closely at some of the details of this process of searching for and prioritizing arenas. A two- or three-dimensional diagram can be used for this search and evaluation (Figure 7.3). Here I use the three dimensions of customer groups, applications, and technologies, which are shown as the X, Y, and Z axes of the diagram. Home base is located, and then other opportunities are identified by moving away from home base in terms of other (but related) customer groups, applications, and technologies.

Chempro is a medium-sized manufacturer of blending and agitation process equipment for the pulp and paper industry. The company's major strength is its ability to design and manufacture rotary hydraulic equipment. The market served is the pulp and paper industry. The application is agitation and blending of liquids and slurries. The company's current or home base is shown as the cube in Figure 7.4.

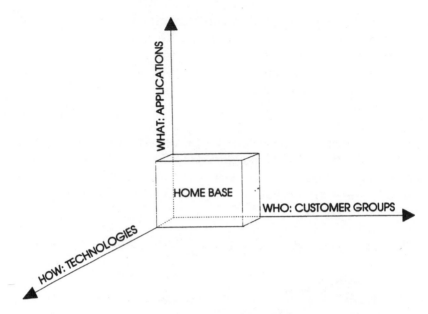

Figure 7.3   Defining New Product Arenas: The Three Dimensions

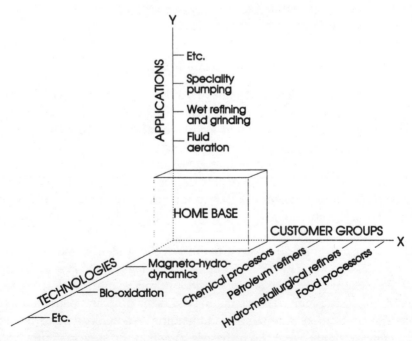

Figure 7.4   The Arena Dimensions for Chempro

What new product arenas exist for the company? Clearly, the home base is one of these, and indeed the firm is active in seeking new product ideas for agitation equipment in the pulp and paper field. Most of these opportunities, however, are limited to modifications and improvements.

One direction that senior management can take is to develop new products aimed at alternative customer groups. These customer groups include the chemical, food-processing, petroleum-refining, and hydro-metallurgical fields. The options are shown on the X or horizontal axis of Figure 7.4.

Similarly, new products in related applications can be sought. These related applications include the pumping of fluids, fluid aeration, and refining and grinding, as shown on the vertical or Y axis of the arena matrix.

Considering these two dimensions—different applications and different customer groups—management now proceeds to define a number of new arenas. Working with a two-dimensional grid (Figure 7.5), recognize that besides the home base arena, there are 12 other arenas that the company can consider for its new product focus.[32] For example, Chempro can develop blending and agitation equipment (same application) aimed at the chemical or petroleum industries (new customer groups). Alternatively, the business can target aeration devices (new application) at its current customers, namely, pulp and paper companies. Each of these possibilities represents a new arena for Chempro.

Chempro might also be able to change its third dimension by moving from its home base of rotary hydraulic technology to other technologies. If the alternatives are superimposed along the third dimension atop the matrix, the result is a much larger number of possible arenas. (This third dimension expansion is not shown in Figure 7.5, as it's a little hard on the eyes!) Possible alternative arenas along the "new technologies" axis include magneto-hydrodynamic pumps and agitators for a variety of end-user groups, bio-oxidation reactors for the food industry, and many others.

Selecting the Right Arenas

The task now is to narrow down the many possible arenas to a target set that will become the focus of the business's innovation strategy. To a certain extent, a prescreening of these arenas has already occurred: the arenas have been identified as being related to the base business on at least one of the three dimensions.

	CURRENT CUSTOMER GROUP	NEW CUSTOMER GROUPS		
	Pulp & paper industry	Chemical process industry	Petroleum refining companies	Metallurgical industry (ore refining)
CURRENT APPLICATION				
Agitation & blending of liquids	Agitators & blenders for pulp & paper industry	Chemical mixers	Blenders for petroleum storage tanks	Hydro-metallurgical agitators
NEW APPLICATIONS				
Aeration of liquids	Surface aerators, P&P waste treatment	Aerators for chemical wastes	Aerators for petroleum waste treatment	Aerators for flotation cells (hdyro-metallurgical)
Wet refining & grinding	Pulpers, repulpers & refiners			
Specialty pumping	High density paper stock pumps	Specialty chemical pumps	Specialty petroleum pumps	Slurry pumps

Figure 7.5 Arena Map—Identification of Possible Strategic Arenas for Chempro

The choice of the right arenas is based on a single must-meet criterion, and two should-meet criteria. The must-meet criterion is an obvious one: does the arena fit within the business's mission, vision, and overall strategy? The two other criteria were identified in my studies of successful new product strategies. These two criteria are *arena opportunity* and *business strength* (see Table 7.2).

Arena opportunity is a strategic dimension that captures how attractive the external opportunity is for that arena. In Table 7.2, arena opportunity consists of:

- *market attractiveness:* the size, growth, and potential of market opportunities within the arena; and
- *technological opportunities:* the degree to which technological and new product opportunities exist within the arena.

In practice, arena opportunity is a composite index constructed from the answers to a number of individual questions. Table 7.2 shows a sample list of questions found in my study of product innovation strategies

Table 7.2   Characteristics of High-Performance New Product Arenas

I. Arena Opportunity (North–South or Vertical Axis)	Weights*

1. Market attractiveness:
- Size of the markets in the arena (dollar volume). — 5
- Number of potential customers for the product in the arena. — 9
- Long-term potential of markets in the arena. — 11
- Growth rates of markets in the arena. — <u>17</u>

Subtotal: Market attractiveness — 42

2. Technological opportunities:
- Technology level of products sold in this arena (high-tech = good). — 12
- Nature of technologies in this arena (leading and state-of-the-art technologies = good). — 19
- Technological elasticity (opportunity for developing new products in this arena; for example, will a dollar spent yield high returns in terms of new product sales and profits?) — <u>27</u>

Subtotal: Technological opportunities — 58

Total for Arena Opportunity — 100

II. Business Strength (East–West or Horizontal Axis)

1. Ability to leverage your technological competencies, strengths, and experience:
- Degree of fit between production processes used in this arena and the production processes and skills of your business. — 11
- Degree of fit between R&D skills/resources required in this arena and the technical skills/resources of your business. — 14
- Degree of fit between engineering/design skills/resources required in this arena and your engineering/technical skills/resources. — <u>4</u>

Subtotal: Technological leverage and synergy — 29

2. Ability to leverage marketing competencies, strengths, and experience:
- Degree of fit between the sales force and/or distribution channel system required for this arena and those of your business. — 8
- Degree of fit between the advertising and promotion approaches and skills required in this arena fit and those of your business. — <u>14</u>

Subtotal: Marketing leverage — 22

continued

Table 7.2 Characteristics of High-Performance New Product Arenas
(continued)

3. Strategic leverage—potential for gaining for product advantage
   or differentiation:
Envision the new products that we would/could develop in this arena . . .

• Magnitude of positive impact on customers.	18
• Degree to which new products will be unique (differentiated from competitive products).	20
• Degree to which new products will meet customer needs better than competitive products.	<u>11</u>
Subtotal: Potential for leverage via product advantage	49
Total for Business Strength	100

*Weights are based on my study of 120 firms' new product strategies and their perfor-
mance results. Advanced statistical analysis (factor analysis and multiple regression
analysis) were used to derive these empirically based weights. You may wish to add or
delete questions, or modify the weights for your own business.

(although this list may not be an exhaustive one). Typically, an arena is
assessed against each question and is given a rating; these ratings are
then multiplied by the question weight shown in the table and added to
yield an *index of arena opportunity*. Arenas that feature large, growing,
and high-potential markets, that are characterized by technological elasticity, and that feature high-tech products based on leading-edge technologies score high on the arena opportunity dimension.

Business strength is the other strategic dimension. Business strength
focuses on the business's ability to successfully exploit the arena. The
ability to leverage the organization's resources and skills to advantage
in the new arena is a key concept here. Business strength is again a composite dimension, consisting of three factors (again from my study of innovation strategies):

- ability to leverage the business's technological competencies;
- ability to leverage its marketing competencies; and
- strategic leverage—the potential to gain product advantage and
  differentiation.

Arenas that build on the business's core and distinctive competencies,
that fit well with the business's marketing and technological strengths
and resources, and that offer the business a solid opportunity to gain

product advantage or achieve product differentiation, are the ones that score high on the business strength dimension.

Mapping the Strategic Arenas

How the various arenas score on the two criteria can be shown pictorially in the arena assessment map of Figure 7.6. Arena opportunity is shown as the vertical or north–south dimension and business strength as the horizontal or east–west axis. The result is a four-sector diagram, not unlike traditional portfolio models, but with different dimensions and different components to each dimension.

Each sector represents a different type of opportunity:

▶ The arenas shown in the northwest sector (the upper left), that feature high arena opportunity and business strength, are clearly the most desirable. These are called the "good bets."

▶ Diagonally opposite, in the southeast (lower right) sector, are the "low-low" arenas—those arenas that neither build on the organization's strengths nor offer attractive external opportunities. These are the "no bets."

▶ The "high-risk bets" are in the northeast (upper right) sector: they represent high-opportunity arenas where the business has no exploitable strengths.

▶ Finally, the southeast (lower left) sector houses the "conservative bets"—arenas where the business can utilize its strengths to advantage, but where the external opportunity is not so attractive. These are opportunities to be pursued at little risk, but offer limited returns.

Using such a map, management can eliminate certain arenas outright (those in the "no bet" sector), and select a reasonable balance of arenas from the three other sectors. The "good bets," in the northwest sector, are usually the top-priority ones.

Assessing the Arenas at Chempro

At Chempro, strategic arena assessment is simplified by recognizing the company's technological and financial resource limitations. Chempro's main asset is its ability to design and engineer rotary hydraulic equipment. Embarking on new and expensive technologies, such as magneto-hydrodynamics or bio-oxidation, is deemed out of bounds. Moreover, having identified its current technology as a field of particular strength, and recognizing that there are many opportunities that can build on this strength, senior management elects to stay with its current technology. Management chooses to *attack from a position of strength,* and so the third dimension, alternative technologies, is deleted. The result is the two-dimensional grid shown previously in Figure 7.5.

Next, the 12 new arenas plus the home base are rated on the two key dimensions of market attractiveness and business position. A list of questions is employed similar to Table 7.2, with each arena rated on each question. The questions are weighted, and a business strength and arena opportunity index are computed for each of the 13 possible arenas. The results for Chempro are shown in Figure 7.6.

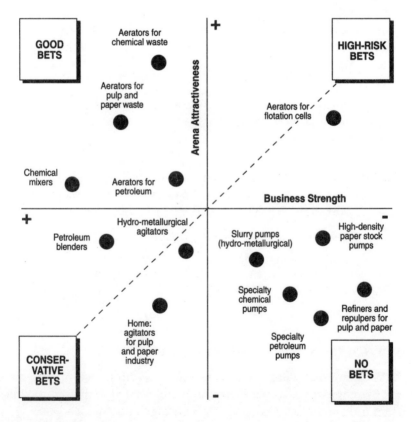

Figure 7.6 Arena Assessment for Chempro

Selecting the Arenas at Chempro

The choice of arenas depends on the risk–return values of management. Selecting only those arenas in the top half of the arena assessment diagram—the good bets and the high-risk bets—emphasizes the attractiveness of the external opportunity, and places no weight at all on the business strength dimension: a high return, but a higher-risk choice. The other extreme—selecting only those arenas on the left of the vertical, the good bets and conservative bets—boils down to a low-risk, low-return strategy: selection of only those arenas in which the company possesses a good business position. Ideally, one looks for a combination of the two: arenas in which the market attractiveness and the business strength both are rated high—the good bets in the northwest sector of Figure 7.6; or perhaps some balance of arenas—some attractive but riskier arenas, some lower risk but less attractive ones.

For Chempro, six arenas were rated positively on both dimensions. In order to quantify or rank-order these opportunities, a cutoff or 45-degree line was drawn (see Figure 7.6). Arenas to the left of and above this line are positive; those to the right and below are negative. The distance of each arena from that line was measured: the greater the distance, the more desirable the arena. Based on this exercise, three good bets and one conservative bet were defined as new arenas for Chempro:

- aerators for the chemical industry (waste treatment);
- blenders for the petroleum industry;
- agitators and mixers for the chemical industry; and
- surface aerators for the pulp and paper industry.

The decision was made to continue seeking new products in the home-base arena as well. Several other arenas were put on hold for future action.

Key Points for Management

The place to begin is with the *strategy of your business*, and flowing from it, *your new product strategy*. Strategy development is the job of the leadership team of the business: you, the senior people, must lead here; indeed, this is how senior people first become engaged in your project selection and portfolio management process—by charting your business's strategy.

After defining the overall goals for your business, spell out your *new product goals:* for example, what percentage of sales or profit or growth new products will contribute. Use gap analysis as Guinness does.

Then move to mapping your battlefields: that is, identify arenas of strategic focus. Draw an arena diagram for your business. Use two dimensions (products and markets, as does Telenor and Agro) or perhaps three dimensions (customer groups, applications, and technologies, like Chempro). Locate your home base, and then move out on each of the three axes, identifying other customer groups, applications, and technologies. This exercise should help you uncover a number of new but related product arenas.

Now that you've identified a list of possible arenas, try to rate each on the two key dimensions of *arena attractiveness* and *business strength.* Develop a list of questions for each dimension (use Table 7.2 as a guide), and score each arena on the questions. Draw an arena assessment map (similar to Figure 7.6) to see where your arenas lie.

Prioritizing: Defining the Spending Splits

Decisions on spending splits must be made in order to translate strategy into reality. Strategic priority decisions should be considered on a *variety of dimensions* other than just by arenas shown in Figure 7.6. But defining and prioritizing arenas provides a good foundation for your leadership team to begin the debate on spending splits. Here are some of the splits that many executive groups consider when developing their business's new product strategy:

> ▶ *Across arenas:* The first and most obvious spending split is across the strategic arenas just defined and prioritized above. That is, having assessed the attractiveness of each, and defined the priorities of each, move to deployment—that is, deciding how many resources each arena or battlefield should receive.

> ▶ *Types of projects:* Decisions or splits can be made in terms of the *types of projects.* For example: "Given our aggressive strategic stance, we target 30 percent of R&D spending to genuine new products and another 20 percent to fundamental research and platform development (technology development for the future); 30 percent will go to prod-

uct modifications and improvements, only 10 percent to cost reductions, with another 10 percent to product maintenance and fixes." (There are various ways to define "project types"—recall the Mercedes star approach and see the examples in Figures 6.8 and 6.9.)

▶ *Project newness:* Decisions or splits can be made in terms of project newness, using the "newness matrix." Recall from Chapter 6 the six-cell matrix with Technology and Market Newness as the key dimensions. Projects might be classed as "defend and/or penetrate" projects through to "new businesses/new ventures" (see Figure 6.4).

▶ *Technologies or technology platforms:* Spending splits can be made across technology types (for example, base, key, pacing, and embryonic technologies) or across specific technology platforms: Platforms X, Y, and Z, and so on.

▶ *By stage or phase of development:* Some businesses distinguish between early-stage projects and projects into Development and beyond: two buckets are created, one for Development projects, the other for early-stage projects. At Company G in Chapter 6, management allocates *seed corn money* to a separate bucket for early stage projects.

In the Chempro's illustration, management prioritizes the four new arenas (defined above) along with the existing arena, namely, home base. The arena map in Figure 7.6 provides a good guide for this prioritization exercise. Also considered are new product opportunities or possible projects that are proposed within each arena. After much discussion and analysis, Target Spending Levels are established for each arena.

Additionally, Chempro's management develops Strategic Buckets for project types: genuine new products versus product improvements and modifications versus cost reductions. No resources are devoted to platform developments or fundamental research. Here, the arenas chosen and the natures of the developments required in each arena help decide the resource split by project types.

Developing Attack Plans

The goals have been decided, and the strategic arenas mapped out and prioritized. Now it's time to determine the *new product attack plan* for each arena. These attack plans tend to be fairly industry- and company-specific. However, there exist a number of frameworks that help guide this effort.

The strategy scenarios or typology offered earlier in this chapter provide a useful way to visualize your attack approach. Recall that these types are:

- *Prospector*—you are the industry innovator, the first in with new products, and the first to adopt new technologies.
- *Analyzer*—you are the fast follower, monitoring competitor entries and bringing superior or more cost-effective products to market.
- *Defender*—you maintain a secure position in a niche or stable market, and protect your position via better service, higher quality, or lower prices.
- *Reactor*—you respond only when forced to.

In deciding your attack plan, also consider the five strategy types I uncovered in my strategy-performance investigation. In particular, take a close look at strategy Types A and B—the Differentiated strategy and the Low-Budget Conservative strategy.

Instead of strategy types (above), your attack plan could focus on the *types of platforms* your business will invest in. For example, having identified certain markets as strategic arenas, in order to win in these market arenas, certain new technology platforms may be envisioned—see below, "Platforms: A Base from Which to Operate."

Platforms: A Base from Which to Operate

Many businesses now look to platforms as a way to think about strategic thrusts in product development. The original notion of a platform was very much *product-based*. For example, the PDMA handbook defines a platform product as "design and components that are shared by a set of products in a product family.[33] From this platform, numerous derivatives can be designed." Thus Chrysler's engine/transmission from its K-car was a platform that spawned other vehicles, including the famous Chrysler minivan.

The notion of platforms has since been broadened to include *technological capabilities*. For example, Exxon's metallocene platform is simply a catalyst that has spawned an entirely new generation of polymers. Thus a platform is like an oil drilling platform in the ocean, which you invest heavily in. From this platform, you can drill many holes, relatively quickly and at low cost. The platform thus leads to many related new product projects in a timely and cost-effective manner.

The definition of platforms has also been broadened to include *marketing or branding concepts* as well as technological capabilities. For example, some consider 3M's Post-It Notes to be a platform, which has created many individual products, while Nabisco's *Snack Well*™ products—indulgent but low-fat dessert food items—is another example of a marketing platform.

The attack plan may also deal with the *split in resources across project types*, as in Chempro's case. For example, having agreed that certain market segments are top-priority ones, what types of developments are needed to win in each arena? Do you need new products, or merely extensions, fixes, and updates? Or are new platforms required in order to win here? The Mercedes star method (Figure 6.9), the Strategic Buckets approach (Table 6.5), and one of the pie charts in Figure 6.8. help translate strategy into resource splits by project types.

Finally, your attack plan may be nothing more than the *specific new products and projects* that are needed in order to be successful in a given arena. For example, once a product category is agreed to as a top-priority one, what new products do you need in order to succeed in a major way in this category? Thus the attack plan may simply be the portfolio of projects aimed at that arena—in effect, a cluster of tactical moves.

> Chempro's attack plan is the same across all arenas: namely, a differentiated approach, focusing on delivering superior products with unique features and benefits to customers. This strategy requires a marriage of Chempro's core technology competency (prowess in the field of rotary hydraulic equipment design) coupled with a customer-orientated, market-driven approach to defining product requirements. Thus the strategy is really a combination of the *Analyzer strategy* and my Type A *Differentiated strategy*.

Contrast Chempro's universal attack plan with National Sea's in Chapter 2. Recall that National Sea's management defined three strategic arenas: national brand (retail), food service, and private label. Management went on to adopt three different attack plans for these three arenas: *innovator* for the branded products arena; *fast follower* for private label; and *value-for-money provider* for the food service arena.

Reflect on Chempro's strategic exercise for a moment. There are several positive points to note:

1. *Senior management leads the way here:* it is the senior people of the business who took up the challenge and mapped out the business's new product strategy. This task was not left to a marketing

or R&D group to do—this is not the time or place for "hands-off" management!

2. Next, this strategy goes beyond vision and mission and nice-sounding words. It was translated into goals and prioritized arenas (defined by application and customer groups), and finally into decisions on resource deployment.

3. The split in resources across arenas, although top-down and strategically driven, also considers opportunities within each arena. This was not a sterile strategic exercise, but an *iterative one* between a top-down, strategic approach, and a bottom-up approach that took into account active as well as proposed projects and opportunities.

4. Finally, attack plans were developed for each arena—how management intends for Chempro to win on each battlefield.

Key Points for Management

Identify your *top-priority arenas*. Start with your arena map as illustrated in Figure 7.6, which identifies possible battlefields. Prioritize your arenas, looking for those in the desirable northwest sector (upper left), but perhaps seeking a balance by including some from the sure-bets and the high-risk bets sectors.

Next, *focus on deployment of resources:* develop spending splits across key dimensions (for example, splits by arenas; or splits on other dimensions such as project types; or pick dimensions that represent strategic thrusts to you). Define Strategic Buckets or Target Spending Levels across dimensions, much like Agro did in Figure 6.11 or as Chempro did.

Finally *define attack plans* for each arena . . . how you plan to win on each battlefield or in each arena. This could be a universal attack plan (as in Chempro's case) or attack plans specific to each arena (as does National Sea).

Putting Your New Product Strategy to Work

The goals and the top-priority arenas for the business's new product strategy have been defined. Let's look at how this new product strategy guides the management of the enterprise's development efforts.

Searching for Product Ideas

The definition of objectives and arenas provides guidance to the idea search effort. Armed with a knowledge of the arenas the business wishes to target, those charged with seeking new product ideas now have a clear definition of where to search. Moreover, it becomes feasible to implement formal search programs—suggestion schemes, contests, sales force programs, creativity methods, and all the other methods outlined in Chapter 4—to generate new product ideas. The search for ideas will be more efficient, generating product ideas that are consistent with the business's focus.

In Chempro's case, all personnel, from the president to sales trainees, gained a clear view of which new product arenas the company wished to concentrate on. These new insights made it possible for good new product ideas in the designated arenas to pour in.

More Effective Project Selection

One of the most critical project selection criteria highlighted in Chapter 5 is whether the new product project is aligned with the business's strategy. All too often the question is answered with blank stares and shrugs. A clear delineation of your business's new product arenas provides the criterion essential to answer the "strategic alignment" question. Either the new product proposal under consideration fits into one of the designated arenas, or it does not. The result is a more effective and efficient screening: precious management time and resources are not wasted on new product proposals that may seem attractive on their own merits, but simply do not mesh with the long-term strategy of the business.

A Guide to Portfolio Management

Effective portfolio management is almost impossible without a well-defined new product strategy in place for the business, complete with goals and prioritized arenas. Target Spending Levels or Strategic Buckets are essential for effective portfolio management—ideal resource splits by market, by product line or category, or by project type—and flow directly from the business's new product strategy. Recall from the Agro case how the business's new product strategy helped decide spending splits across both markets and products (the pie charts in Figure 6.11). Additionally, the ideal balance of projects (bubble diagrams) and the identification of strategic imperative projects—must-do-now projects—are similarly driven by the business unit's new product strategy.

Personnel and Resource Planning

Resources essential to new products—R&D, engineering, marketing, production—cannot be acquired overnight. Without a definition of which arenas the business intends to target, planning for the acquisition of these resources is like asking a blindfolded person to throw darts.

For Chempro, aerators for the pulp and paper industry were defined as a top-priority arena. R&D management hired researchers in the field of biochemistry and waste treatment; the engineering department acquired new people in the field of aeration equipment design and aeration application engineering; and plans were made to add aeration experts to the sales force. Finally, several exploratory technical and market research programs were initiated in aeration and bio-oxidation.

Some Final Thoughts on New Product Strategy

With the increasing importance of new product warfare also comes the desire to more effectively manage innovation, hence the wish to develop new product innovation strategies. Developing a new product strategy for your business is not easy. In spite of the challenge, however, a new product strategy is a must for all businesses that are serious about building new products into their long-range plans. Many businesses operate without such a strategy, and the senior managements know the problems all too well. There is no direction to the idea search, or there is no idea search at all. Much time is wasted in screening proposed projects and agonizing over the same question: should we be in this business? Portfolio management is almost impossible, and there are difficulties in making a long-term, sustained budget commitment to new products. And personnel, resource and technology acquisition planning is hit-and-miss.

Methods for defining the new product strategic direction have been outlined in this chapter. I began with a recognition of the need for and rewards of having such a strategy. Goals are defined that give the business's new product effort a sense of purpose, and tie it firmly to the business's overall objectives. Strategic arenas—the target battlefields or arenas of strategic thrust—are identified and pared down to a set of top-priority fields for exploitation. These arenas give the new product effort direction and focus—ingredients that are critical to a successful innovation strategy. These arenas are prioritized, and from these priorities, spending splits are decided, as the business's new product strategy begins to drive portfolio management. Finally, attack plans are developed for each arena. And so the new product strategy evolves to guide your business's new product war effort.

8

Taking Action—
An Executive Summary

Executive summaries usually are located at the beginning of a report. I'm doing a reversal here: you've read the book, and you've seen many concepts and prescriptions on how to win at new products in the previous seven chapters. It's a daunting list, but no one said that leading at new products was going to be simple or could be boiled down to a handful of quick fixes! In this final chapter, I do try to simplify—to reduce some of the complexity, and to distill the essence of the book into a handful of key messages and major calls to action: a fast summary of the book.

It's War and Winning Is Everything

1. *New product development is a war, where victory ultimately decides the fate of your business.*

Do you and the other members of your leadership team recognize that you are indeed at war, and that this war merits your undivided time and attention? And are you leading your business the way generals would run their warfare operations?

- Have you mapped out a strategy for this war—a new products and/or technology strategy?
- Have you defined the battlefields or strategic arenas where you wish to fight?
- Have you thought about tactics—about the details of how you'll drive new products to market quickly and effectively?

279

2. *Businesses that boast the three cornerstones of successful product innovation fare much better in this new products war.*

These cornerstones are:

- a clearly articulated new product strategy for your business;
- the right resources devoted to new products in light of your strategy and goals; and
- a superb and systematic new product process to drive projects to market.

3. *There are five major actions that you, the leadership team, must take in order to win the new products war:*

▶ *Commitment:* Embrace a long-term commitment to product development. Look beyond a short-term, financial focus and ensure that resources are committed for the longer term (not off again, on again), and that your development portfolio contains a certain proportion of longer-term and platform projects (not just quick, one-year hits).

▶ *Strategy:* Develop a vision, objectives, and strategy for your new product effort driven by (and linked to) your business's overall objectives and strategy. This means new product goals, defined and prioritized strategic arenas, deployment of resources, and attack plans.

▶ *Implement a* Stage-Gate™ *process:* Install a systematic, high-quality new product process in your business, and practice discipline, following the principles of the process. Demonstrate that you're committed to the process by your actions, not just your words. Walk the talk!

▶ *Commit the resources:* Make available the necessary resources. There is no free lunch here: businesses that commit the money and people on average are blessed with much higher new product performance. Take a direct role in resource deployment and allocation, via your actions at gates and portfolio reviews.

▶ *Foster innovation in your organization:* Create an innovative, positive climate for product development—one that supports, rewards, and recognizes new product efforts in your business. Empower project teams, and support committed champions: act as godfathers, sponsors, or executive champions for major new product projects.

4. *The place to begin is with an* audit *of your new product performance and practices.*

How well is your business performing in terms of the three cornerstones of new product performance? And how do you rate on the 13 success factors outlined in Chapters 2 and 3? I began the book by urging you to keep score—to start tracking your new product performance. But go beyond that. Undertake internal benchmarking by lowering the microscope on your current new product practices and performance: rate your practices in terms of the three cornerstones and the 13 success factors. In this way, you pinpoint your relative strengths and weaknesses— an excellent way to probe what needs fixing and overhauling in your new product process. Use our *ProBE* methodology (or something similar to it) (see Appendix A).

Understanding What Separates Winners from Losers

5. *Build in the six critical success factors when you revitalize or overhaul your new product process.*

Recall the six success factors that are process-related and that distinguish winning new products and businesses (from Chapter 2):

1. Emphasize doing the up-front homework—both market and technical assessments—*before projects move into the Development phase.* Take a hard look at your new product process. If homework is typically lacking, you have no one to blame but yourselves. *Homework doesn't get done because senior management does not demand it!*
2. Adopt a slavelike dedication to a market orientation, and build in the voice of the customer throughout. If you have an unbalanced new product process, one that is dominated by technology and excludes the customer, first, probably you are underperforming; and second, the solution is within your grasp! Put in place *a rigorous, balanced new product process*—one that strikes the right balance between *technology push* and *market pull.* And make sure that the needed marketing resources are in place.
3. Demand sharp, early, and stable product definition, before Development work begins. Build a *product definition stage* into your new product process, followed by a *definitional checkpoint or gate,* where your leadership team signs off on the product/project definition. Make it a rule: no project enters Development without a product

definition, based on facts, agreed to by the project team, and signed off by you, the senior management team.

4. Build in gates—tough Go/Kill decision points in the process, where senior management really does kill projects. There are about five gates in the typical new product process. Gates are where you, the leadership team, review the project in depth and decide whether you wish to continue to fund it. Focus and a funneling approach are the results.

5. Focus on quality of execution, where activities in new product projects are carried out in a quality fashion. Demand that best practices be built in at *every stage* of your process; emphasize quality of execution throughout; and set high standards at gate checkpoints, where deliverables are scrutinized, with gates becoming the quality control checkpoints in your process. Make "doing it right the first time" a rule. As a senior gatekeeper, *you* are the *quality controller* here!

6. Make your new product process complete and thorough, where every vital activity is carried out—no hasty corner-cutting. But the process should also be flexible, where stages and decision points can be skipped or combined, as dictated by the nature and risk of the project. Flexibility and shortcuts can be built in, especially for lower-risk projects and when the risks of omission are understood. But for significant and higher-risk projects, adhere to a disciplined, thorough new product process.

Seven Additional Keys to Victory

6. *Embrace the seven additional success factors that, while not process factors per se, nonetheless impact strongly on your new product results.*

Recall from Chapter 3 what these seven factors are:

1. Put in place the needed resources to undertake new products. Top-performer firms do: senior management makes the *necessary resource commitment and keeps it.* Tell-tale signs that your new product effort is underresourced include:

   - when projects seem to take forever to get to market;
   - when vital up-front homework isn't done;

- when market information seems badly lacking;
- when there are problems moving the typical project into operations/manufacturing and Launch or roll-out: and
- when quality of work seems not what it should be.

If these symptoms exist, likely the problem is simply a lack of resources—trying to do too much with too little. Undertake an *audit of resource adequacy,* and probe the impact that resource adequacy (or its lack) is having on your performance. Next, have a *resource requirements assessment* undertaken, where you translate your new product goals into numbers of major and minor launches, and finally to resources needed (people and dollars).

2. Make the quest for an *unbeatable product* top priority: a superior, differentiated product that delivers unique benefits and better value to the customer. Make product superiority and differentiation a key issue at gate reviews: challenge the project team—what have they done to gain insights that will lead to a product that delights the customer? At gate meetings, use product superiority as a key criterion to rate and rank projects. Use the seven items that comprise product superiority (Chapter 3) as criteria against which to rate and rank projects.

3. Don't forget the people side. Design your organization for product innovation. Utilize true cross-functional teams as described in Chapter 3: empowered teams, lead by a defined, dedicated leader, accountable from beginning to end of project, and with players from various functions, with appropriate release times for the project.

   Set the stage for effective project teams, providing the means for good team communication: small, dedicated teams; physically close to each other, or via co-location or a team office; electronic communication facilities and IT support (with training); and team training—for members and the leader.

   Foster the right climate and culture: reward and recognize teams and team members; avoid punishment for failure; provide resources for creative work (time off or scouting time), and bootstrapping money and facilities.

4. Look to the world product: an *international orientation* in product design, development, and target marketing provides the edge in product innovation. Recognize that international products— global and glocal—aimed at regional or world markets are the most profitable. This means adopting a *transnational new product*

process with international checks built in, and incorporating international commitment points in the process. It also requires using international project teams; doing market research and field trials in multiple countries; utilizing global criteria at gates, and establishing a global or regional structure to handle Go/Kill or gate decisions.

5. Leverage your *core competencies*. Synergy with the base business and its strengths is vital to success; "step-out" projects tend to fail more often. The ability to leverage core competencies (or having strong synergy between the new product project and your base business) is an important criterion in the selection of projects. At minimum, build synergy criteria—marketing, technological, and operations—into your list of criteria for making Go/Kill and prioritization decisions.

6. Seek *attractive markets*—ones that are sufficiently large and growing to make the product development effort worthwhile. Make market attractiveness a key criterion for project selection and prioritization.

7. Speed is everything . . . but not at the expense of quality of execution. Speed is important because it yields competitive advantage; it means less likelihood that the market has changed; and it means a quicker realization of profits. But there is also a dark side to speed: there is not a one-to-one link between speed and profits, while many of the actions people take in the interest of reducing cycle time have very negative effects. Finally, the quest for cycle time reduction may bias your new product portfolio towards short-term, limited projects to the long-run detriment of your business.

The *Stage-Gate*™ New Product Process—A Roadmap to Success

*7. Adopt a systematic, formal new product process in your business—a **Stage-Gate**™ process.*

Many leading companies do and the results seem to be worth the effort. So, either . . .

▶ design and install a systematic new product process in your business; or if you already have a process . . .

▶ audit your current process and begin its overhaul.

If you currently have a new product process, take a critical look at it. Answer the following questions:

- Are your stages clearly defined?
- Are best practices built in and key activities outlined for each stage (is your process a roadmap, or just a list of templates and requirements)?
- Can you identify which stage each of your projects are in?
- Are gates clearly described, complete with . . .

  - gatekeepers defined—who the decision makers are?
  - a standard menu of deliverables for each gate (can you produce the list)?
  - visible criteria for making Go/Kill and prioritization decisions?
  - defined gate outputs?

If not, maybe your process is an *imaginary process,* and lacks substance. Perhaps it's time to make your process a little more concrete and real.

8. *Merely having a formal, documented process leads to* **no improvements in performance;** *rather, it is the nature and quality of that process that makes all the difference. There are seven characteristics of a superb new product process.*

So you've decided either to develop a new product process or to overhaul your existing one, and have set up a task force to do so. Make sure that your task force understands clearly these seven vital characteristics. *Make these the goals of your process and a part of your task force's mandate:*

- Quality of execution.
- Sharp focus, rigorous project prioritization.
- A strong market orientation.
- Solid up-front homework and sharp, early product definition.
- Fast-paced parallel processing.
- A *true* cross-functional team approach.
- Products with competitive advantage—differentiated products, unique benefits, superior value for the customer.

9. *If you already have a new product process in place, then move to my third-generation* **Stage-Gate™** *process. It features six Fs:*

1. flexibility—where stages can be combined, gates collapsed, activities omitted.
2. fuzzy gates—conditional Go/Kill decisions at gates, conditional on some future event or information.
3. fluidity—where stages overlap and long lead-time activities can be brought forward.
4. focus—where the emphasis is on focusing resources on the great projects (project prioritization and portfolio management).
5. facilitation—where you provide a process manager or gate meister to ensure that the process works.
6. forever green—where your *Stage-Gate™* process is constantly being renewed and improved. Audit and overhaul your process if it's more than two years old!

Effective Gates and Gatekeeping—Picking the Winners

10. *As go the gates, so goes the process! The gates must work. And you, the leadership team, are the principal gatekeepers.*

The gates are the quality-control checkpoints in the process, where you make tough decisions: culling out poor projects and focusing resources on the right ones. Weak, inconsistent gates are prevalent in many businesses, however, which results in many other problems: poor homework and minimal customer input; unstable product definitions; long times-to-market; and higher failure rates.

If there is one area in new products warfare where you, the leadership team, must be 100 percent engaged and lead, it is here . . . at the gates.

11. *Your gates should have three main components: deliverables, criteria, and outputs.*

More specifically . . .

- a menu of deliverables, defined for each gate—clear expectations!
- criteria on which the Go/Kill and prioritization decisions will be made.
- outputs—Go/Kill/Hold/Recycle and resources approved.

Use a set of must-meet questions in a checklist format as culling questions, followed by a list of should-meet questions in a scoring model format to help determine relative project attractiveness. Employ these criteria at your gate meeting, discussing each question and reaching closure on it. If you do this, chances are your leadership team or gatekeeping group will make more objective, more reasoned, and better decisions.

12. *Adopt a formal and consistent project selection method (and don't rely solely on a financial analysis) to make your Go/Kill decisions.*

▶ Checklist and scoring models have much going for them for use at gate meetings: they yield better decisions: high-value projects; solid Go/Kill decisions; and a good balance of projects. Further, they fit management's decision-making style and are time-efficient.

▶ Financial methods should be part of your new product selection method, especially at Gates 3, 4, and 5 in the process, where expenditures are large and revenue and cost estimates are more reliable. But words of caution:

- Don't rely exclusively on financial methods for project selection—the businesses that do achieve inferior results.
- Financial estimates may be somewhat reliable by Gate 3, but they're still a long way from being very predictive. So continue to use these projections with caution.
- Don't rely on financial methods too early or for step-out projects.
- Consider switching from traditional NPV or DCF methods to the more suitable ECV or option pricing theory approaches, which recognize the incremental nature of the investment decisions, especially when evaluating higher-risk projects.

13. *The* **greatest change in behavior** *usually occurs not at the project team level, but* **with the gatekeepers.**

As a member of your leadership team, endorse the needed discipline and move toward professional gatekeeping in your business. Define your roles as a gatekeeping group, and spell out some *rules of the game* that you agree to live by. And try to refrain from the practices outlined in my "ten ways to ruin gate meetings" (Chapter 5).

Manage Your New Product Portfolio

14. *New products are the leading edge of your business strategy. The product choices you make today determine what your business's product offerings and market position will be in five years.*

Effective portfolio management and new product project selection are fundamental to business success (Chapter 6). Portfolio management is important for a number of vital reasons, most notably: to maximize financial return on R&D spending; to maintain the competitive position of the business; to properly allocate scarce resources; and to forge the link between project selection and the business's strategy.

15. *Your portfolio management process should strive to achieve three main goals:*

- maximize the value of your portfolio;
- achieve the right balance of projects; and
- ensure that projects are on-strategy and that your spending breakdowns mirror your business's strategy.

There exist effective tools to achieve each of these goals: scoring models, financial approaches, bubble diagrams, Strategic Buckets, and so on. Make use of these, and move toward an integrated portfolio management process.

Moving from Battle Plan to War Plan: A New Product Strategy for Your Business

16. *Doing business without strategy is like trying to sail a ship without a rudder. New product strategy pays off.*

Those businesses that lack goals for their total new product effort, where arenas or areas of strategic thrust have not been defined, where the strategy and projects are short-term in nature, and where the strategy is not well communicated to all, are at a decided performance disadvantage. If your organization does not have an explicit, written new product strategy, complete with measurable goals and specification of arenas as a guide to your business's new product efforts, now is the time to begin developing one.

17. *Envision your new product strategy or strategic approach.*

What strategy type is your business—prospector, analyzer, defender, or reactor? Which type should you be? Recall that these are:

▶ *Prospector*—you are the industry innovator, the first in with new products, and the first to adopt new technologies.

▶ *Analyzer*—you are the fast follower, monitoring competitor entries and bringing superior or more cost-effective products to market.

▶ *Defender*—you maintain a secure position in a niche or stable market, and protect your position via better service, higher quality, or lower prices.

▶ *Reactor*—you respond only when forced to.

Four major strategic thrusts are the common denominators in businesses that are successful at new products. These thrusts are:

- technological sophistication;
- a strong market orientation and a market-driven process;
- focus; and
- an offensive (versus a defensive) stance.

Build these orientations or thrusts into your new product strategy.

18. *Strategy development is the job of the leadership team of the business. This is how senior people become engaged in project selection and portfolio management processes—by charting your business's strategy.*

Here's how to proceed (Chapter 7):

▶ Spell out your *new product goals:* for example, what percentage of sales or profit or growth new products will contribute. Use gap analysis.

▶ Map your battlefields: that is, identify arenas of strategic focus. Draw an arena grid for your business—use two dimensions (products and markets) or three dimensions (customer groups, applications, and technologies). Locate your home base, and move out on each of the three axes, identifying other customer groups, applications, and technologies.

- Now that you've identified a list of possible arenas, try to rate each on the two key dimensions of *arena opportunity* and *business strength*. Draw an arena assessment map to see in which sectors your arenas lie.

- Prioritize your arenas or battlefields, looking for those in the desirable best bets sector, but perhaps seeking a balance by including some from the sure bets and the high-risk bets sectors.

- Next, deploy your resources: develop spending splits across key dimensions (for example, splits by arenas; or splits on other dimensions such as project types; or pick dimensions that represent strategic thrusts to you). Define Strategic Buckets or Target Spending Levels across dimensions.

- Finally define attack plans for each arena . . . how you plan to win on each battlefield or in each arena.

The War Plan and the Battle Plan

Define the goals of your new product effort. Choose the strategic arenas that you wish to attack. Deploy the resources. Decide the attack plans. These are the ingredients of the war plan—your product innovation strategy. Then move toward the battle plan: a step-by-step sequence of actions or a *Stage-Gate*™ process to bring products from mere ideas to money-making successes in the marketplace. This is the new product process, the tactics or battle plan.

There are no guarantees, of course. Even the best war plans and battle plans have been laid to waste by bad luck, unforeseen events, and poor execution. Product innovation is a future-oriented, hence an uncertain and high-risk endeavor. Having no plan or no process at all, however, is simply begging disaster to strike. Product innovation is too important to be left totally to chance. The processes outlined in this book provide a discipline that builds the success ingredients into product innovation by design rather than by chance. By doing so, they increase your odds of *becoming the leader in new products.*

Appendix A

The *ProBE* Diagnostic Tool

How well are you doing at new product development? And how do your methods and approaches compare with industry best practices? *ProBE* is a diagnostic tool that helps provide answers to these vital questions. (*ProBE* stands for *Pro*duct *B*enchmarking and *E*valuation.)

ProBE was originally developed in response to repeated requests by companies, whose management wanted to compare their business to those scores of companies in our database. Recall the benchmarking study we undertook, where we looked at hundreds of businesses in an attempt to learn what the drivers of new product performance are.[1] In this study, almost 100 drivers of performance were considered. The result was that we amassed a huge database—many companies rated on the numerous drivers of performance.

ProBE enables your business to assess its new product performance and practices versus those companies in the database. This is a questionnaire-based method, where a number of people in your organization answer a detailed, tested questionnaire. The questions are relatively simple ones—zero-to-ten scales with anchor phrases—that seek subjective opinion from these knowledgeable people. Questions cover many topics in your business, from culture and climate through to whether your new product process is functioning well, and even how well important activities are executed in typical new product projects.

Using our *ProBE* software, we analyze your questionnaire data and produce an initial report. This report—essentially a set of bar and pie charts—pinpoints your areas of strengths and weaknesses and helps identify areas needing fixing. Figure A.1 shows a sample output page (there are 14 such pages of output). *ProBE* benchmarks your practices and performance against industry averages, and also against the 20 percent best firms.

Next, the *ProBE* consultants conduct a diagnostic session with you and your people. They review the results and identify the causes of substandard performance. Finally, they develop a plan of action with you to correct the causes.

ProBE is an ideal way to begin your new product internal audit. That is, before you embark on a major overhaul or redesign of your new product process or new product efforts in your business, consider using *ProBE* or a similar structured technique to pinpoint what needs fixing. Remember: the beginning of a solution is understanding the problem!

ProBE is commercially available from number of sources. For more information, see the outline at the Product Development Institute's web page: www.prod-dev.com.[2]

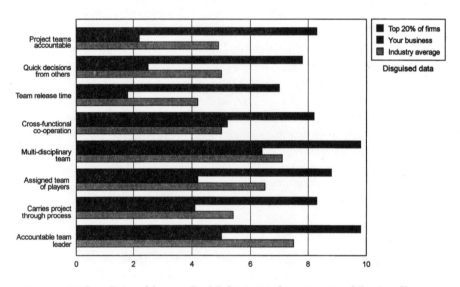

Figure A.1 One Page of Sampe *ProBE* Output—Organizational Design (Project Teams)

Appendix B

A Sample Scoring Model (Gates 2 & 3)

Nineteen Key Questions Scored on 1–10 Scales
(a major chemical company)

Reward:

1. Absolute contribution to profitability (five-year cash flow: cumulative cash flows less all cash costs, before interest and taxes).
2. Technological payback: the number of years for the cumulative cash flow to equal all cash costs expended prior to the start-up date.
3. Time to commercial start-up.

Business Strategy Fit:

4. Congruence: how well the program fits with the strategy (stated or implied) for the product line, business, and/or company.
5. Impact: the financial and strategic impact of the program on the product line, business, and/or company (scored from "minimal" to "critical").

Strategic Leverage:

6. Proprietary position (from "easily copied" to "well protected").
7. Platform for growth (from "one of a kind" to "opens up new technical and commercial fields").
8. Durability: the life of the product in the marketplace (years).
9. Synergy with other operations/businesses within the corporation.

Probability of Commercial Success:

10. Existence of a market need.

---

11. Market maturity (from "declining" to "rapid growth").
12. Competitive intensity: how tough or intense the competition is.
13. Existence of commercial applications development skills (from "new" to "already in place").
14. Commercial assumptions (from "low probability" to "highly predicable").
15. Regulatory/social/political impact (from "negative" to "positive").

Probability of Technical Success:
16. Technical gap (from "large gap" to "incremental improvement").
17. Program complexity.
18. Existence of technological skill base (from "new to us" to "widely practiced in company").
19. Availability of people and facilities (from "must hire/build" to "immediately available").

Each criterion (question) is scored 1–10; 1, 4, 7, and 10 are "anchored" that is, phrases are provided to define scale-points 1, 4, 7 and 10.

The five factors are calculated via weightings × ratings.
They are added in a weighted fashion to yield a project score.

Source: Hoechst-U.S.[1]

Appendix C

The Right Procedure to Ensure High-Quality Gate Meetings

- The deliverables are submitted and delivered to gatekeepers approximately one week ahead of the gate meeting. Consider using a standard format for deliverables (for example, templates).
- If major questions and show-stoppers arise, gatekeepers should contact the gate facilitator or the project team leader in advance of the meeting.
- Hold the meeting! Cancellation or postponements are unacceptable unless the deliverables are not ready. And hold the meeting even if the project team recommends a Kill decision. This achieves closure; you agree on the lessons learned; and you celebrate success, namely, a "correct Kill" decision. If gatekeepers cannot attend, they must use video- or teleconferencing from whatever city they are in.
- The *entire* project team should be present, where physically possible and convenient. (Some businesses only invite the project leader to gates; this may be efficient, but communication to the entire team is hampered.) Other attendees should be limited— no cheering sections and *gate-crashers!*
- Some businesses nominate a *head gatekeeper* for each gate meeting—a rotating position. One of her roles is to follow up with the project team leader on any outstanding items or "loose ends" following the gate meeting. This eliminates the need for the entire gatekeeping team to reconvene, and helps speed up the process.
- The procedure at the meeting goes like this: The project team has 15 minutes to present, uninterrupted. Give the team a chance to

finish their presentation before you dive in with questions! Next follows a question-and-answer session by the gatekeepers. Then the *gate facilitator* walks the gatekeepers through the list of criteria. The must-meet items are agreed to; then the should-meet items are scored by gatekeepers, ideally using a scorecard. The "scores" are recorded on an overhead or video projector, and differences debated. Consensus is reached and a decision is made: Go/Kill/Hold/Recycle.

▶ Next, a prioritization level is established. That is, the project in question is compared to the existing projects in the pipelines as well as against other projects on hold to establish its priority level. Various portfolio models and displays are used to achieve this prioritization. The end result is a decision to resource the project immediately (Go) or to put the project on hold, awaiting resources. If Go, an immediate resource commitment decision is made by the gatekeepers: people, their time, and money.

▶ The proposed action plan is discussed and modified if necessary. Agreement is reached on the action plan and the deliverables for the next gate. A date is set for next gate review.

▶ The project team is brought back into the gate meeting (normally they are asked to leave the room while the gatekeepers have a frank discussion on difficult issues). They are informed of the decision and reasons why—face to face.

Notes

Chapter 1

1. C. F. von Braun, *The Innovation War*. Upper Saddle River, N.J.: Prentice-Hall, 1997.

2. R. G. Cooper, "Developing new products on time, in time," *Research & Technology Management* 38, 5, September–October 1995, 49–57.

3. These NewProd studies began in 1975. Publications include: R. G. Cooper, "Pre-development activities determine new product success," *Industrial Marketing Management* 17, 3, 1988, 237–247; R. G. Cooper, "Debunking the myths of new product development," *Research & Technology Management* 37, 4, July–August 1994, 40–50; R. G. Cooper, "New products: What separates the winners from the losers," in *PDMA Handbook for New Product Development*, ed. Milton D. Rosenau Jr. New York: John Wiley & Sons Inc., 1996; R. G. Cooper, "Overhauling the new product process," *Industrial Marketing Management* 25, 6, November 1996, 465–482; R. G. Cooper & Kleinschmidt, E. J., "An investigation into the new product process: Steps, deficiencies and impact," *Journal of Product Innovation Management* 3, 2, 1986, 71–85; R. G. Cooper & Kleinschmidt, E. J., "New products: What separates winners from losers," *Journal of Product Innovation Management* 4, 3, 1987, 169–184; R. G. Cooper & Kleinschmidt, E. J., *New Products: The Key Factors in Success*. Chicago: American Marketing Association, 1990, monograph; R. G. Cooper & Kleinschmidt, E. J., "Major new products: What distinguishes the winners in the chemical industry," *Journal of Product Innovation Management* 2, 10, March 1993, 90–111; R. G. Cooper & Kleinschmidt, E. J., "New product success in the chemical industry," *Industrial Marketing Management* 22, 2, 1993, 85–99; R. G. Cooper & Kleinschmidt, E. J., "Uncovering the keys to new product success," *Engineering Management Review* 21, 4, Winter 1993, 5–18.

4. These benchmarking studies were undertaken by the author and his colleague, Professor Elko Kleinschmidt, and are reported in: R. G. Cooper & Kleinschmidt, E. J., "Benchmarking the firm's critical success factors in new product development," *Journal of Product Innovation Management* 12, 5, November 1995, 374–391; R. G. Cooper & Kleinschmidt, E. J., "Benchmarking firms' new product performance and practices," *Engineering Management Review* 23, 3, Fall 1995, 112–120; R. G. Cooper & Kleinschmidt, E. J., "Winning businesses in product development: Critical success factors," *Research-Technology Management* 39, 4, July–August 1996, 18–29.

5. Based on a survey of the new product (R&D management) literature undertaken at Cranfield University (U.K.) in 1996. See Leslie T. Falkingham and Richard Reeves, "Context analysis—a technique for analyzing research in a field, applied to literature on the management of R&D at the section level," working paper SWP-1197. Bedford, U.K.: Cranfield University, Research Office, School of Management.

6. Benchmarking studies: see note 4.

7. Benchmarking studies: see note 4.

8. R. G. Cooper, *Winning at New Products: Accelerating the Process from Idea to Launch.* Reading, Mass.: Perseus Books, 1993.

9. This list of prescriptions for senior management comes from our benchmarking studies: see note 4 above; see also Booz-Allen & Hamilton, *New Product Management for the 1980s.* New York: Booz-Allen & Hamilton Inc., 1982.

10. R. G. Cooper, "Third-generation new product processes," *Journal of Product Innovation Management* 11, 1994, 3–14. See also not 13.

11. Benchmarking studies: see note 4.

12. This paragraph taken from a book co-authored by the author: R. G. Cooper, Edgett, S. J., & Kleinschmidt, E. J., *Portfolio Management for New Products.* Reading, Mass.: Perseus Books, 1998.

13. PDMA best practices study; see Abbie Griffin, *Drivers of NPD Success: The 1997 PDMA Report.* Chicago: Product Development & Management Association), 1997.

14. PDMA study: see note 13.

15. See R. G. Cooper & Kleinschmidt, E. J., "Performance topologies of new product projects," *Industrial Marketing Management* 24, 1995, 439–456; see also NewProd studies in note 3, specifically two articles: *IMM* 1993 and *JPIM* 1993.

16. Based on NewProd studies, unpublished results: note 3. See also note 15.

17. R. G. Cooper, "Stage-gate systems: A new tool for managing new products," *Business Horizons* 33, 3, May–June 1990.

18. E. A. Robinson, "America's most admired corporations," *Fortune,* March 3, 1997, 68.

19. Brian O'Reilly, "Secrets of America's most admired corporations: New ideas, new products," *Fortune,* March 3, 1997, 60–66.

20. 1994 data, the most recent year reported by the OECD. *Main Science and Technology Indicators, no. 2, 1995.* OECD, 1996.

21. Source is note 1.

22. Booz-Allen & Hamilton, *New Product Management for the 1980s.* New York: Booz-Allen & Hamilton Inc., 1982.

23. Source is note 1.

24. C. M. Crawford, "New product failure rates—facts and fallacies," *Research Management,* September 1979, 9–13.

25. Failure rates taken from several of our studies: R. G. Cooper, "The performance impact of product innovation strategies," *European Journal of Marketing* 18, 5, 1984, 5–54; also R. G. Cooper, "Overall corporate strategies for new product programs," *Industrial Marketing Management* 14, 1985, 179–183. See also note 15.

26. PDMA study: see note 13.

27. D. S. Hopkins, *New Product Winners and Losers.* Conference Board Report no. 773, 1980.

28. See note 22.

29. See note 22.

30. A. L. Page, "PDMA new product development survey: Performance and best practices," paper presented at PDMA Conference, Chicago, November 13, 1991.

31. PDMA study: see note 13.

32. See note 22.

33. See note 22.

34. E. J. Kleinschmidt & Cooper, R. G., "The impact of product innovativeness on performance," *Journal of Product Innovation Management* 8, 1991, 240–251.

35. See note 34.

Chapter 2

1. Parts of this chapter are taken from other works by the author and co-authors. In particular, see references in notes 3 and 4 in Chapter 1 (the New-Prod projects studies and the benchmarking studies). Also: R. G. Cooper, "Overhauling the new product process," *Industrial Marketing Management* 25, 6, November 1996, 465–482.

2. Benchmarking studies: see note 4 in Chapter 1.

3. NewProd projects studies: see note 3 in Chapter 1.

4. NewProd projects studies: see note 3 in Chapter 1.

5. Benchmarking studies: see note 4 in Chapter 1.

6. Havelock and Elder as cited in Everett M. Rogers, "The R&D/Marketing interface in the technological innovation process," in Massoud M. Saghafi and Ashok K. Gupta, eds., *Managing the R&D Interface for Process Success: The Telecommunication Focus,* vol. 1, *Advances in Telecommunications Management.* Greenwich, Conn.: JAI Press Inc., 1990.

7. See R. G. Cooper, "Stage-gate systems: A new tool for managing new products," *Business Horizons* 33, 3, May–June 1990; also R. G. Cooper, *Winning at New Products: Accelerating the Process from Idea to Launch.* Reading, Mass.: Perseus Books, 1993.

8. R. G. Cooper, "Developing new products on time, in time," *Research & Technology Management* 38, 5 September–October 1995, 49–57; also R. G. Cooper & Kleinschmidt, E. J., "Determinants of timeliness in new product development," *Journal of Product Innovation Management* 11, 5, November 1994, 381–396; R. G. Cooper & Kleinschmidt, E. J., "New product performance: Keys to success, profitability and cycle time reduction," *Journal of Marketing Management* 11, 1995, 315–337.

9. NewProd projects studies: see note 3 in Chapter 1.

10. Benchmarking studies: see note 4 in Chapter 1.

11. E. A. Von Hippel, *The Sources of Innovation.* New York: Oxford University Press, 1988.

12. NewProd projects studies: note 3 in Chapter 1; also note 8 above.

13. C. M. Crawford, "Protocol: New tool for product innovation," *Journal of Product Innovation Management* 2, 1984, 85–91.

14. Edith Wilson, *Product Development Process, Product Definition Guide, Release 1.0,* internal Hewlett-Packard document, Palo Alto, Calif., 1991.

15. Benchmarking studies: see note 4 in Chapter 1.

16. See R. G. Cooper & Kleinschmidt, E. J., "An investigation into the new product process: Steps, deficiencies and impact," *Journal of Product Innovation Management* 3, 2, 1986, 71–85; also R. G. Cooper & Kleinschmidt, E. J., "Winning businesses in product development: Critical success factors," *Research-Technology Management* 39, 4, July–August 1996, 18–29.

17. These weaknesses were identified in our benchmarking studies: see note 4 in Chapter 1; also in a recent study on portfolio management and project selection practices, undertaken by the author and colleagues Professors Scott Edgett and Elko Kleinschmidt. See R. G. Cooper, Edgett, S. J., Kleinschmidt, E. J. *Portfolio Management for New Products.* Hamilton, Ont., Canada: McMaster University, 1997; and: R. G. Cooper, Edgett, S. J., & Kleinschmidt, E. J., *Portfolio Management for New Products.* Reading, Mass.: Perseus Books, 1998; also the two-part article series by the same authors: "Portfolio management in new product development: Lessons from the leaders," *Research-Technology Management* 40, 5 September–October 1997 and 40, 6, November–December 1997.

18. R. G. Cooper, Edgett, S.J., & Kleinschmidt, E. J., *R&D Portfolio Management Best Practices Study.* Hamilton, Ont., Canada McMaster University, 1997; report also available from the Industrial Research Institute (IRI), Washington, D.C.

19. NewProd projects studies: see note 3 in Chapter 1.

20. Benchmarking studies: see note 4 in Chapter 1.

21. See NewProd and benchmarking studies: notes 3 and 4 in Chapter 1; also R. G. Cooper & Kleinschmidt, E. J., "An investigation into the new prod-

uct process: Steps, deficiencies and impact," *Journal of Product Innovation Management* 3, 2, 1986, 71–85.

22. R. G. Cooper & Kleinschmidt, E.J., "An investigation into the new product process: Steps, deficiencies and impact," *Journal of Product Innovation Management* 3, 2, 1986, 71–85.

23. Benchmarking studies: see note 4 in Chapter 1.

24. Benchmarking studies: see note 4 in Chapter 1.

25. Benchmarking studies: see note 4 in Chapter 1; see also R. G. Cooper & Kleinschmidt, E. J., *Formal Processes for Managing New Products: The Industry Experience.* Hamilton, Ont., Canada: McMaster University, 1991; and R. G. Cooper & Kleinschmidt, E. J., "New product processes at leading industrial firms," *Industrial Marketing Management* 10, 2, May 1991, 137–147.

26. NewProd projects studies: see note 3 in Chapter 1.

Chapter 3

1. Parts of this chapter are taken from other works by the author and co-authors. In particular, see references in notes 3 and 4 in Chapter 1.

2. Benchmarking studies: see note 4 in Chapter 1.

3. See results of a study that investigated the cost of different stages and activities in the new product process: R. G. Cooper & Kleinschmidt, E. J., "Resource allocation in the new product process," *Industrial Marketing Management* 17, 3, 1988, 249–262.

4. See note 3.

5. NewProd projects studies: see note 3 in Chapter 1.

6. M. A. Maidique & Zirger, B. J., "A study of success and failure in product innovation: The case of the U.S. electronics industry," *IEEE Trans. in Engineering Management* EM-31, November 1984, 192–203; also B. J. Zirger & Maidique, M. A., "A model of new product development: An empirical test," *Management Science* 36, 7, 1990, 867–883.

7. See note 6.

8. NewProd projects studies: see note 3 in Chapter 1.

9. Benchmarking studies: see note 4 in Chapter 1.

10. E. W. Larson & Gobeli, D. H., "Organizing for product development projects," *Journal of Product Innovation Management* 5, 1988, 180–190.

11. T. J. Peters, *Thriving on Chaos.* New York: Harper & Row, 1988.

12. NewProd projects studies: see note 3 Chapter 1.

13. Booz-Allen & Hamilton, *New Product Management for the 1980s.* New York: Booz-Allen & Hamilton Inc., 1982.

14. M. E. Porter, *Competitive Advantage: Creating and Sustaining Superior Performance.* New York: Free Press, 1985.

15. See *The Product Portfolio*, pamphlet no. 66. Boston: The Boston Consulting Group, 1970; also B. Heldey, "Strategy and the business portfolio," *Long Range Planning*, 1977. For information on the GE portfolio approach, see

George Day, *Analysis for Strategic Marketing Decisions*. St. Paul, Minn.: West Publishing, 1986; and La Rue Hosner, *Strategic Management*. Englewood Cliffs, N.J.: Prentice-Hall.

16. See note 3, Chapter 1. Also M. A. Maidique & Zirger, B. J., "A study of success and failure in product innovation: The case of the U.S. electronics industry," *IEEE Trans. in Engineering Management* EM-31, November 1984, 192–203.

17. This section taken from an article by the author: R. G. Cooper, "Developing products on time, in time," *Research-Technology Management* 38, 5, September–October 1995, 40–50.

18. See C. M. Crawford, "The hidden costs of accelerated product development," *Journal of Product Innovation Management* 9, 3, September 1992, 188–199.

19. See G. L. Lillien and E. Yoon, "The timing of competitive market entry: An exploratory study of new industrial products," *Management Science* 36, 5, May 1990, 568–584; also W. T. Robinson, "Product innovation and start up business market share performance," *Management Science* 36, 10, October 1990, 1279–1289.

20. See R. G. Cooper & Kleinschmidt, E. J., "Major new products: What distinguishes the winners in the chemical industry," *Journal of Product Innovation Management* 2, 10, March 1993, 90–111.

21. See B. Dumaine, "How managers can succeed through speed," *Fortune*, February 13, 1989, 54–59.

22. See R. P. Nayak, "Planning speeds technological development," *Planning Review* 18, November–December 1990, 14–25.

23. See Crawford, note 18.

24. See M. L. Patterson, "Accelerating innovation: A dip into the meme pool," *National Productivity Review* 9, 4, Autumn 1990, 409–418.

25. R. Cordero, "Managing for speed to obsolesce: A survey of techniques," *Journal of Product Innovation Management* 8, 4, December 1991, 283–294.

26. PDMA best practices study; see Abbie Griffin, *Drivers of NPD Success: The 1997 PDMA Report*. Chicago: Product Development & Management Association, 1997.

27. Ibid.

28. See Peters, note 11.

Chapter 4

1. A. quotation describing the quality process, which has equal applicability to the new product process. See Thomas H. Berry, *Managing the Total Quality Transformation*. New York: McGraw-Hill Inc., 1991.

2. This chapter is based on material from four sources: R. G. Cooper, "A process model for industrial new product development," *IEEE Trans. on Engineering Management* EM-30, February 1983, 2–11; R. G. Cooper, "The new product process: A decision guide for managers," *Journal of Marketing Manage-*

ment 3, 3, 1988, 238–255; R. G. Cooper, "Stage-gate systems: A new tool for managing new products," *Business Horizons* 33, 3, May–June 1990; and R. G. Cooper & Kleinschmidt, E. J., "Stage gate systems for new product success," *Marketing Management* 1, 4, 1993, 20–29. For more detail on *Stage-Gate™* approaches, see R. G. Cooper, *Winning at New Products: Accelerating the Process from Idea to Launch.* Reading, Mass.: Perseus Books, 1993.

3. Some of these examples are taken from (all updated): R. G. Cooper, "Stage-gate systems: A new tool for managing new products," *Business Horizons* 33, 3, May–June 1990; and R. G. Cooper & Kleinschmidt, E. J., "Stage gate systems for new product success," *Marketing Management* 1, 4, 1993, 20–29.

4. Quotation taken from PDMA best practices study; see Abbie Griffin, *Drivers of NPD Success: The 1997 PDMA Report.* Chicago: Product Development & Management Association, 1997. The references cited in her report are: R. G. Cooper, "Stage-gate systems: A new tool for managing new products," *Business Horizons* 33, 3, May–June 1990; and R. G. Cooper, "Third-generation new product processes," *Journal of Product Innovation Management* 11, 1994, 3–14.

5. See note 4.

6. Parts of this section are taken from an article by the author. See R. G. Cooper, "Overhauling the new product process," *Industrial Marketing Management* 25, 6, November 1996, 465–482.

7. B. Uttal, "Speeding new ideas to market," *Fortune,* March 1987, 62–66.

8. R. G. Cooper, "Third-generation new product processes," *Journal of Product Innovation Management* 11, 1994, 3–14.

9. See note 2, specifically: R. G. Cooper, "The new product process: A decision guide for managers"; and R. G. Cooper, "Stage-gate systems: A new tool for managing new products."

10. This early work is reported in R. G. Cooper, "Identifying industrial new product success: Project NewProd," *Industrial Marketing Management* 8 May 1979, 124–135; also R. G. Cooper, "The new product process: An empirically derived classification scheme," *R&D Management* 13, January 1983, 2–11.

11. Early versions of *Stage-Gate™* were published in a variety of sources by the author; see note 2.

12. *Stage-Gate™* based on material in: R. G. Cooper, *Winning at New Products: Accelerating the Process from Idea to Launch.* Reading, Mass.: Perseus Books, 1993.

13. Ron Sears & Barry, M., "Product Value Analysis^SM—product interaction predicts profits," *Innovation,* Winter 1993, 13–18.

14. For more information on the use of lead users in idea generation, see Eric Von Hippel, Sonnack, M., & Churchill, J., *Developing Breakthrough Products and Services: The Lead User Method.* Minneapolis, Minn.: LUCI Press. See also C. Herstatt & Von Hippel, E. A., "From experience: Developing new product concepts via the lead user method: A case study in a 'low tech' field," *Journal of Product Innovation Management* 9, 1992, 213–221; and G. L. Urban & Von Hippel, E. A., "Lead user analyses for the development of new industrial

products," *Management Science* 34, 5, May 1988, 569–582. See also: E. A. Von Hippel, *The Sources of Innovation.* New York: Oxford University Press, 1988.

15. See PDMA study in note 4. For a thorough description of third-generation new product processes, see note. 8.

16. See PDMA study, note 4.

17. See "Third generation new-product processes," note 8.

Chapter 5

1. R. G. Cooper, "The NewProd system: The industry experience," *Journal of Product Innovation Management* 9, 1992, 113–127.

2. Benchmarking studies: see note 4 in Chapter 1.

3. R. G. Cooper & Kleinschmidt, E. J., "An investigation into the new product process: Steps, deficiencies and impact," *Journal of Product Innovation Management* 3, 2, 1986, 71–85.

4. See Abbie Griffin, *Drivers of NPD Success: The 1997 PDMA Report.* Chicago: Product Development & Management Association, 1997; also Booz-Allen & Hamilton, *New Product Management for the 1980s.* New York: Booz-Allen & Hamilton Inc., 1982.

5. N. R. Baker, "R&D project selection models: An assessment," *IEEE Trans. Engineering Management,* EM-21, November 1974, 165–171; see also N. R. Baker & Freeland, J., "Recent advances in R&D benefit measurement and project selection methods," *Management Science* 21 1975, 1164–1175.

6. Baker, "R&D project selection models"; see note 5.

7. A good summary article on such methods is: Byron Jackson, "Decision methods for selecting a portfolio of R&D projects," *Research Management,* September–October 1983, 21–26.

8. P. Roussel, Saad, K. N., & Erickson, T. J., *Third Generation R&D, Managing the Link to Corporate Strategy.* Harvard Business School Press & Arthur D. Little Inc., 1991.

9. R. G. Cooper, Edgett, S. J., and Kleinschmidt, E. J., *R&D Portfolio Management Best Practices Study,* Industrial Research Institute (IRI), Washington, D.C., 1997.

10. See Baker; Baker & Freeland, note 5.

11. See portfolio management best practices study: note 9.

12. For more information on this issue and options pricing in general, refer to R. Deaves & Krinsky, I., "New tools for investment decision-making: Real options analysis," McMaster University Working Paper, April 1997; T. Faulkner, "Applying 'options thinking' to R&D valuation," *Research-Technology Management,* May–June 1996, 50–57; T. Luehrman, "What's it worth? A general manager's guide to valuation," *Harvard Business Review,* May–June 1997, 1321–142.

13. T. Faulkner, "Applying 'options thinking' to R&D valuation," *Research-Technology Management* May–June 1996, 50–57.

14. See portfolio management best practices study: note 9.

15. W. E. Souder, "A system for using R&D project evaluation methods," *Research Management* 21, September 1978, 21–37.

16. G. L. Lilien & Kotler, P., *Marketing Decision Making: A Model-Building Approach.* New York: Harper & Row Publishers, 1983; also W. E. Souder & Mandakovic, T., "R&D project selection models," *Research Management*, 29, 4, 1986, 36–42; also F. Zahedi, "The analytic hierarchy process—A survey of the method and its applications," *Interfaces*, 16, 4, 1986, 96–108.

17. Hoechst example taken from another recent book, which the author co-authored: R. G. Cooper, Edgett, S. J., & Kleinschmidt, E. J., *Portfolio Management for New Products.* Reading, Mass.: Perseus Books, 1998.

18. For more information on the *NewProd™* model, contact the author. See also R. G. Cooper, "Selecting winning new products: Using the NewProd system," *Journal of Product Innovation Management* 2, 1987, 34–44; and R. G. Cooper, "The NewProd system: The industry experience," *Journal of Product Innovation Management* 9, 1992, 113–127.

19. For example, Procter & Gamble uses the *NewProd™* model, and reports a predictive ability of about 84 percent. See Robert E. Davis, "The role of market research in the development of new consumer products," *Journal of Product Innovation Management* 10, 4, 309–317; see also J. A. M. Bronnenberg & van Engelen, M. L., "A Dutch test with the NewProd model," *R&D Management* 18, 4, 1988, 321–332.

20. S. B. Graves & Ringuest, J. L., "Evaluating competing R&D investments," *Research & Technology Management*, July–August 1991, 32–36.

21. T. Faulkner, "Applying 'options thinking' to R&D valuation," *Research-Technology Management*, May–June 1996, 50–57.

22. ECC example taken from another book, which the author co-authored: see note 17.

23. A. Albala, "Stage approach for the evaluation and selection of R&D projects," *IEEE Trans. Engineering Management*, EM-22, November 1975, 153–162.

24. R. G. Cooper, "A process model for industrial new product development," *IEEE Trans. on Engineering Management*, EM-30, February 1983, 2–11.

25. See Albala, note 23.

26. See Albala, note 23.

27. Firmness of resources taken from another book, which the author co-authored: see note 17.

28. Based on unpublished work of Dr. Larry Gastwirt, Stevens Institute of Technology, N.J.

Chapter 6

1. Much of this chapter is taken from two articles, that the author wrote with co-authors, Professors Elko Kleinschmidt and Scott Edgett: R. G. Cooper, Edgett, S. J., & Kleinschmidt, E. J., "Portfolio management in new product

development: Lessons from the leaders—Part I," *Research-Technology Management,* September–October 1997; and R. G. Cooper, Edgett, S. J., & Kleinschmidt, E. J., "Portfolio management in new product development: Lessons from the leaders—Part II," *Research-Technology Management,* November–December 1997. For more detail on portfolio management, see the recent book by the same authors on the topic: R. G. Cooper, Edgett, S. J., & Kleinschmidt, E. J., *Portfolio Management for New Products.* Reading, Mass.: Perseus Books, 1998.

   2. A. Griffin, *Drivers of NPD Success: The 1997 PDMA Report.* Chicago: Product Development & Management Association, 1997.

   3. See "Portfolio management in new product development," Part I: note 1.

   4. R. G. Cooper, Edgett, S. J., & Kleinschmidt, E. J., *R&D Portfolio Management Best Practices Study,* Industrial Research Institute (IRI), Washington,, D.C., 1997.

   5. Portfolio study: see note 4.

   6. Taken from the Strategic Decisions Group (SDG). For more information, refer to David Matheson, Matheson, James E., & Manke, Michael M., "Making excellent R&D decisions," *Research Technology Management,* November–December 1994, 21–24; and Patricia Evans, "Streamlining formal portfolio management," *Scrip Magazine,* February 1996.

   7. For more information on these corporate planning portfolio models, see the Boston Consulting Group's Growth-Share Matrix in B. Heldey, "Strategy and the business portfolio," *Long Range Planning,* 1977; for the approach used by GE, refer to George Day, *Analysis for Strategic Marketing Decisions.* St. Paul, Minn.: West Publishing, 1986; and La Rue Hosner, *Strategic Management.* Englewood Cliffs, N.J.: Prentice-Hall.

   8. Portfolio study: note 4.

   9. The A. D. Little model is outlined in: P. Roussel, Saad K., & Erickson, T., *Third Generation R&D, Managing the Link to Corporate Strategy.* Boston, Mass.: Harvard Business School Press & Arthur D. Little Inc., 1991.

   10. The SDG method: see note 6.

   11. Source: internal 3M documents: Dr. Gary L. Tritle, "New Product Investment Portfolio."

   12. Adapted from E. Roberts & Berry, C. "Entering new businesses: Selecting strategies for success," *Sloan Management Review,* Spring 1983, 3–17.

   13. R. G. Cooper & Kleinschmidt, E. J., "Winning businesses in product development: Critical success factors," *Research-Technology Management* 39, 4, July–August 1996, 18–29.

Chapter 7

   1. Benchmarking studies: see note 4 in Chapter 1.

   2. Booz-Allen & Hamilton, *New Product Management for the 1980s.* New York: Booz-Allen & Hamilton Inc., 1982.

   3. C. M. Crawford, "Defining the charter for product innovation," *Sloan Management Review,* 1980, 3–12.

4. D. J. Luck & Prell, A. E., *Market Strategy*. Englewood Cliffs, N.J.: Prentice-Hall, 1968, 2.

5. I. H. Ansoff, *Corporate Strategy*. New York: McGraw-Hill, 1965.

6. R. E. Corey, "Key options in market selection and product planning," *Harvard Business Review*, September–October 1978, 119–128.

7. Some sections in this chapter are taken from a recent book, where the author was one of the co-authors: R. G. Cooper, Edgett, S. J., & Kleinschmidt, E. J., *Portfolio Management for New Products*. Reading, Mass.: Perseus Books, 1998.

8. Crawford: see note 3.

9. J. B. Quinn, "Formulating strategy one step at a time," *Journal of Business Strategy* 1, 1981, 42–63.

10. Booz-Allen & Hamilton: see note 2.

11. See H. Nystrom, "Company strategies for research and development," in *Industrial Innovation*, edited by N. Baker. New York: Macmillan, 1979; also H. Nystrom, *Company Strategies for Research and Development*, Institute for Economics and Statistics, Uppsala, Sweden, Report S-750 07, 1977; H. Nystrom & Edvardsson, B., *Research and Development Strategies for Swedish Companies in the Farm Machinery Industry*, Institute for Economics and Statistics, Uppsala, Sweden, 1978; and H. Nystrom & Edvardsson, B., *Research and Development Strategies for Four Swedish Farm Machine Companies*, Institute for Economics and Statistics, Uppsala, Sweden, 1980.

12. The Cooper strategy studies: R. G. Cooper, "The performance impact of product innovation strategies," *European Journal of Marketing* 18, 5, 1984, 5–54; also R. G. Cooper, "How new product strategies impact on performance," *Journal of Product Innovation Management* 1, 1984, 5–18; R. G. Cooper, "The strategy–performance link in product innovation," *R&D Management* 14, October 1984, 151–164; R. G. Cooper, "New product strategies: What distinguishes the top performers," *Journal of Product Innovation Management* 2, 1984, 151–164; R. G. Cooper, "Industrial firms' new product strategies," *Journal of Business Research* 13, April 1985, 107–121; and R. G. Cooper, "Overall corporate strategies for new product programs," *Industrial Marketing Management* 14, 1985, 179–183.

13. M. M. Menke, "Essentials of R&D strategic excellence," *Research-Technology Management* 40, 5, September–October 1997, 42–47.

14. Paragraph taken from: R. G. Cooper, "Benchmarking new product performance: Results of the best practices study," *European Management Journal*, 16, 1, Feb. 1998, 1–17.

15. Benchmarking study: see note 4 in Chapter 1.

16. R. E. Miles & Snow, C. C., *Organizational Strategy, Structure and Process*. New York: McGraw-Hill, 1978.

17. These definitions are taken from an article by Griffin and Page, who provide a breakdown of project types by strategy elected. See: Abbie Griffin & Page, Albert L., "PDMA success measurement project: Recommended measures for product development success and failure," *Journal of Product Innovation Management* 13, 6, November 1996, 478–495.

18. Ibid.

19. Strategy studies: see note 12.

20. R. C. Bennett & Cooper, R. G., "The product life cycle trap," *Business Horizons*, September–October 1984, 7–16.

21. Booz-Allen & Hamilton: see note 2.

22. Ibid.

23. Griffin & Page: see note 17.

24. G. S. Day, "A strategic perspective on product planning," *Journal of Contemporary Business*, Spring 1975, 1–34.

25. Strategy studies: see note 12.

26. Booz-Allen & Hamilton: see note 2.

27. Day: see note 24.

28. Corey: see note 6.

29. D. F. Abell, *Defining the Business*. Englewood Cliffs, N.J.: Prentice-Hall, 1980.

30. Crawford: see note 3.

31. The original concept for developing a new product strategy for the business is found in: R. G. Cooper, "Strategic planning for successful technological innovation," *Business Quarterly* 43, Spring 1978, 46–54. See also R. G. Cooper, "Defining the new product strategy," *IEEE Trans. on Engineering Management*, EM-34, 3, 1987, 184–193; and R. G. Cooper, "Identifying and evaluating new product opportunities," in *The Interface of Marketing and Strategy* by G. S. Day, B. Weitz, & R. Wensley, vol. 4 of the series: *Strategic Management Policy and Planning: A Multivolume Treatise*. Greenwich, Conn.: JAI Press Inc., 1990.

32. Grid in Figure 7.5 adapted from: R. G. Cooper, *Winning at New Products*, 1993, where it was reproduced with permission of the *Business Quarterly*, Western Business School, the University of Western Ontario, London, Canada. The original figure appeared in Cooper, *Business Quarterly*, 1978 (note 31).

33. The PDMA definition of "platform" is found in the glossary of *The PDMA Handbook of New Product Development*, M. D. Rosenau Jr., editor. New York: John Wiley & Sons, 1996. See also: M. H. Meyer and Lehnerd, A. P., *The Power of Product Platforms*, New York: The Free Press, 1997.

Appendix A

1. See benchmarking studies: note 4 in Chapter 1.

2. *ProBE* was developed jointly by Jens Arleth of U3 Innovation Management (Copenhagen), and Robert Cooper and Scott Edgett of Product Development Institute Inc. Website www.prod-dev.com.

Appendix B

1. More details of this scoring model are in the Portfolio book, see note 12 in Chapter 1.

Index